C000246806

Ypres

Ypres

THE FIRST BATTLE, 1914

Ian F.W. Beckett

Harlow, England • London • New York • Boston • San Francisco • Toronto
Sydney • Tokyo • Singapore • Hong Kong • Seoul • Taipei • New Delhi
Cape Town • Madrid • Mexico City • Amsterdam • Munich • Paris • Milan

Pearson Education Limited
Edinburgh Gate
Harlow CM20 2JE
United Kingdom
Tel: +44 (0)1279 623623
Fax: +44 (0)1279 431059
Website: www.pearsoned.co.uk

First edition published in Great Britain in 2004
© Pearson Education Limited 2004

The right of Ian F.W. Beckett to be identified as author of this work has been
asserted by him in accordance with the Copyright, Designs and Patents Act 1988.

ISBN 0 582 50612 3

British Library Cataloguing-in-Publication Data
A CIP catalogue record for this book can be obtained from the British Library

Library of Congress Cataloging-in-Publication Data
Beckett, I.F.W. (Ian Frederick William)
  Ypres : the first battle, 1914 / Ian F.W. Beckett.—1st ed.
      p. cm.
  Includes bibliographical references and index.
  ISBN 0–582–50612–3
    1. Ypres, 1st Battle of, Ieper, Belgium, 1914. 2. Great Britain. Army—History—World
War, 1914–1918. I. Title.

  D542.Y6B43 2004
  940.4′21—dc22

                                                        2004050396

10 9 8 7 6 5 4 3 2 1
08 07 06 05 04

Set by 35 in 9/13.5pt Stone Serif
Printed and bound in Great Britain by Biddles Ltd, King's Lynn

The Publishers' policy is to use paper manufactured from sustainable forests.

'We were only clinging to the ground by our eyelids'

Major General E.S. Bulfin, Diary, 31 October 1914

Contents

Acknowledgements

This book was researched and written while I was privileged to hold the visiting chair of Major General Matthew C. Horner Professor in Military Theory at the US Marine Corps University, Quantico, Virginia for 2002–2003 and 2003–2004. I am most grateful for the support of the then Chief Executive of the Marine Corps University Foundation, Major General Don Gardner, USMC (Ret'd), who has since become President of the University, and his staff, especially the Chief Operating Officer, Lieutenant Colonel John Hales, USMC (Ret'd), and the Director of Business Operations, Julie Sledd. I am also grateful for the support of the academic and military staff of the University's constituent colleges including the Command and Staff College, the War College and the School of Advanced Warfighting. Within the General Alfred M. Gray Marine Corps Research Centre, I received equal support from the Director, Dr Kurt Sanftleben, and his staff, including the Director of Research Archives, Kerry Strong, the Director of the Library, Carol Ramkey, and Catherine MacLaren of the Reference Service Centre, who was indefatigable in pursuit of inter-library loans on my behalf.

I also owe my particular thanks to Rod Suddaby and the staff of the Department of Documents at the Imperial War Museum; Dr Alastair Massie and the staff of the National Army Museum; Mitch Yockelson of the US National Archives; the staff of the Special Collections at the Brotherton Library of the University of Leeds; and Dr Jan Dewilde and his staff at the In Flanders Fields Museum, Ypres. Rob and Sue Perry were very helpful hosts at their excellent bed and breakfast establishment, Essex Villa, at Langemarck, when I was conducting my research in Ypres.

At Longman Pearson, as always, Heather McCallum has been a sympathetic and supportive commissioning editor. I am also grateful to the senior editor, Melanie Carter, for seeing the book through press and to the copy editor, Heather Ancient.

Quotations from the Royal Archives appear by gracious permission of Her Majesty the Queen. Those from Crown copyright sources in the National Archives (formerly the Public Record Office) and elsewhere appear by permission of Her Majesty's Stationery Office. I am also indebted for permission to use and/or quote from archives to Earl Haig and the Trustees of the National Library of Scotland; the Trustees of the British Library Board, the Churchill Archives Centre, Churchill College, Cambridge; the Brotherton Library, University of Leeds (Liddle Collection); the Trustees fo the Liddell Hart Centre for Military Archives, King's College, University of London; the US National Archives; the Service Historique de l'Armée de Terre, Vincennes; the Trustees of the Imperial War Museum; Katherine Dean; Lord Clinton; Comtesse de Roany; Lady Patricia Kingsbury; Henry F. Waddy; Mrs Denise Boyes; John Pym; Kate Grimond; David McLennan; Davina Loch; Captain Hugh Owen, RN; Mrs Diana Stockwood; Mrs Ann Smallman; and Colonel P.N.M. Jebb.

As always my greatest debt is to my wife, Trina, who on this occasion had to bear my attempts to complete the manuscript while we were supposedly on holiday on the otherwise enchanting island of Eleuthera in the Bahamas.

IFWB

Maps

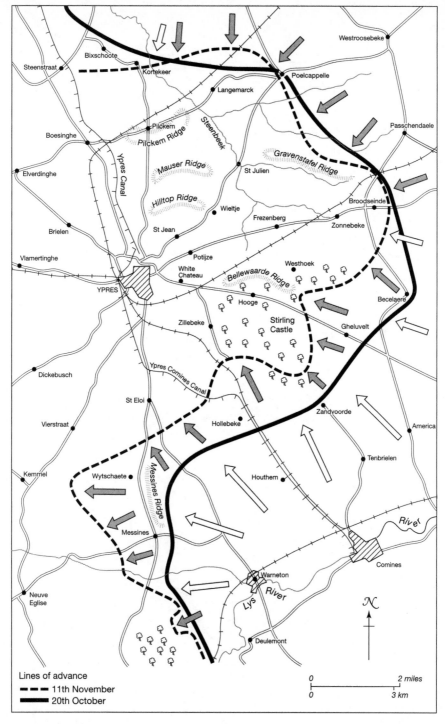

Westroosebeke

Steenstraat
Bixschoote
Kortekeer
Poelcappelle
Langemarck
Passchendaele

Boesinghe
Pilckem
Pilckem Ridge
Steenbeek
Gravenstafel Ridge

Elverdinghe
Ypres Canal
Mauser Ridge
St Julien
Broodseinde

Hilltop Ridge
Wieltje
Frezenberg
Zonnebeke

Brielen
St Jean

Vlamertinghe
Potijze
Westhoek

White Chateau
Bellewaarde Ridge
Becelaere

YPRES
Hooge
Stirling Castle
Gheluvelt

Zillebeke

Dickebusch
Ypres Comines Canal
Zandvoorde
America

St Eloi
Hollebeke
Tenbrielen

Vierstraat
Houthem

Kemmel
Wytschaete
Messines Ridge

Messines
River

Neuve Eglise
Warneton
Comines
River
Lys

Deulemont

N

Lines of advance
— — — 11th November
————— 20th October

0   2 miles
0   3 km

Map 1 Flanders, 1914

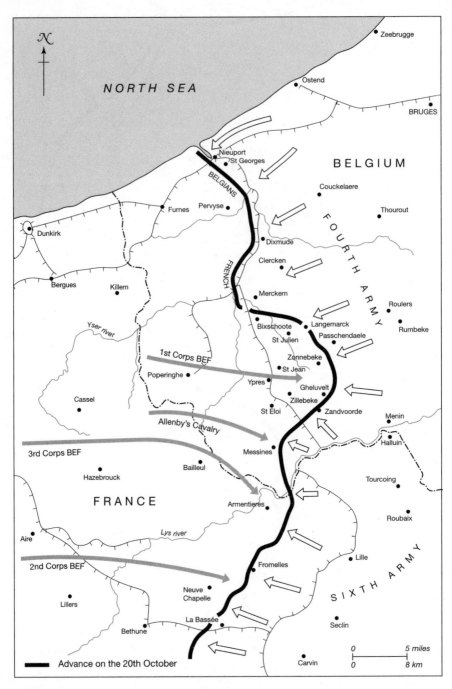

NORTH SEA

Zeebrugge

Ostend

BRUGES

BELGIUM

Nieuport
St Georges

Couckelaere

Thourout

BELGIANS

Furnes Pervyse

Dunkirk

FRENCH

Dixmude

Clercken

F
O
U
R
T
H

A
R
M
Y

Roulers

Bergues Killem

Merckem

Rumbeke

Yser river

Bixschoote
St Julien

Langemarck
Passchendaele

1st Corps BEF

Poperinghe

Ypres

St Jean

Zonnebeke

Gheluvelt
Zillebeke

Cassel

St Eloi

Zandvoorde

Menin

Allenby's Cavalry

Halluin

3rd Corps BEF

Messines

Tourcoing

FRANCE

Bailleul

Armentieres

Roubaix

Hazebrouck

Aire

Lys river

S
I
X
T
H

A
R
M
Y

2nd Corps BEF

Fromelles

Lille

Lillers

Neuve
Chapelle

Bethune

La Bassée

Seclin

0   5 miles

Advance on the 20th October

Carvin

0   8 km

Map 2 Advance to contact, 20 October 1914

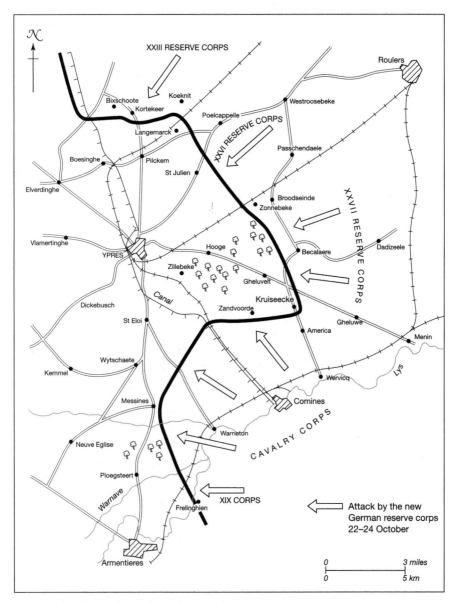

Map 3 Kindermord, 22–4 October 1914

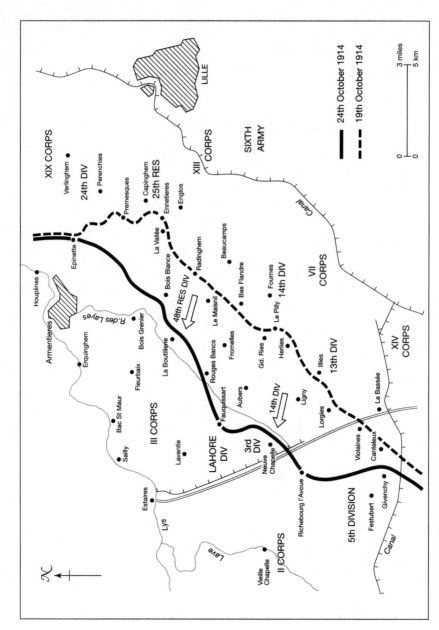

Map 4 The South, 19–24 October 1914

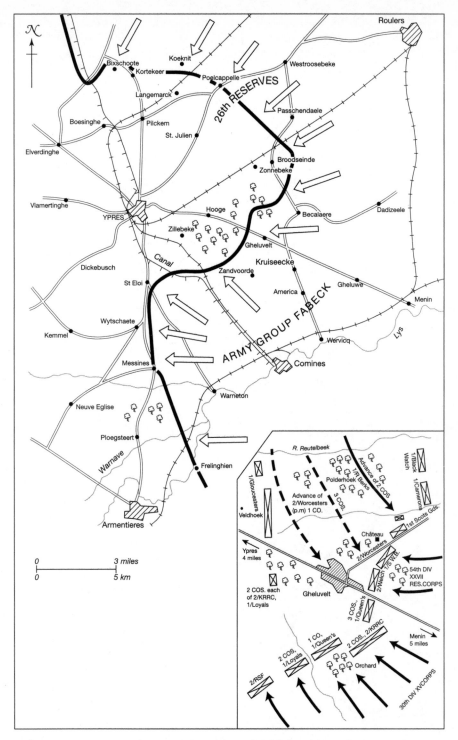

Map 5 Army Group Fabeck and the struggle for Gheluvelt, 31 October 1914

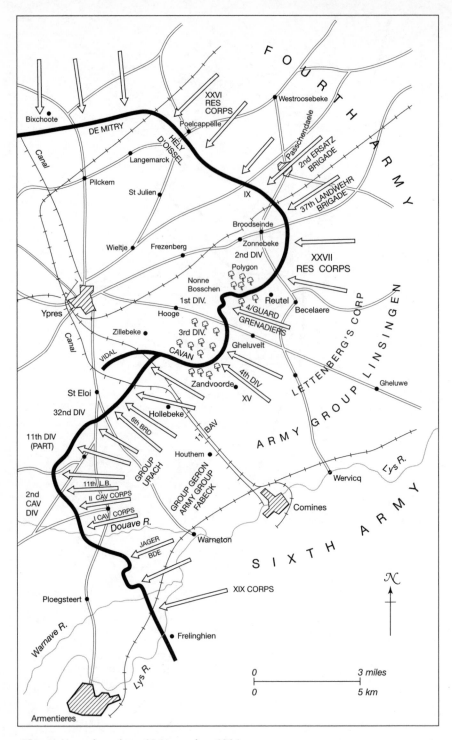

Map 6 Nonnebosschen, 11 November 1914

Illustrations

Abbreviations

Text

AA&QMG Assistant Adjutant and Quartermaster General
ADC Aide de camp
AOK Armee-Oberkommando (Austro-Hungarian High Command)
BBC British Broadcasting Commission
BEF British Expeditionary Force
CID Committee of Imperial Defence
CIGS Chief of the Imperial General Staff
CinC Commander-in-Chief
CO Commanding Officer
CRA Commander, Royal Artillery
CRE Commander, Royal Engineers
CTA County Territorial Association
GHQ General Headquarters (British)
GQG Grand Quartier Général (French High Command)
GSO General Staff Officer
NCO Non Commissioned Officer
OBLI Oxfordshire and Buckinghamshire Light Infantry
OHL Oberste Heeresleitung (German High Command)
POW Prisoner of War
QF Quick Firing (Gun)
RA Royal Artillery
RE Royal Engineers
RFA Royal Field Artillery
RFC Royal Flying Corps
RGA Royal Garrison Artillery
RHA Royal Horse Artillery
RNAS Royal Naval Air Service

SA Sturmabteilung ('Storm Detachment')
SS Schutzstaffel ('Guard Unit')
TF Territorial Force
VC Victoria Cross

Endnotes

BL British Library
CCA Churchill College Archives Centre
HPG Hubert Gough Mss
IWM Imperial War Museum
JEG John Gough Mss
LHCMA Liddell Hart Centre for Military Archives
LUBLLC Leeds University Brotherton Library – Liddle Collection
NAM National Army Museum
NLS National Library of Scotland
OFH British Official History
PRO National Archives (formerly Public Record Office)
SHAT Service Historique de l'Armée de Terre

Note

The text follows the usual convention of rendering German formations in italics to distinguish them from allied formations. Flemish place names are rendered in the version most familiar to British readers both at the time and since so that, for example, Ypres, Messines and Wytschaete are used in preference to Ieper, Mesen and Wijtschate. Times are given according to the twenty-four-hour clock and on British time, contemporary German time being an hour earlier than that of the British.

Introduction

It was early October 1914 and the British Expeditionary Force (BEF) was finally moving forward again. Bathed by bright autumn sunshine, the men of General Sir Horace Smith-Dorrien's II Corps (3rd and 5th Divisions) were marching up the hard, granite-blocked pavé roads of northern France towards the Belgian frontier, which they had last crossed during the great retreat to the south in August 1914. Trains had brought them north from the River Aisne to detrain at Abbeville on 8 and 9 October, and motor buses found by the French had helped speed them to Béthune by 11 October. Ahead of them moved the patrols of Major General Beauvoir de Lisle's 1st Cavalry Division and Major General Hubert Gough's 2nd Cavalry Division, together comprising Lieutenant General Edmund Allenby's newly designated Cavalry Corps, which had marched up from the Aisne in stages starting on 3 October. When Allenby's Cavalry Corps had been instituted, Allenby had picked up the list of new appointments, muttering to his assembled subordinates, 'I see you have become a brigadier. My God, you have been made a brigadier' and so on, until he reached Noel 'Curly' Birch, a gunner who had acted as his GSO1 and who would later be Douglas Haig's CRA: 'Curly, they have actually made you a brigadier too: seems to me they make every bloody fool in France a brigadier nowadays.'[1]

On 10 October Major General William Pulteney's III Corps (4th and 6th Divisions) also began to arrive, detraining at St Omer and beginning to move towards Hazebrouck. Some 50 miles to the north-east of St Omer, Lieutenant General Sir Henry Rawlinson's newly constituted IV Corps (7th Division and 3rd Cavalry Division) was around Ghent following its abortive mission to assist in the defence of Antwerp, which fell to the Germans on 10 October. As yet, Lieutenant General Sir Douglas Haig's I Corps (1st and 2nd Divisions) remained on the Aisne, awaiting relief by the French, so that it, too, could move north: it would begin to do so on 16 October.

Things did not always go perfectly to plan. On the train taking the 2nd Oxfordshire and Buckinghamshire Light Infantry in 5th Brigade north, one man who had climbed on to a 'look-out' on top of a truck was seriously injured when the train entered a tunnel. A coupling on another train broke in a tunnel north of Boulogne, causing a collision and damage to twelve trucks. When about 700 men and all the company officers of the 2nd Coldstream Guards got out at Calais for breakfast in the expectation of having at least half an hour, the train pulled off without them almost at once. As a result, they had to get on the next available train, which proved very crowded. On arrival at Perles, however, Captain Harry Pryce-Jones was able to enjoy his first bath since 11 August. There was also a 'sumptuous dinner' with 'pâté de foie gras, beef and rice, roast mutton, cheese soufflé, champagne, white and red wine, and liqueurs, and coffee'. Comfortably billeted, the Coldstream played cricket in a bowling alley behind their mess.[2] Similarly, Charles Deedes, then attached to GHQ Operations Staff, found a 'delightful', recently vacated, house in Abbeville while en route, occupying the room of one of the family's daughters: 'It was a treat to sleep between sheets again, although it was rather sad to look at all the little pictures on the walls and girlish trifles on the tables, and one wondered what had become of the rightful occupant.' Many men, indeed, enjoyed what they later described as the best period of the whole war.[3]

This was so because, as the marching columns advanced, men were initially struck by the apparent calm of the towns and villages through which they passed. Indeed, when Smith-Dorrien and his staff billeted in a girls' boarding school in Abbeville overnight on 7 October, they discovered the following morning that it was the first day of the new autumn term and that mothers and their daughters were turning up unaware that the school had been taken over. Sergeant Reeve of 16th Battery, Royal Field Artillery (RFA), attached to I Corps had earlier noted of the rail journey north, the 'fine reception all along the line, especially from the women cheering and throwing kisses and getting very excited'. Moving now through Hazebrouck, he found 'all the shops open and business going on as usual', the first time he had seen such scenes since disembarking at Le Havre back in August.[4]

Also at Hazebrouck, and while noting the peaceful scenes, Major 'Ma' Jeffreys of the 2nd Grenadier Guards was astonished at the reaction when one of the battalion's horses broke a leg and had to be shot: 'No sooner was he dead than crowds of inhabitants came rushing with knives and plates and dishes from every direction and in an incredibly short time he was cut up and every bit of meat taken away! Apparently they are great horse eaters hereabouts.' At Bailleul, Captain A.G. Ritchie of the 1st Cameronians (The Scottish Rifles), temporarily attached to 6th Division, passed 'through crowds of smiling friendly people, who poured out coffee and wine and beer for the men'.[5] The GSO1 of 1st Cavalry Division, Archibald Home, similarly found the inhabitants in Belgium 'quite friendly'. Offered lunch in one town, Home and his colleagues discovered their hostess 'very talkative and spent the time cursing the Germans, pressing food and wine on us and scolding her daughter for not waiting properly'. Private Harry Osborne of the 1st East Lancashire Regiment in 4th Division, to whom punctuation was something of a mystery, would certainly have agreed with Home's assessment of the Belgians, finding that 'tobacco is dirt cheap here get handfuls given from every civilian we meet also cigars and food & coffee much cheaper than in France'.[6]

Yet, as the British troops advanced further, and as the fighting began, there was a steady stream of refugees fleeing south. Reeve of the Royal Field Artillery (RFA) saw, 'All classes and conditions and every description of conveyance, prams, bikes, carriages, and even old people being trundled along in wheelbarrows.' Similarly, Major D.G.H.H. Scott-Tucker of the 1st Kings (Liverpool) Regiment, serving in 2nd Division, moving up beyond Hazebrouck after fighting had already occurred, remembered a biblical-like trek of families, fathers leading wagons, mothers and children walking alongside, cows tied to the wagon or driven along behind it, and the wagons 'piled high with all the household goods and the grandfather & mother perched on the top'. These, however, were the better off, the poor being 'in a much worse plight with just the clothes they stood in which was very little and no food most of them weeping & crying out against the Germans . . .' Another officer from 2nd Division, the Hon. J.F. Trefusis of the 1st Irish Guards, later killed while commanding 20th Brigade in October 1915, also noted the refugees: 'All the women had terribly hunted expressions on their faces, and that perhaps more than any other thing else I have seen made one realise the horrors of war.' In the case of the 2nd King's Royal Rifle Corps, the battalion found itself sharing a barn and cottages at Boesinghe with refugees, some cottages having as many as forty-three people inside.[7]

It was also increasingly apparent that the Germans had done great damage to the villages through which they had passed. At Romarin, Osborne of the 1st East Lancashires noted, German *Uhlans* had 'been in here horses in bedrooms and everything upside down have killed their cows etc. ruined home everywhere'. At Steenwerck, the 2nd Royal Welch Fusiliers found the streets littered with clothing, furniture and other household effects, some fouled with excrement. Two girls had been clearly raped and the only house untouched, which had been used as a German staff billet, had an angry crowd of villagers outside it. The Welch put a guard over the house and its woman owner, the regiment's chronicler wryly noting that two years later, when the battalion passed this way again, she was running the BEF Officer's Club.[8]

Not all, however, were entirely sympathetic towards the Belgians. Indeed, the Royal Welch found the Belgians had padlocked their wells at Vlamertinghe to prevent the British using them. While noticing how different the churches were from the 'funny little white-washed things' in France and the different look to the inhabitants, Captain James Patterson, the adjutant of the 1st South Wales Borderers in 3rd Brigade of 1st Division, was enraged by the 'number of able-bodied men in Belgium who are doing nothing. They ought to be able to make a good Division of all those we have seen alone, not to mention the thousands there must be elsewhere.' E. Craig Brown of the 1st Queen's Own Cameron Highlanders, who began the campaign as a company commander and ended it in temporary command of his battalion, was scathing for a different reason. Occupying one farm in October, he noted the Belgians 'were not fond of ventilation'. Staying a few days later in a cottage prompted him to write, 'Cleanliness is not the strong point of these people. Their houses have garrets which look like rag & bone stores you never saw such a collection of filthy rubbish as they collect.'[9]

So the BEF marched north towards what was to become an all too familiar landscape in Flanders, the culmination of the 'race to the sea' around Ypres marking the real transition between the mobile warfare that had been anticipated by European armies prior to the outbreak of war, and the onset of the deadlock that was to characterise the Western Front for the next four years. In July 1920 the War Office's Battles Nomenclature Committee identified four separate battles as having taken place in Flanders in October and November 1914. These comprised the battle of La Bassée from 10 October to 2 November; the battle of Armentières from 13 October to 2 November; the battle of Messines from 12 October to 2 November; and the battle of Ypres from 19 October to 22 November. The latter itself was capable of being subdivided into the three significant battles: Langemarck from 21–24 October, Gheluvelt from 29–31 October and Nonnebosschen on 11 November. As the British Official Historian, Sir James Edmonds, later pointed out, however, it was more appropriate to consider the operations as a whole as one of two phases, the initial advance of the BEF from 12–18 October and the defence of the resulting line against the German Flanders offensive between 19 October and 22 November. The Germans themselves referred to three battles in Flanders: Lille between 15 and 28 October, the Yser between 18 and 30 October, and Ypres between 30 October and 24 November.[10]

Whatever the chosen definition, however, the actions in Flanders between 10 October and 22 November 1914 were of immense significance in closing the last opportunity for open, mobile warfare on the Western Front. On the one hand they were characterised by hand-to-hand combat as evinced by the 'charges' of the 2nd Worcestershire Regiment at Gheluvelt, the 14th London (London Scottish) Regiment at Messines, and the 2nd Oxfordshire and Buckinghamshire Light Infantry at Nonnebosschen, providing traditional artistic images of gallantry. On the other, all combatants became increasingly aware of the shell shortages concomitant with the failure to comprehend the production demands of modern mass industrialised warfare. In the process, the old British regular army was largely destroyed in the defence of Ypres, although the battle also saw the introduction to combat of the Territorial Force (TF) and of an Indian Corps in a European theatre for the first time since a small expeditionary force had been briefly deployed to Malta and Cyprus in 1878.

Ground held at such cost could not thereafter be surrendered lightly and, in any case, the Flanders theatre accorded with the pre-war strategic predilection of many in Britain for a 'Belgian option' conveying a substantial element of independence from the French, then the more significant partner in the allied coalition in terms of land power. While two further battles for Ypres in 1915 and 1917 were to add yet more British blood to the salient, it was still that first battle with its association to the old army that arguably did most to establish the concept of the 'immortal salient'. Indeed, the mythologising of the BEF's struggle to defend Ypres has obscured the major French role let alone that of the Belgians, whose own desperate battle on the Yser was equally dramatic. If there is a degree of mythology in the case of the British, however, Ypres was also of similar significance for the German army. The so-called *kindermord* ('slaughter of the innocents') of the 'school-boy corps' at Langemarck proved in itself an enduring and usable myth kept alive into the Nazi era by the participation of Adolf Hitler serving with the *16th (Bavarian) Reserve Infantry Regiment.*

The First Battle of Ypres, then, is a story worth re-examination, especially as it is one that has not been substantially retold since the publication of Anthony Farrar-Hockley's book, *Death of an Army*, in 1967.[11] Inevitably, many new sources have become available in the last thirty-seven years, not least a considerable body of unpublished primary sources. As the ninetieth anniversary of First Ypres approaches, it seems appropriate to look once more at the moment of transition between war as it had been and war as it would become.

Notes and references

1 Hubert Gough Mss (hereafter HPG), *Beddington Memoirs*, pp. 80–1.

2 A.F. Mockler-Ferryman (ed.) (1920), *The Oxfordshire and Buckinghamshire Light Infantry Chronicle, 1914–1915*, London: Eyre & Spottiswoode, p. 172; Imperial War Museum (hereafter IWM), Horne Mss, Horne to wife, 17 October 1914; 'A Guards Officer at War: The Diary and Letters of Lieutenant Colonel H.M. Pryce-Jones', *The Great War, 1914–1918* 3(3) 1991, pp. 93–4, diary for 15 and 18 October, and letter from Pryce-Jones to his wife, 16 October 1914.

3 General Sir Charles Deedes, 'The View from GHQ', *Stand To* 12, 1984, p. 28; Marquess of Anglesey (1996), *A History of the British Cavalry, 1816–1919 VII: The Curragh Incident and the Western Front, 1914*, London: Leo Cooper, p. 201.

4 General Sir Horace Smith-Dorrien (1925), *Forty-Eight Years' Service*, London: John Murray, p. 440; IWM, Reeve Mss, 90/21/1, diary, 14 and 17 October 1914.

5 J.M. Craster (1976), *Fifteen Rounds a Minute*, London: Macmillan, p. 106; Leeds University Brotherton Library, Liddle Collection (hereafter LUBLLC), Ritchie Mss, GS1361, diary, 14 October 1914.

6 IWM, Home Mss, 82/18/1, diary, 14 October 1914; LUBLLC, Osborne Mss, GS1206, journal, 15 October 1914.

7 IWM, Reeve Mss, 90/21/1, diary, 20 October 1914; ibid., Scott-Tucker Mss, 90/7/1, account; ibid., Trefusis Mss, 82/30/1, diary, 20 October 1914; CQMS H.J. Hopper, 'The Diary of an Old Contemptible' *Stand To* 12, 1984, p. 15.

8 LUBLLC, Osborne Mss, GS1206, journal, 16 October 1914; J.C. Dunn (ed.) (1987), *The War the Infantry Knew, 1914–19*, 2nd edn., London: Jane's, with introduction by Keith Simpson, p. 71.

9 *War Infantry Knew*, p. 71; LUBLLC, Patterson Mss, GS1232, diary, 20 October 1914; IWM, Craig Brown Mss, 92/23/2, diary, 26–28 and 30 October 1914.

10 Brigadier General Sir James Edmonds (1925), *Official History of the Great War: Military Operations France and Belgium, 1914: Volume II: Antwerp, La Bassée, Armetières, Messines, and Ypres October–November 1914* (hereafter OFH) II, London: HMSO, pp. 125–6.

11 Anthony Farrar-Hockley (1967), *Death of an Army*, London: Arthur Barker. Second edition published as *Ypres 1914: Death of an Army*, London: Pan, 1970.

chapter 1

The Belgian option and the race to the sea

Writing to a young woman – Venetia Stanley, with whom he was obsessed – on 2 August 1914, the British Prime Minister, Herbert Asquith, set down, as much for his own benefit as hers, the respective obligations and interests underlying the British position in relation to the deteriorating diplomatic situation in Europe. In his own mind at least there was an obligation to defend Belgium but no actual obligation to France and Russia beyond the 'long standing and intimate relationship' with the former although, in fact, even this really dated only from 1904 and 1907 respectively. Britain's interests, however, in preventing the elimination of France as a great power and in preventing Germany from establishing any hostile bases on the Channel coast were paramount.[1] Britain, indeed, had become a guarantor of Belgian neutrality under the Treaty of London of 1839 but this did not require Britain to act in all circumstances. Moreover, while Britain had grown closer to France, there was still considerable debate as to the appropriate role for a British expeditionary force in any European conflict. The nascent General Staff, gradually established between 1904 and 1906, generally favoured placing the BEF alongside the French army, a view firmly held by the first two Directors of Military Operations in the new structure, Major Generals Sir James Grierson and Sir John Spencer Ewart. Grierson and Ewart, indeed, were careful to maintain unofficial contacts with the French General Staff following the first brief official contacts in 1905.[2]

It was also an end to which the third Director of Military Operations at the War Office, the then Brigadier General Sir Henry Wilson, assiduously worked in drawing up detailed mobilisation schedules and plans between 1910 and 1914. Under these plans, which had been co-ordinated with the French, the BEF would be concentrated at Mauberge, a general assumption being that any German advance into Belgium would be confined to the area south of the Meuse. Ironically, in view of the British government's seemingly wavering commitment to continental involvement, the French had not actually assigned the BEF any specific role once it had reached Mauberge.[3] Neither the existence of Wilson's schedules nor his machinations, however, did of themselves commit the British government to military intervention. Moreover, the French option did not go unchallenged. Even those politicians such as the First Lord of the Admiralty, Winston Churchill, who favoured intervention on the continent, had been made wary by the opposition among many of their own colleagues when the nature of the contacts between the British and French General Staffs had been revealed to the Cabinet in November 1911.[4] Indeed, at a famous meeting of the Committee of Imperial Defence (CID) on 23 August 1911, no actual decision had been reached in terms of any definite commitment of the BEF for all Wilson's skill in presenting the case for the so-called WF ('With France') Plan.

To some, a more attractive option appeared to be sending the BEF into Belgium, a notion that, in August 1914, had the support of the 61-year-old Commander-in-Chief of the BEF, Field Marshal Sir John French. The seeming image of the later 'Blimp' figure, Sir John French was certainly 'un beau sabreur', as James Edmonds once described him, and a man capable of inspiring great affection among ordinary soldiers. The womanising French, who liked to think himself Anglo-Irish, was no intellectual and prone to displays of emotion but, in many respects, he was more imaginative than his eventual successor, Haig. French was also perceptive enough to recognise the changing nature of battle on the Aisne in September 1914 with the onset of siege-type warfare rather than the war of manoeuvre that he had anticipated, though he was anxious to attempt to make movement possible by committing the BEF to the north. French, however, was at best mercurial in temperament and could also be vindictive and more than capable of carrying personal animosities to an extreme. Indeed, his feud with Horace Smith-Dorrien, which dated from at least 1907, was a case in point. Moreover, his apparent backing for the Liberal government at the time of the Curragh incident in March 1914 had greatly damaged his reputation among many of his subordinates. Faced with an apparent order to coerce Ulster into accepting Irish Home Rule, the then Brigadier General Hubert

Gough and fellow officers of the 3rd Cavalry Brigade had threatened to resign their commissions. The depth of support for Gough then forced the Secretary of State for War, J.E.B. Seely, together with French as CIGS and the Adjutant General, Spencer Ewart, to issue a document rejecting any possibility of coercion, the subsequent repudiation of the agreement by the Cabinet compelling all three men to resign. The divisions within the army on what might or might not constitute legitimate orders, however, had been deep, with the ramifications rumbling on well into July 1914.[5]

Prior to his resignation, French had held the post of CIGS since 1912 and had been a permanent member of the CID since 1905. French's strategic ideas did not always display consistency but, having begun his career in the Royal Navy as a naval cadet at Dartmouth at the age of 14, French was more open than some to the notion of amphibious operations. Indeed, Admiral Sir John Fisher once suggested that French was 'almost solitary amongst all the Generals, who all want to play at the German Army'.[6] French had taken part in the deliberations of the CID subcommittee on strategic choices that had examined the Belgian option in 1905 and that had also actually initiated the first staff conversations with the French. Though he had kept in touch with Grierson, however, French did not take part in the subsequent discussions that led to the General Staff concluding the French option preferable due to the Belgians rebuffing British approaches for fear of it compromising their neutrality. The difficulty with the 'Belgian option', indeed, lay in the general uncertainty as to Belgian intentions, the Belgians again rebuffing British approaches in 1912. Moreover, the preliminary planning that was undertaken suggested that the BEF would still need to disembark at French ports whatever the final destination and there were serious doubts as to the efficiency of the Belgian army.[7]

Before the war, Sir John had invariably appeared sufficiently friendly in contacts with French officers observing British manoeuvres for them to assume his general support for close co-operation. In many respects, however, Sir John was motivated rather more by the wish to maintain independence from the French High Command, since Britain would clearly be the junior partner in a wartime alliance. Indeed, he had expressed just such a belief during the deliberations of another CID subcommittee in January 1909, at which point he also favoured holding the BEF in reserve, perhaps at Amiens or even Reims, so that it might be available for operations in Belgium. French, like Churchill, had also questioned Wilson closely at the celebrated meeting in August 1911 and also appears to have convinced Asquith of the merits of the Belgian option. It was French, who as CIGS, initiated the second approach to the Belgians. In short, though French was a continentalist, he was also a nationalist intent on using the BEF in British rather than French interests.[8]

Irrespective of whether Britain was or was not propelled into war primarily by the treaty obligation to Belgium, it certainly let Asquith off the hook with regard to opposition among the Liberals to a continental involvement, and in terms of establishing general popular support for war.[9] It did not resolve the strategic debate, however, and 5 August 1914 saw an extraordinary meeting of a so-called War Council. A variety of prominent military and naval officers – eighteen persons were present – were summoned to meet with Asquith, Churchill and the acting Secretary of State for War, Haldane, and debate the options afresh, notwithstanding the fact that all mobilisation plans were geared to a concentration at Mauberge. To the dismay of Wilson, who characterised the assembly as 'an historic meeting of men, mostly entirely ignorant of their subject', French was able to resurrect the Belgian option by arguing for landing the BEF at, or marching it to, Antwerp although he also suggested that it might be concentrated in a reserve deployment at Amiens in order to see how matters developed. Haig, too, suggested delaying the dispatch of the BEF albeit on the grounds that it would be beneficial to await the arrival of British and imperial forces from overseas. Though Wilson admitted that some thought had now been given by the General Staff to a concentration at Amiens, Antwerp was deemed impossible both on logistic grounds and also through naval fears of operating in confined waters. It was tentatively agreed to send the BEF to France but to leave any decision as to its line of operations until after the French had been consulted. A second meeting of the council on 6 August endorsed an earlier Cabinet decision that day to dispatch only four of the six infantry divisions of the BEF in case the Germans attempted an invasion before the defence of Britain had been properly secured. French as well as Field Marshal Lord Kitchener, who was appointed Secretary of State for War on 5 August, continued to press for concentration at Amiens. On 12 August, however, Wilson and a French delegation finally persuaded Sir John and Kitchener to concentrate at Mauberge as originally intended.[10] Arguably, therefore, British strategic interests were sacrificed to wider alliance considerations, but French was invested by Kitchener with instructions that made clear that his command was an independent one and that he had direct recourse of appeal to the British government in the event of difficulties.

The episode, however, demonstrated Sir John French's continuing commitment to the idea of operating on the allied left flank, a concept revived with the movement of the BEF to Belgium in September 1914 amid the German operations to seize Antwerp.

The German withdrawal from the Marne had begun on 9 September, the army consolidating on the Aisne. The Chief of the German General Staff, Helmuth von Moltke, however, was even prepared to withdraw further if necessary. On 14 September the Prussian minister of war, Erich von Falkenhayn, succeeded Moltke as Chief of Staff though the appointment was not formally announced until 3 November. Falkenhayn remained minister of war.[11] Noticed by the Kaiser for his service in China during the Boxer Rebellion, Falkenhayn had then held a number of staff positions before obtaining the command of the *4th Foot Guards* in 1911. Two years later, the 51-year-old became a surprising choice as minister of war. Falkenhayn was undoubtedly clever but also possessed an arrogant and aloof nature that did not endear him to many within the German army.

Assisted by Colonel Gerhard von Tappen, who remained head of the General Staff's Operations Section, Falkenhayn considered the available options on the night of 14–15 September, particularly in the light of the available railway capacity. He then met the Chancellor, Theobald von Bethmann-Hollweg, and the Secretary of State from the Foreign Office, Gottlieb von Jagow, on the following day to pronounce his judgement on the situation. It was clear that there was a crisis in the West while there was equal uncertainty on the Eastern Front, notwithstanding the German success at Tannenberg between 27 and 30 August and at the Masurian lakes between 9 and 10 September because the Austro-Hungarian army had been checked in Galicia. Both Bethmann-Hollweg and Jagow were insistent that there had to be a swift resolution of the situation in the West in view of the increasing difficulties in the East but neither were optimistic. Falkenhayn, however, still had absolute confidence in the ability of the army to win through, as suggested by the tone of his first order of the day to the army on 15 September.

The key seemed to be moving the *Sixth Army* from the already dead-locked front in Alsace-Lorraine to the north of the *First Army*, whose flank lay largely open between Compiègne and the forces investing Antwerp. Some had favoured using the *Sixth Army* around Verdun, but Falkenhayn opted to commit it to a new quasi-Schlieffenesque envelopment of the allied left. Accordingly, while intending the *First*, *Second* and *Seventh Armies* to consolidate by a partial withdrawal, Falkenhayn ordered a series of local attacks by the *Third, Fourth* and *Fifth Armies* to keep the French occupied so that they did not have the opportunity to pull forces out of the line to be sent to the open flank to the north. The General Staff's railway specialist, Wilhelm Groener, wanted to shift even more corps from the south. However, Lieutenant General Hermann von Kuhl later claimed that, with the exception of General Karl von Bülow of the *Second Army*, the German army commanders were extremely reluctant to release any formations from their own fronts for operations further north.

Falkenhayn's faith in the superiority of the German soldier over his British, French and Belgian opponents was absolute, despite the obvious advantage of the allies in terms of being able to send their own forces north by rail rapidly. Indeed, von Bülow was supported by Tappen, who visited both *First* and *Second Armies* on 15 September, in arguing that the French could always shift troops north faster than the Germans given the north-south alignment of most of the railway lines and that some caution should be exercised. Consequently, while agreeing that troops should be shifted north, von Bülow and Tappen wanted to use the men released for a new effort between Soissons and Reims, especially as rail transport would not be available to begin moving German units north until at least 18 September. Belgian and French lines in German occupied areas had not yet been sufficiently repaired to be of any real use and, in effect, the Germans had only one operational line to carry and supply troops operating in the north. Von Bülow and Tappen also argued that the partial withdrawal Falkenhayn was contemplating would send the wrong signals to Germany's potential allies, Italy and Romania. Faced by these arguments, Falkenhayn momentarily wavered in his resolve and allowed von Bülow to launch an offensive in the Soissons-Reims area on 16 September. With the failure of the *Second Army* to make any progress, however, he ultimately confirmed the move to the north on 25 September, the same day he moved the headquarters of the German High Command or *Oberste Heeresleitung* (OHL) from Luxembourg to Mézières.[12]

Yet, Falkenhayn still allowed himself to be drawn to events in the centre through late September: it was only on 6 October as the offensive of the *Sixth Army* around Arras stalled that he fully committed himself to the seizure of Antwerp and an offensive in Flanders for a drive on the Channel ports. The latter would be undertaken by a new *Fourth Army* drawn from formations which would be released once Antwerp had fallen and from the reserve corps, the creation of which, as minister of war, he had authorised on 16 August. Falkenhayn subsequently rationalised his choice by the suggestion that, believing it impossible to secure any favourable decision on the Eastern Front in view of the advanced state of the year, he was conscious of the importance of threatening Britain through seizure of the Channel coast for operations by submarines, aircraft and airships. At the same time, it would secure his own line of communications through Belgium. The intention was thus to achieve a decision in the north 'as soon as possible and with forces as strong as possible'. At the time, however, it would appear that Falkenhayn was contemplating only the means to bring about a decision in the West rather than embracing any longer-term strategic vision. Moreover, given the fact that the Germans had secured Antwerp, Zeebrugge and Ostend by 10 October, it is not clear what further purpose would have been served by the seizure of Calais and Dunkirk beyond extending the advantage already gained.[13]

As the German *Sixth Army* began its move to the north, initially around Compiègne, it ran into French forces, for the French Commander-in-Chief, Joseph Joffre, had anticipated him to some extent in eyeing the open flank. A man of conviction and strength of character, if also obstinate, Joffre had begun withdrawing divisions from the line before Falkenhayn's spoiling attacks began. These formations were deployed north of the Oise, first as part of General Noel de Castelnau's Second Army on the Somme on 17 September, and then more as Louis de Maud'huy's Tenth Army further north on 2 October. Some four-fifths of the French cavalry was also deployed north of the Oise by the end of September, though those troops furthest to the north were mostly French Territorials. On 26 September Joffre had tried to appoint Ferdinand Foch as his deputy to co-ordinate the actions of Second and Tenth Armies. Solidly set on short and powerful but almost bandy legs, and square-chested, with piercing eyes set beneath a furrowed and wrinkled brow, Foch displayed an extravagant range of hand gestures, and was prone to speaking so rapidly that Englishmen found it hard to understand him. Now 62 – he would turn 63 in November – Foch visibly buzzed with energy. His determination to prevail over the Germans appeared all the stronger from the fact that he had lost both his son, Germain, and his son-in-law, killed in action in August 1914. A devout Catholic, Foch had been all but exiled from his teaching post at the École de Guerre in 1901 for his supposed lack of sympathy with the Republic but had returned to head the school in 1908. He had been commanding a corps in August 1914, being promoted to Tenth Army at the end of August despite sustaining heavy losses.

A number of other French generals, however, were suspicious of the Joffre-Foch axis and, as a result, Foch was merely named Assistant Chief of Staff rather than as Joffre's designated successor on 4 October.

Foch was told, 'Go and see the situation, and do your best.' Arriving at de Castelnau's headquarters at Breteuil at 0400 on 5 October, Foch found the Second Army commander, who had also lost two of his sons in action, engaged in heavy fighting between Arras and the Oise and contemplating a withdrawal south of the Somme. De Castelnau, previously Foch's superior, was roundly directed to 'search his mind and call upon his imagination for means which will enable his troops to hold out until the crisis is over'. Subsequently, Joffre, who was also alarmed at de Castelnau's state of mind, removed the Second Army's Chief of Staff, Anthoine, feeling that an army he had intended to envelop the Germans was itself being enveloped. Foch then moved on to meet a more optimistic de Maud'huy some 60 miles away at Aubigny at 0900. Some of de Maud'huy's staff overheard Foch telling their chief that the only three ways to fight were to attack, hold on, or clear out and the last he forbade. By the time he reached his own new headquarters at Doullens on 6 October, Foch had driven 530 miles in 57 hours.[14]

On 11 October Foch became head of the French Northern Army Group and, though he had no formal powers in this respect, it was clear that Joffre intended Foch also to co-ordinate the operations of the Belgians and British, the latter of course also now moving north. Indeed, it was a measure of the problem that, while marching north with his cavalry, Hubert Gough had been told by Sir John not to accede to any request for help from the French 'which would draw me into action on their behalf'. In the event, de Castelnau arrived to see Gough in company with his British liaison officer, C.B. Thompson, on 7 October to ask for help and Gough agreed to stay his march for a day to help out the French behind Roye.[15]

French had wanted for some time to withdraw the BEF from the Aisne to the north, which would greatly ease the supply problems by positioning it closer to the Channel ports as well as enabling the British to support Antwerp. The lines of communication had certainly been disrupted to a major extent during the retreat in August and the French had not always proved amenable to giving the BEF any kind of priority in the use of the railway system on the Aisne. A move would also enable French to 'regain my original position on the left flank' of the French armies. Moreover, with the 7th and 8th Divisions being readied for embarkation and the Indian Corps en route to France, it would make sense to concentrate the BEF. It has also been suggested that, as a cavalryman, French wanted a more open theatre of operations for his cavalry than the crowded Aisne.[16] French himself later suggested he had become anxious about the security of the Channel coast on 16 September when Thompson, then acting as liaison officer with the French Sixth Army, reported that the Germans were already on the allied left flank. Churchill, with whom French discussed the move on 27 September, strongly favoured the scheme, seeing the value of the BEF regaining an independent offensive role and operating on the coast with the support of his own 'Dunkirk circus' of marines and Royal Naval Air Service (RNAS) armoured cars and aircraft and the guns of the Royal Navy's monitors. So, too, had Henry Wilson when consulted three days earlier. Indeed, Wilson, who drafted a suitable document to be put to Joffre, seems also to have discussed the move to the left with Churchill even earlier than French.[17] French therefore raised the issue with Joffre, writing on 29 September that with the BEF consolidated, 'my freedom of action, field of operations, and power of initiative will increase out of all proportion to the numerical increase in Corps'. According to Asquith, French would be able to carry out 'a great outflanking march' and sweep to a line across Belgium from Brussels to Cologne, relieving Antwerp en route.[18]

Accepting the logic but disagreeing with the timing, not least because the French armies on both flanks of the BEF were still under attack and he was also dealing with de Castelnau's anxieties, Joffre somewhat reluctantly gave his consent once he understood that he could not block a move supported by the British government. Suggesting Lille as the area for the BEF's concentration, Joffre insisted, however, that the BEF move by instalments in a way which would actually strengthen his own planned envelopment of the Germans rather than allow Sir John a fully independent role. Joffre finally agreed to the move on 1 October but no railway transport was immediately available.[19] Thus, II Corps entrained on 4 October and III Corps on 7 October. It had been intended to go as far as St Omer before detraining but it was already apparent that the Germans were also active in the area, hence the decision to put the troops off the trains at Abbeville.[20]

Subsequently, though the BEF's move did fulfil his strategic purpose to some extent, Joffre was to complain in his memoirs that the French were forced back on the Aisne following the departure of the British. Moreover, the key railway junction of Lille was lost on 12 October with some 4500 men taken prisoner, because the allocation of the available trains to the

BEF prevented him from sending French troops north to secure the city, disrupting all rail transport for ten days. Joffre was also somewhat suspicious of having the BEF operating out on the left with no French troops between it and the Channel ports.[21] In fact, rail transport was critical to the 'race to the sea', some seventy allied divisions totalling some 800,000 men being carried north between 14 September and 17 November over distances varying from 40 to 350 miles in over 6000 train movements at an average of twenty-three movements a day. The rail transport of I Corps alone involved fifty-one trains for combatants and thirteen for supplies, each train consisting of fifty wagons and trucks. That of the Lahore Division involved eighteen troop and fourteen supply trains.[22]

Joffre had only ever been really interested in maximising the British commitment to France under French strategic direction, which did not equate to safeguarding British as opposed to French strategic interests. Relations had become strained under the pressure of the 'great retreat' in August 1914, not least when French had interpreted his obligation to ensure the safety of the BEF and of the Channel ports in terms of continuing to retreat towards Amiens and Le Havre rather than participating in Joffre's planned counter-offensive. In the event, political necessity had led the Cabinet to dispatch Kitchener on 1 September to order French to remain in the line. The meeting did little to ameliorate French's antagonism towards Kitchener, who chose to wear his Field Marshal's uniform for the occasion, or to reverse the mutual distrust between French and Joffre. Now, on 10 October, Wilson noted that Sir John was getting 'decidedly more difficult in his attitude to the French', demanding that Joffre send I Corps north at once and also refusing another request to help out de Maud'huy around Béthune.[23]

As both sides endeavoured to move to the north in search of an open flank, the position of the Belgian army at Antwerp appeared ever more problematic, attempted sorties by the Belgians from the fast-decreasing perimeter around the city failing on 24 August and 11–12 September. As described somewhat melodramatically by one American war correspondent on the latter occasion, the Belgians advanced into a virtual trap: 'The whole German front, which for several hours past had replied but feebly to the Belgian fire, spat a continuous stream of lead and flame. The rolling crash of musketry and the ripping snarl of machine guns were stabbed by the vicious pom-pom-pom of the quick-firers. From every window of the three-storied [Linterport] chateau opposite us the lean muzzles of mitrailleuses poured out their hail of death. I have seen fighting on four continents but I have never witnessed so deadly a fire as that which wiped out the head of the Belgian column.'[24]

The German *III Reserve Corps* of General Hans von Beseler, a 64-year-old Pomeranian former chief of the engineer corps and inspector general of fortifications who had won the Iron Cross in the Franco-Prussian War, began to bombard the city on 28 September. In addition, Beseler had a naval force, an *Ersatz* division and three *Landwehr* brigades. Heavy German artillery had already demonstrated its potential at Liège in August and again at Mauberge, which, having been isolated behind German lines for some weeks, finally surrendered on 8 September. The obsolete fortifications of Antwerp presented little obstacle to the formidable array of guns available to Beseler though his actual attacking force was relatively weak in numbers. Indeed, Beseler had only six divisions when, prior to the war, German planning had anticipated five corps being required to take Antwerp. However, under the punishing artillery fire, the Belgians made early preparations for a retreat to Ostend, warning the British ambassador, Sir Francis Villiers, as well as the French ambassador, on 30 September, that a German breach of the line of the outer forts would precipitate withdrawal. In the hope of at least prolonging the defence until the BEF was deployed to the north and might mount a relief, the Cabinet agreed on 1 October to send the 7th Division provided Joffre also provided a regular division. Despite the French Minister of War, Alexandre Millerand, impressing on Joffre the political necessity of supporting the Belgians, Joffre promised only the 87th Territorial Division and a marine fusilier brigade, leading Kitchener to counsel that it would be better to keep back the British force rather than risk its loss.[25]

Joffre felt the enterprise doomed from the beginning but the British intention to put in troops exerted pressure. Accordingly, Joffre sent General Paul Pau to report on the situation, in the hope that Pau could persuade the Belgians to release their field army from the city for operations in conjunction with the French and British to the south. Insisting on 7 October that the real purpose should be to facilitate a junction of the allied armies, Joffre limited the 87th Territorial Division to the Poperinghe area and sent only the marine fusiliers into the city itself. Indeed, Joffre did not believe that any relief attempt should interfere with his strategy of envelopment, especially when both de Castelnau and de Maud'huy were actually losing ground. As far as Joffre was concerned, the British desire to save Antwerp was merely 'traditional dogma' regarding keeping the city out of hostile hands while, having shut itself up in Antwerp when superior in numbers to its opponents, the Belgian army had forfeited any role commensurate with its strength. In some respects Joffre was justified, for Antwerp could only have been realistically maintained if the allies had supplied it by sea and thus violated Dutch neutrality.[26]

With the German assault intensifying on 1 and 2 October, the Belgian government was evacuated from the city though no decision was actually taken with regard to the Belgian field army. On 3 October, however, the field army withdrew to a second defensive line between Termonde and the Nèthe. King Albert I of the Belgians, who was his own CinC, was determined to stay to the last and, indeed, to share the fate of the garrison. His Prime Minister, Baron Charles de Broqueville, who also acted as war minister, and the King's private secretary, Jules Inglenbleek, tried to persuade Albert otherwise.[27] De Broqueville, however, apparently told Villiers that the army would begin its withdrawal on 3 October, conveying this to London by telegram. While Joffre welcomed this as a means of uniting the allied armies in the field, the reaction in London was very different. With Asquith absent, fulfilling a political engagement at Cardiff, a hasty meeting between Churchill, Kitchener, the Foreign Secretary, Sir Edward Grey, and the First Sea Lord, Prince Louis of Battenberg, decided to send immediate reinforcements to Antwerp, with Churchill himself also going to Antwerp. The First Lord had been on his way for a weekend inspection visit to Dunkirk when recalled to London and appears to have decided on his mission despite the advice of Grey and Kitchener to the contrary. Indeed, it was suggested at the time that even Villiers was not informed of Churchill's mission and had begun burning his files. Churchill had been concerned about Antwerp and the Channel ports for some weeks, having raised the possibility of sending British Territorials to reinforce the Belgians, and even making the improbable suggestion to transport Russian troops there from Archangel.[28]

On arrival at Antwerp, Churchill made an arrangement with de Broqueville. The defence of the city would be prolonged for at least ten days. But, if the British government could not state definitely what steps they would undertake to relieve the city within three days, the Belgians were free to evacuate it, upon which British troops would be sent to Ghent to cover the withdrawal. Having been briefly sent to Ostend by Churchill in late August, a Royal Marine Brigade – many of them aged reservists or new recruits – and the Queen's Own Oxfordshire Hussars, the first Territorial Force unit to see active service, had been landed at Dunkirk in early September.

According to Asquith, Kitchener had been glad to be rid of the yeomen, who included Churchill's brother, Jack.[29] On 28 September one of the marine battalions had been sent forward to Lille with the remainder pushing forward to Cassel two days later. Patrols were sent out in buses and on bicycles while the RNAS armoured cars of Commander C.R. Samson motored further afield, engaging advanced German cavalry patrols. The marines would now be sent to Antwerp with the addition of two naval brigades. The latter would be taken from the newly constituted Royal Naval Division – Churchill's 'Sea-dogs' as the former First Sea Lord, Sir John Fisher, called them – and drawn from those naval reservists surplus to manning ship requirements on mobilisation, supplemented by New Army volunteers. They were, however, only partially trained as infantrymen and lacked equipment of all kinds including ammunition pouches, greatcoats, and water bottles, some even reportedly having to slip bayonets through their belts or tying them on belts with string. Asquith himself considered it 'idle butchery' to send the marines to Antwerp but this did not apparently induce him to make any objection, possibly because he was wrongly informed by Churchill that all recruits would be left behind and only 'seasoned reservists' taken. The American military attaché in London, Lieutenant Colonel Thomas Treadwell, who had concluded a little unjustly that the BEF as a whole was not ready for war in August 1914, was especially critical of the dispatch of the marines to Antwerp.[30]

The 7th Division with the addition of the 3rd Cavalry Division was to land at Ostend. The French would also provide the territorial division and marine brigade they had previously pledged. In all, some 53,700 men and seventy-five guns would be available once all had arrived, the French providing 23,500 men and forty guns and the British the remainder. Conceivably prompted by the favourable evaluation of such a possibility by the War Office representative in Antwerp, Colonel A.G. Dallas, Kitchener also appears to have hoped that Antwerp could be held long enough for the BEF formations coming north to be thrown directly into a relief effort, a mission that would actually have negated the intended outflanking operation.[31]

In typically extravagant style Churchill sent a telegram to Asquith at 0800 on 5 October offering his resignation as First Lord in order to take personal command of the British forces at Antwerp. Asquith indicated he must return to the Admiralty, despite Kitchener's apparent willingness to make Churchill a Lieutenant General. Indeed, when Churchill's telegram was read in the Cabinet, it produced merely 'a Homeric laugh'. Rawlinson was ordered to take command of British forces at Antwerp and Ostend.[32] With the three days stipulated in Churchill's agreement with the Belgians expiring on 6 October and without any British troops having thus far reached Ghent, the Belgians began to withdraw to the left bank of the Schelde. Before leaving Antwerp for Ostend that day, Churchill directed the 53-year-old Brigadier General Archibald Paris, acting commander of the Royal Naval Division following the illness of Sir George Aston, that he must not be caught in any capitulation of the city.

Meanwhile, Major General Thompson Capper's 7th Division was disembarking at Zeebrugge. Most recently Inspector of Infantry, Tommy Capper was the epitome of the 'offensive spirit'. Almost ludicrously brave, Capper was to be killed at Loos in September 1915. Considered by Haig 'too full of nerves and too much of a crank to get the best out of officers', Capper was certainly not the easiest of commanders, spectacularly falling out with his Chief of Staff, Hugo Montgomery, in November 1914 and demanding his removal after having already threatened to remove all his three brigade commanders in October.[33] Mindful of his orders not to get shut up in Antwerp, Capper declined to entrain immediately for the city as the Belgian authorities in Zeebrugge wished. In any case, he soon received Rawlinson's instructions to proceed to Bruges, Albert having requested that the British secure Ghent and the Belgian line of retreat.[34] No other allied troops had yet appeared. Joffre had the French 87th Territorial Division landed at Dunkirk and then sent it to Poperinghe to facilitate the Belgian field army's retirement rather than to relieve the city. Consequently, no advance to the relief of Antwerp could be realistically contemplated with a single division. The 51-year-old Major General the Hon. Julian Byng's understrength 3rd Cavalry Division finally began to disembark on 8 October, much of the harness being deficient or too small: the 1st Royal Dragoons and the 10th Hussars had only arrived back in England from overseas garrisons four days earlier. Like Capper, Byng was also extraordinarily courageous, ordering some coffee in a café near Kemmel on 21 October and insisting on drinking it at a table set up in full view of the Germans.[35]

That same day, Paris concluded that the defence of the city could not be carried on much longer and informed the Belgians that, in compliance with his instructions, he would withdraw. Churchill, whom Paris contacted personally by telephone, was furious with the decision, which effectively forced the hand of the senior Belgian commander in Antwerp, General Deguise.[36] In fact, Kitchener had already made a similar deduction to Paris and his orders for the withdrawal of the Royal Naval Division crossed with Paris's call to London. Unfortunately, three battalions of the 1st Naval Brigade lost contact with the remainder of the force and, rather than surrender to the Germans, marched into internment across the Dutch frontier. Part of the rearguard battalion of the Royal Marine Brigade was also forced to surrender on 9 October. The city was formally surrendered on 10 October, freeing Beseler to march on Zeebrugge and Ostend, the latter being occupied on 15 October. Subsequently, however, the first attempt by Beseler's *III Reserve Corps* to force the Belgian positions on the Yser failed on 18 October. Nieuport with the vital locks and sluices that controlled the drainage of the low-lying area next to the sea remained in Belgian hands.

Dixmude, not much more than a large village, dependent before the war on salt-marsh mutton and butter, was held by the French Marine Fusilier Brigade commanded by Rear Admiral Pierre Ronarc'h. Ronarc'h was a short and sturdy 49-year-old Breton torpedo and mine specialist who had seen land-based service in the China Relief Expedition of 1900 and was the youngest general officer in the navy. Composed of some 6000 surplus seamen – mostly Breton reservists – rather than trained marines and hastily put together in just two weeks, it had been previously intended for the defence of Antwerp but, as with the French Territorials, Joffre had had no intention of committing it to a relief operation. For the Frenchmen, Dixmude was to become a 'raft of suffering at the entrance to the delta of marshes, watched over by ancient windmills with shattered wings'.[37]

Albert, who had been persuaded not to stay in the city by his Queen, left Antwerp on horseback in the company of Pau. He had decided to lead his army towards the coast since there were clearly German forces between the Schelde and the Lys. But he also distrusted the French and preferred to keep in touch with the British, though he and his military adviser, Emile Galet, had placed too much faith in the British ability to sustain the defence of Antwerp. Above all, Albert believed it vital to remain on Belgian soil and, of course, Belgium was still technically a neutral, not having declared war on Germany, and therefore an associated rather than an allied power. On 9 October Pau presented a demand from Joffre to the Belgian government that the Belgian army should not retreat to the coast. At a meeting at Ostend on the following day attended by Rawlinson, de Broqueville and the Belgian Deputy Chief of Staff, Lieutenant Colonel Wielemans, who had formerly been head of de Broqueville's military cabinet, Pau attempted to persuade Albert to give up personal command of his army and send it into

France to operate between Calais and St Omer with Boulogne as its base. When rebuffed, Pau insisted that the Belgians mount an offensive towards the line Poperinghe-Ypres-Poelcappelle after 48 hours' rest, which Albert also resisted, despite de Broqueville's support for the Frenchman, on the grounds that the army was incapable of offensive operations without more rest. By this time, too, Albert, who already enjoyed a stormy relationship with de Broqueville, had taken a violent dislike to the French military attaché at his headquarters, Eugène Génie, whom he described as an untrustworthy dog. Génie's predecessor, Colonel Aldebert, had resigned when Albert had declined to follow his advice and had retired with his army into Antwerp. The Belgian ministers, however, did agree to ask the French government to extend their hospitality to them by allowing them to install a government in exile at Le Havre, whence they proceeded without Albert on 13 October.[38]

In the meantime, Albert had agreed on 12 October to accept general directions from the French High Command or Grand Quartier Général (GQG) on the same basis as did the BEF, namely the right to retain independence if it was considered national interests were at stake.[39] On the same day his ministers left Ostend, Albert issued a proclamation to his army, indicating that anyone who spoke of retreat would be considered a traitor. On 15 October Albert also met every divisional commander to warn them they would be dismissed if they abandoned their positions.

There was then a meeting at Furnes on 16 October between Albert and Foch, newly tasked by Joffre with co-ordinating the allied armies in the north. According to Albert's account, Foch asked if the Belgians would continue to resist, to which the King replied that he would but that a major effort was not possible and that help was needed. Foch, who insisted the German forces in the area were second-class formations, promised help within 48 hours though it was not until 23 October that the 42nd Division arrived. Even then Albert did not believe his own army capable of an offensive and he deplored the continuing French commitment to such a course of action. Nonetheless, Foch found Albert far more resolute than any of his subordinates though he wrote to Joffre that it would be best to have some French troops on the left of the Belgians, hence Joffre's readiness to dispatch the 42nd Division under the 55-year-old taciturn and imperturbable Corsican, Grossetti. On one occasion, indeed, Grossetti was to be found during the subsequent battle on the Yser calmly directing his men while sitting on a chair in the middle of a crossroads under fire. According to the account of the only Frenchman present with Foch, Lieutenant Colonel Brécard, Albert expressed his high regard for Foch, but an account by Galet suggested Albert had a less laudatory opinion of the Frenchman and his demands.[40]

The British generally blamed the lack of French co-operation for the loss of Antwerp.[41] Certainly, the same failures of allied co-operation that had already marked the conduct of the campaign in August and September had resulted in both the fall of Antwerp and also the loss of any opportunity of freeing a larger area of Belgium from German occupation through securing the northern flank. Allied intentions were too divergent, their military efforts too dissipated as a result, condemning them for the next four years to the increasingly costly endeavour to regain the territory they might have so easily won.

Meanwhile, while Sir John French had, initially reluctantly, accepted the need to relieve Antwerp and had tried unsuccessfully to use the situation to pressure Joffre into agreeing to a quicker transit north for the BEF, he doubted the wisdom of putting mobile forces into Antwerp. He also feared that heavy guns sent to the city would be lost and, in any case, felt his move to the left flank would be the best way of relieving the city.[42] French was also frustrated by Kitchener's involvement and Rawlinson's apparently independent role, claiming not to have been kept fully informed. Indeed, French not only complained to Churchill about Kitchener's 'pinpricks' on 5 October but also sent Rawlinson an ill-natured telegram on 11 October, 'I really do not understand whether you regard yourself as under my orders or not; but if you do, please be good enough to explain your situation clearly without delay . . .' Similarly, Henry Wilson noted that a telegram from Kitchener on 6 October about the deployment of the BEF infuriated French who 'lost his temper & stormed up & down like an idiot' while Smith-Dorrien had noted on 11 October that French was 'displeased at times by Lord K's desperate interference'. Kitchener, however, tried to mollify French by indicating that the Cabinet had initially refused to allow the 7th Division to be used for more than a few days at Antwerp, but that circumstances then resulted in a change of policy, enabling it to be put at French's disposal.[43]

Significantly, this came two days after Rawlinson had formally passed under the direct command of French, Kitchener feeling obliged to leave Rawlinson's force in Belgium when he had originally intended to withdraw it once Antwerp was safe.[44] Rawlinson's two divisions – now formally constituted as IV Corps – were ordered to hold Ghent and Bruges as long as possible then retire on the line St Omer-Dunkirk. With the Belgian field army that had escaped Antwerp beginning to reconcentrate around Ostend and Dixmude, then retiring on the line Dixmude-Furnes with its base at Dunkirk, Rawlinson began to pull back from Ghent as there was at least a 10-mile gap between him and the Belgians. He reached Ypres on 14 October, linking with Allenby's cavalry in advance of the BEF arriving from the Aisne.

German cavalry and cyclists had briefly passed through Ypres on 7 October. Informing the burgomaster that they would be there for three days, the Germans had levied a sum of 70,000 francs for the town's good behaviour, this representing 5000 more than was available in the municipal treasury. The Germans also wrecked the town's telegraph system but, on arriving with Rawlinson's force, 7th Signal Company was able to patch through a telephone line the Germans had missed at the railway station to Poperinghe. Supposedly, the local inhabitants had placed straw in the mouths of the two stone lions on either side of the passageway through the old ramparts known as the Menin Gate in the belief that the Germans would not enter the town until the lions had eaten the straw.[45] Though the straw had not prevented the brief occupation, the Germans were not to enter the town again.

Notes and references

1 Michael and Eleanor Brock (eds.) (1982), *H.H. Asquith: Letters to Venetia Stanley*, Oxford: Oxford University Press, pp. 145–7.

2 Hew Strachan (2002), 'The Continental Commitment, 1904–14' in David French and Brian Holden Reid (eds.), *The General Staff: Reform and Innovation, 1890–1939*, London: Frank Cass, pp. 75–94.

3 William Philpott (1996), *Anglo-French Relations and Strategy on the Western Front, 1914–1918*, Basingstoke: Macmillan, p. 6.

4 Keith Wilson (1977), 'The War Office, Churchill and the Belgian Option, August to December 1911', *Bulletin of the Institute of Historical Research* **50**, pp. 218–28 (also reproduced in Keith Wilson (ed.), *Empire and Continent*, London: Mansell, 1987, pp. 126–40).

5 See Ian F.W. Beckett (1986), *The Army and the Curragh Incident, 1914*, London: Bodley Head for Army Records Society.

6 Ian F.W. Beckett, 'Selection by Disparagement: Lord Esher, the General Staff and the Politics of Command, 1904–14' in Holden Reid and French, *British General Staff*, pp. 41–56; ibid., 'Haig and French' in Brian Bond and Nigel Cave (eds.) (1999), *Haig: A Reappraisal 70 Years On*, Barnsley: Leo Cooper, pp. 51–63.

7 William Philpott, 'The General Staff and the Paradoxes of Continental War' in French and Holden Reid, *British General Staff*, pp. 95–111.

8 William Philpott (1989), 'The Strategic Ideas of Sir John French', *Journal of Strategic Studies* 12, pp. 455–78.

9 Michael Brock (1990), 'Britain enters the War' in R.J.W. Evans and H. Pogge von Strandemann (eds.), *The Coming of the First World War*, 2nd edn., Oxford: Oxford University Press, pp. 145–78; Keith Wilson (1995), 'Britain' in Keith Wilson (ed.), *Decisions for War, 1914*, London: UCL Press, pp. 175–208; Trevor Wilson (1979), 'Britain's Moral Commitment to France in July 1914', *History* 64, pp. 380–90.

10 Philpott, *Anglo-French Relations*, pp. 8–11; R.A. Prete (1989), 'French Strategic Planning and the Deployment of the BEF in France in 1914', *Canadian Journal of History* 24, pp. 42–62.

11 Erich von Falkenhayn (1920), *The German General Staff and its Decisions, 1914–16*, New York: Dodd, Mead & Co., pp. 1–2.

12 *Der Weltkrieg 1914–1918 dem deutschen Volke dargestelt von Hermann von Kuhl*, Berlin: Verlag Tradition Wilhelm Kolk (1929) I, Pt. II, p. 71; Robert Foley (2000), 'East or West: General Erich von Falkenhayn and German Strategy, 1914–15' in Matthew Hughes and Matthew Seligmann (eds.), *Leadership in Conflict, 1914–18*, Barnsley: Leo Cooper, pp. 117–38; Jean Ratinaud (1967), *La Course à la Mer*, Paris: Fayard, pp. 46–9, 131; Hew Strachan (2001), *The First World War: To Arms*, Oxford: Oxford University Press, pp. 265–6.

13 Falkenhayn, *German General Staff*, pp. 13, 17, 30; Reichsarchiv (1929), *Der Weltkrieg, 1914–1918*, Berlin: Mittler & Sohn, V, pp. 63, 272–82; Holger Afflerbach (1996), *Falkenhayn: Politisches Denken und Handeln im Kaiserriech*, 2nd edn., Munich: R. Oldenbourg Verlag, pp. 190–4; Strachan, *First World War*, p. 270.

14 Basil Liddell Hart (1931), *Foch: The Man of Orleans*, London: Eyre & Spottiswoode, p. 123; Ferdinand Foch (trans. by T. Bentley Mott) (1931), *The Memoirs of Marshal Foch*, New York: Doubleday, pp. 120, 123; Marshal Joseph Joffre (trans. by T. Bentley Mott) (1932), *The Personal Memoirs of Joffre*, I, New York: Harper & Brothers, pp. 293–8; Sir George Aston (1930), *The Biography of the Late Marshal Foch*, London: Hutchinson, pp. 128–9, 137.

15 General Sir Hubert Gough (1931), *The Fifth Army*, London; Hodder & Stoughton, p. 55.

16 Joffre, *Memoirs*, I, pp. 299–300; Everard Wyrall (1921), *The History of the Second Division, 1914–18*, I, London: Thomas Nelson & Sons, pp. 101–2; Farrar-Hockley, *Ypres 1914*, p. 41; Ian Malcolm Brown (1998), *British Logistics on the Western Front, 1914–19*, Westport: Praeger, p. 62.

17 Field Marshal Lord French (1919), *1914*, Boston: Houghton Mufflin, pp. 157, 166; IWM, Wilson Mss, DS/MISC/80, diary, 24 September 1914; ibid., HHW 2/73/62, Note by Wilson, 29 September 1914 and French to Joffre, 29 September 1914.

18 IWM, French Mss, 75/46/6, French to Kitchener, 28 and 29 September 1914; French, *1914*, pp. 167–8; Brock and Brock, *Asquith*, p. 256.

19 IWM, Wilson Mss, HHW 2/73/63 and 65, Joffre to French, 30 September and 1 October 1914; National Archives, formerly Public Record Office (hereafter PRO), WO95/1, CinC's War Diary, 30 September, 2 and 3 October 1914; ibid., Kitchener Mss, PRO30/57/49, WA29, French to Kitchener, 1 October 1914; French, *1914*, pp. 167–74; Joffre, *Memoirs*, I, pp. 300–4; Philpott, *Anglo-French Relations*, p. 36.

20 IWM, Wilson Mss, HHW 2/73/69, Joffre to French, 4 October 1914; Smith-Dorrien, *Forty-Eight Years*, p. 440.

21 Joffre, *Memoirs*, I, pp. 303–4; IWM, Wilson Mss, HHW 2/73/69, Joffre to French, 4 October 1914.

22 Ratinaud, *Course*, p. 72; Service Historique de l'Armée de Terre (hereafter SHAT), 18N 134, Joffre to Foch, 11 October and 15 October 1914.

23 Philpott, *Anglo-French Relations*, pp. 15–30; IWM, Wilson Mss, DS/MISC/80, diary, 10 October 1914; National Library of Scotland (hereafter NLS), Haig Mss, Acc 3155/98, diary, 11 October 1914.

24 Léon Van Der Essen (1917), *The Invasion and the War in Belgium from Liège to the Yser*, London: T. Fisher Unwin, p. 225.

25 Martin Gilbert (1972), *Winston S. Churchill*, Vol. III 1914–16, Companion Pt. I, London: Heinemann, pp. 153–4; Brock and Brock, *Asquith*, pp. 257–8.

26 Ministère de la Guerre, État-Major de l'Armée – Service Historique (1934), *Les Armées Françaises dans la Grande Guerre*, I, Pt. IV, Paris: Imprimerie Nationale, pp. 285–7; Joffre, *Memoirs*, I, pp. 305–7; Strachan, *First World War*, p. 272.

27 Marie-Rose Thielemans (ed.) (1991), *Albert Ier: Carnets et Correspondance de Guerre, 1914–1918*, Paris and Louvain: Éditions Duculot, p. 40; Marie-Rose Thielemans and Emile Vandewoude (eds.) (1982), *Le Roi Albert: Au Travers de ses lettres inédites, 1882–1916*, Brussels: Office International de Librairie, pp. 525–8.

28 OFH, pp. 39–40; Gilbert, *Churchill Companion*, pp. 156–7, 174–5; Essen, *Invasion and War in Belgium*, pp. 249–50; Philpott, *Anglo-French Relations*, pp. 32–3; Winston S. Churchill (1923), *The World Crisis*, I, New York: Scribner's Sons, pp. 366–8.

29 Gilbert, *Churchill Companion*, pp. 160–1; Brock and Brock, *Asquith*, p. 247.

30 Essen, *Invasion and War in Belgium*, p. 254; Brock and Brock, *Asquith*, pp. 257–8, 275–6; US National Archives, War College Division File 8759–36, Entry 296, Record Group 165, Report by Treadwell, 18 November 1914.

31 Gilbert, *Churchill Companion*, p. 162; PRO, WO32/5086, Kitchener to French, 2 and 3 October 1914; Dallas to Kitchener, 4 October 1914.

32 Churchill to Asquith, 5 October 1914 in Gilbert, *Churchill Companion*, p. 163; Brock and Brock, *Asquith*, pp. 262–3.

33 PRO, WO95/1627, Montgomery to Edmonds, 4 February 1921; National Army Museum (hereafter NAM), Rawlinson Mss, 5201-33-17, Capper to Rawlinson, 7 November 1914; Churchill College Archives Centre (hereafter CAC), Rawlinson Mss, RWLN 01/001, Wilson to Rawlinson, 30 and 31 October 1914; Keith Simpson (1973), 'Capper and the Offensive Spirit', *Journal of the Royal United Services Institute for Defence Studies* **118**, 2, pp. 51–6.

34 C.T. Atkinson (1927), *The Seventh Division, 1914–18*, London: John Murray, p. 10; Thielemans, *Albert*, p. 174.

35 Anglesey, *History of Cavalry*, p. 204; Toby Rawlinson (1925), *Adventures on the Western Front: August 1914 to June 1915*, London: Andrew Melrose, p. 201.

36 Brock and Brock, *Asquith*, pp. 267–8.

37 Charles Le Goffre (1916), *Dixmude*, Philadelphia: J.B. Lippincott, pp. 2–3, 26, 42, 48.

38 Thielemans, *Albert*, pp. 41–2, 174–6; Thielemans and Vandewoude, *Roi Albert*, pp. 527–9; William Philpott, 'Britain, France and the Belgian Army' in Brian Bond (ed.) (1999), *Look To Your Front: Studies in the First World War*, Staplehurst: Spellmount, pp. 121–36; Emile Cammaerts (1935), *Albert of Belgium: Defender of the Right*, New York: Macmillan, pp. 182–5.

39 *Armées Françaises* I, Pt. IV, p. 265.

40 Thielemans, *Albert*, p. 179; Thielemans and Vandewoude, *Roi Albert*, pp. 531–2, 534; Foch, *Memoirs*, p. 136; Joffre, *Memoirs*, I, p. 314; Ratinaud, *Course*, pp. 267, 282.

41 Gilbert, *Churchill Companion*, pp. 183–8; IWM, French Mss, 75/46/11, Kitchener to French, 10 and 11 October 1914; ibid., PP/MCR/C33, Kitchener to French, 11 October 1914; Brock and Brock, *Asquith*, pp. 267–8.

42 PRO, WO33/713, French to Kitchener, 6 and 7 October 1914; IWM, Smith-Dorrien Mss, 87/47/10, diary, 10 October 1914.

43 IWM, French Mss, 75/46/6, French to Rawlinson, 11 October 1914; ibid., PP/MCR/C32, diary, 10, 11 and 12 October 1914; ibid., PP/MCR/C33, Kitchener to French, 10 October 1914 (also PRO30/57/49, WA30); ibid., Wilson Mss, DS/MISC/80, diary, 6 October 1914; ibid., Smith-Dorrien Mss, 87/47/5, Smith-Dorrien to wife, 11 October 1914; Gilbert, *Churchill Companion*, p. 168; French, *1914*, pp. 178–89.

44 Philpott, *Anglo-French Relations*, p. 46.

45 Beckles Willson (1920), *Ypres: The Holy Ground of British Arms*, Bruges: Charles Beyaert, p. 30; IWM, Garwood Mss, 91/23/1, diary, 15 October 1914; Dominiek Dendooven (2001), *Menin Gate and Last Post: Ypres as Holy Ground*, Koksijde: De Klaproos, p. 53.

chapter 2

Four armies in Flanders Fields

The four armies – those of Britain, Germany, France and Belgium – now about to be engaged in Flanders were very different, one from another. All had begun to grapple with the demands of a new kind of war beyond previous expectations, not least in terms of the extraordinary expenditure of ammunition and the heavy losses, but also with the onset of stagnation when all had anticipated a war of movement.

The BEF, of course, was an exception to the continental model in that it was enlisted in peacetime by voluntary means. There had been temporary and limited legislation on occasions in the early eighteenth century for impressment into the British army but only the militia, raised for home defence, had been conscripted, and only between 1757 and 1831. Prior to 1914, advances in professionalism had been accomplished without the British army becoming any more representative of society as a whole. Officers were still drawn largely from the traditional landed elite and, in any case, the majority of candidates for commission were products of the public schools. At the other extreme, the rank and file were still largely recruited from the lowest elements of society. Overwhelmingly English in nationality, the army was also largely urban in origin, with unskilled labourers the largest single category of pre-war recruit. The army did not keep statistics of the numbers of its recruits who were unemployed, but a report in 1909 revealed that 90 per cent of those presenting themselves for medical examination prior to enlistment were out of work. There was in effect what Field Marshal Lord Nicholson in 1906 called a 'compulsion of destitution' about recruitment with the burden of military service falling wholly unequally.[1]

Behind the regulars stood the small army and special reserves and the part-time Territorial Force. While embracing middle-class elements, the Territorials were largely dependent for recruits upon the working class, albeit skilled manual workers in receipt of regular wages rather than the casually employed found in the ranks of the army.[2]

Pre-war militarisation in Britain fell far short of any popular support for conscription and the greater proportion of the BEF would have to be found upon mobilisation from the reserves and these would also make up wastage for the first six months. Indeed, something like 60 per cent of the BEF had been made up of reservists in August. Thereafter, the Territorials would be the means of expansion. Unfortunately, while it had been intended originally that the Territorials would be available for overseas service after six months' wartime training, political compromises during the creation of the force in 1906–8 had resulted in the emphasis being switched wholly to home defence. Territorials were only liable for overseas service if they chose to take the so-called imperial service obligation. In 1914, just over 18,000, or only some 7 per cent, had done so, although at least the County Territorial Associations (CTAs) provided a ready-made machinery for wartime expansion.

Whatever assumptions had been made prior to the war, however, all were set aside by the appointment of Kitchener as Secretary of State for War. Kitchener, who often paradoxically came to the right conclusions for the wrong reasons, had not served at home since 1883. He was wholly unfamiliar with any pre-war arrangements although he was certain that the war would be prolonged and that Britain must have a sufficiently large army to be able to dictate the terms of any post-war settlement. The Unionist politician, Leo Amery, aptly described him as a 'great improviser but also a great disorganiser'. This was particularly seen in Kitchener's distaste for the Territorials, whom he regarded as amateurs and a 'town clerk's army'. His attitude effectively spelled the end of any pre-war plans to expand through the CTAs, as Kitchener resolved to raise his 'Kitchener' or 'New' Armies through the War Office.[3]

Nevertheless, there was more to Kitchener's reasoning than simple prejudice. There were no actual practical plans for expansion through the associations and Kitchener believed they would be swamped by having to train and recruit simultaneously. Similarly, the Territorials were not liable to go overseas unless they took the imperial service obligation and Kitchener was reluctant to put pressure on married men to volunteer for service abroad. Most significant of all was his preoccupation with possible German invasion, against which the Territorials were the principal defence. Indeed, as previously indicated, two regular divisions – the 4th and 6th – had been initially kept back from the BEF for home defence.[4]

Having taken the decision, Kitchener would not be swayed, although he did allow some Territorials, who had taken the obligation, to go overseas in September 1914 to relieve imperial garrisons. He was eventually reluctantly persuaded to allow Territorials to 'fill the gap' in France and Flanders before his New Armies were ready to do so. In fact, there were difficulties in persuading many pre-war Territorials to take the obligation, many being either older, married men with family responsibilities, or younger than the age of nineteen at which overseas service was permissible. Territorials could and did continue to enlist for home service only until March 1915 and pre-war Territorials also could and did seek their discharge at the end of their original term of service until May 1916. Yet the failure to utilise the CTAs clearly resulted in duplication of effort and competition, both in recruitment and in finding equipment, damaging to both Territorials and New Armies. Unfortunately, it was also the case that the raising of the New Armies was almost entirely haphazard in the absence of any coherent manpower policy.[5]

The pattern of military participation, as a result of voluntary enlistment, was quite arbitrary. In Britain, 15 per cent of all wartime enlistments did indeed take place in the first two months but the 'rush to the colours' was not immediate and it has been almost precisely dated to the period between 25 August and 9 September 1914. Initial confusion was not assisted by a lack of news from France until the publication of a sensational 'Amiens dispatch' on 30 August by two journalists reporting the retreat from Mons. German atrocity stories had also surfaced and on 24 August the Earl of Derby approached the War Office with a suggestion to raise so-called 'Pals' battalions of men from the same communities, factories and so on. The idea had actually originated in the War Office as early as 14 August and the 'Stockbrokers Battalion' of the Royal Fusiliers had begun to recruit on 21 August.[6]

Together, these factors seem to have accounted for the sudden increase in recruitment. Only 51,647 men had enlisted in Britain prior to 15 August 1914, but 174,901 were enlisted between 30 August and 5 September. The highest total for a single day, of 33,204 recruits on 3 September, exceeded the average pre-war annual total of recruits for the whole army. However, the most fruitful recruiting period was over by 9 September as the news from France improved and there were increasing rumours that recruits were suffering discomfort in improvised accommodation. It also appeared that men were no longer required, deferred enlistment having been introduced in view of the accommodation problems and with the War Office also trying to regulate the flow by arbitrary variations in age and physical requirements. By the time the height requirement was lowered to 5 feet 4 inches and the upper age limit raised to 35 on 23 October, it was too late to revive enlistment and further adjustments made no appreciable impact.[7]

All this lay in the future, of course, and the struggle for Ypres would be fought primarily by the old regular army and its reservists. The strength of the regular British army was its regimental system, but it also had disadvantages. In theory, one of each regiment's two regular battalions was intended to serve overseas and the other at home to supply drafts. In practice, an equal balance had never been achieved since the establishment of this system of linked battalions back in 1871 and, in any case, most of the home battalions were understrength with either young recruits or servicemen reaching the end of their term of service. Regulars were volunteers, recruited between the ages of 18 and 25, mostly for seven years with the colours and five with the reserve, the exception being the Army Service Corps which enlisted men for three years with the companies. After eleven years an individual could re-engage up to a total of twenty-five years. In fact, in 1914, British regulars were not that experienced, only 4192 men having over fifteen years' service, with 46,291 men registering under two years' service with the colours.[8]

In theory, each of the six divisions of the original BEF comprised some 12,000 infantry, its twelve battalions (in three brigades) having two machine guns each. The standard infantry weapon, of course, was the .30 calibre Lee-Enfield magazine rifle. Attached to the division were also 4000 artillerymen with seventy-six guns, comprising three field artillery brigades (each of three batteries with six 18-pounders), a field howitzer brigade (of three batteries, each with six 4.5-inch howitzers) and a heavy battery (four 60-pounders) and, in addition, a cavalry squadron, a cyclist company, a supply train, an ammunition column, and two field companies of Royal Engineers. In all, an infantry division comprised 18,073 men and 5592 horses. A cavalry division had four brigades, each of three regiments, approximating to 9000 men. Attached were twenty-four machine guns, twenty-four 13-pounders, signal troops, an engineer field squadron, a supply column, and field ambulances.[9]

Slightly different from the first six divisions, Capper's 7th Division was composed mostly of units withdrawn from overseas garrisons. Four battalions had been stationed in the United Kingdom in August 1914 – the 1st

Grenadier Guards, 2nd Scots Guards, 2nd Green Howards, and 2nd Border Regiment. Two battalions came from Gibraltar – the 2nd Royal Scots Fusiliers and 2nd Wiltshire Regiment – and two from Malta – the 2nd Royal Warwickshire Regiment and 1st Royal Welch Fusiliers. Three others were from South Africa – 2nd Queen's Regiment, 2nd Bedfordshire Regiment and 1st South Staffordshire Regiment – and one from Egypt – the 2nd Gordon Highlanders. Divisional artillery units came from South Africa as well as home stations, but the division had only forty-eight field guns instead of fifty-four and only eight 4.7-inch guns instead of eighteen howitzers, and four 60-pounders. Other supporting services were also drawn from far and wide, the divisional cavalry squadron being provided by the yeomen of the Northumberland Hussars.[10] At least the units drawn from overseas were experienced regulars, with few reservists required to make them up to war establishment as battalions on overseas service enjoyed higher peace establishments than those at home. Rather similarly, the 3rd Cavalry Division consisted initially of only two rather than three brigades: the 6th Cavalry Brigade drawn from units previously in South Africa and Egypt and the 7th Cavalry Brigade from the Household Cavalry. Its supporting units were entirely improvised and much of the divisional equipment did not appear for some days after it had disembarked at Ostend and Zeebrugge.

British field artillery was initially attached to infantry brigades but, as the campaign went on, it was drawn back from brigades and combined with the heavier artillery designated for corps use to give direct support where required to the infantry. The number of heavy guns available to the BEF totalled just fifty-four. They comprised twenty of the heavy 60-pounders, sixteen of the 4.7-inch QF (quick-firing) guns first adopted at the time of the South African War and notoriously unreliable in accuracy, sixteen of the old 6-inch howitzers, a single 6-inch gun and a single experimental 9.2-inch howitzer that arrived in France on 19 October. Batteries depended upon telephone to co-ordinate their fire and upon forward observation to direct that fire, there being no wireless available for reconnaissance aircraft. Counter-battery work was primarily the role of a Royal Navy armoured train mounting one 6-inch and two 4.7-inch guns since naval ammunition was more plentiful than any other. Indeed, initially the 18-pounders had only shrapnel and no high explosive shells were supplied until 19 October.[11]

Firepower had been emphasised since the South African War, with increasing stress after 1909 on a more offensive spirit though with appropriate fire support from the artillery. The method of infantry advance was, by small groups, to build a firing line some 200 yards from the enemy, which would be steadily reinforced until the volume of fire permitted a bayonet assault. Individual short-range fire was preferred to collective fire at medium range with more initiative allowed to platoon and section commanders. At the same time, the adoption of a four rather than an eight-company structure had made company training itself more viable.[12]

After many internal debates, there was something of a move towards a mounted infantry role for the British cavalry immediately after the South African War, the lessons of which had been ambiguous. Indeed, cavalry traditionalists such as French and Haig saw little reason to alter their views of the efficacy of sword and lance as a result. French had worked on a new edition of the manual *Cavalry Drill* in the 1890s and then contributed a preface to an English translation of Friedrich von Bernhardi's *Cavalry in Future Wars* in 1906. His reputation as a cavalry theorist of some prominence was established largely through his success at Elandslaagte in October 1899 and subsequent performance with the Cavalry Division in the relief of Kimberley in February 1900. Haig had contributed to a new edition of the *Cavalry Drill Book* in 1896 and to *Cavalry Training* in 1904, also writing *Cavalry Studies* in 1907 with the assistance of Colonel Lonsdale Hale. Both French and Haig had earned reputations as dynamic modernists, though they were most progressive in terms of the most conservative and traditional arm of the service. Thus, they led a reversion to shock action, though the cavalry embarked on war largely trained for a dual role of mounted and dismounted action to a much greater extent than either the French or German cavalry.[13]

An Indian Corps of some 15,700 men, dispatched from India on 27 August 1914, joined the BEF in October. In 1914 there were thirty-nine cavalry regiments and 126 infantry regiments in the Indian army, each of one battalion with the exception of the Garwhal Rifles and the ten Gurkha regiments, which each had two battalions. The majority of battalions were of mixed native 'classes' but with companies being of one class only, a potential problem in finding reinforcing drafts. Indian battalions also had fewer men, averaging thirteen officers and 764 other ranks compared to the twenty-eight officers and 816 other ranks of a British battalion. The paucity of British officers was a distinct disadvantage, rendering the Indians vulnerable to disintegration should officer casualties prove high despite the recruitment of supposed 'martial classes', who were loyal but invariably poorly educated. Moreover, the native junior officers, of whom there were on average seventeen in a battalion, fulfilling in effect the role of NCOs, became commissioned only after long service in the ranks. Fears of improper relations being formed between Indian troops and European women were to lead to severe restrictions being placed on the men once they reached France, adding to tensions arising from the unfamiliarity with conditions on the Western Front. Moreover, British officers of the Indian army tended to be less well professionally educated than their British counterparts, the Indian Staff College at Quetta dating only from 1905 with only 218 officers having graduated from it by 1914. Over 250 officers of the Indian army on home leave were pressed into service for battalions of Kitchener's New Armies in August and September 1914, involving at the very least a potential further reduction of the supply of trained staff officers for formations leaving India.

Another problem was that since the Mutiny, Indian troops had been armed with less advanced weapons than their British counterparts, newer weapons with which the troops were not familiar being issued on their arrival in France. The Indian divisions were also weaker in artillery than British divisions as they had only one field artillery brigade and a mountain brigade, all British, this deficiency also having to be made up upon deployment.[14]

By comparison with the small British regular army, the Germans had a mass conscript army in 1914. Germany was eventually to mobilise 13.2 million (or 41.4 per cent of the male population) during the war but, initially, in anticipation of a short war, about two million German reservists were not recalled in August 1914, the initial field strength being about five million. Additionally, there were perhaps 5.4 million men of military age, who had not previously been trained through past exemption. However, an estimated 308,000 *kriegsfreiwillige* (wartime volunteers) in Germany at the start of the war did not wait to be conscripted. The *kriegsfreiwillige* have been characterised as being motivated not only by a mixture of patriotism and adventurism, but also with a highly idealistic commitment to re-establishing a sense of *volksgemeinschaft* (national community). It has been argued that this was a conscious attempt to escape from modernity, the 'bondage' of class and status and the 'unnatural' constraints of the market place.[15]

After 1893, Germany had a basic two-year term of military service from the age of 17, but three years in the cavalry and horse artillery. In practice, however, peacetime training began only when a man reached his twentieth year. The basic conscript term was followed by five years in the first line reserve, a reservist being liable to fourteen days' training annually; five years in the first levy or 'ban' of the *Landwehr*, in which a man would be liable for seven or fourteen days' training twice during his service; and seven years in the second *Landwehr* levy or 'ban', also known as the *Ersatz* reserve, in which there would be no training. The latter also included those not called up prior to the age of 23, those who had postponed their initial conscript service, and those with physical deficiencies of a minor character, these men serving for twelve years. There was then further service to the age of 45 in the secondary militia force known as the *Landsturm* again without any annual training. In addition, there was provision for the better educated to become one-year volunteers, most of whom were likely to receive commissions in the reserve after their service. Regular NCOs were invariably taken from the products of special schools or volunteer entrants, while regular officers were derived from cadet schools or, through a process of examination, from high schools. All officer candidates initially entered the ranks, but those from cadet schools as NCOs, before being commissioned after two or three years, with admission to a particular regiment by vote of its officers.[16]

In August 1914 the Germans activated thirty-one trained reserve divisions to join fifty-one active divisions. In addition, four *Landwehr* and six *Ersatz* divisions were formed but subsequent reserve formations were improvised. As previously suggested, the creation of six new reserve corps was ordered on 16 August, five of them – General von Falkenhayn's *XXII*, General von Kleist's *XXIII*, General von Loden's *XXIV*, *XXV* (which went to the Eastern Front) and General von Hügel's *XXVI*, being Prussian, and General von Carlowitz's *XXVII Corps* a mixture of Saxon and Württemberg units: Falkenhayn was the elder brother of the Chief of the German General Staff. In addition, Bavaria formed its *6th Bavarian Reserve Division* on the same date.

It proved difficult to equip these formations, some helmets for example being obtained from the Berlin Police and weapons from replacement training units, who then had to be given captured Russian and Belgian rifles. Indeed, equipment of all kinds was in short supply in a manner highly reminiscent of the Kitchener 'New Armies' in Britain. The *239th Reserve Infantry Regiment*, for example, was 1500 rifles short of establishment on 7 September and the *240th Reserve Infantry Regiment* still some 500 short three days later. Falkenhayn, who recognised at least some of the deficiencies of the reserve formations, was to complain later of shortages of troops and supplies. Indeed, he adopted a policy of *notbehelfe* (makeshift) using ammunition of the dead and wounded, taking food from land and so on. The French similarly talked of *pis-aller* (also makeshift).

Traditionally, it has been suggested that 75 per cent of the men in these new formations were *kriegsfreiwillige* volunteers when it is more accurate to say that 75 per cent were either *kriegsfreiwillige* volunteers or untrained, under-aged and over-aged men, the remaining 25 per cent being trained reservists from the *Landwehr, Ersatz* reserve, and *Landsturm*. Each battalion and company had a cadre of trained men, while many of the volunteers were well educated. In the case of the *51ˢᵗ Reserve Division* of *XXVI Reserve Corps*, all the NCOs were reservists, many of them being schoolmasters, while officers were a mixture of reservists, *Landwehr* officers, or those brought back from retirement. Certainly, many of the officers were manifestly unfit for the physical requirements of campaign, the *208ᵗʰ Reserve Infantry Regiment* losing its commanding officer and its three battalion commanders: all broke down within five days between 22 and 26 October.[17]

It was by no means the case, however, that these men were all students as implied by the popular impression of 'school-boy corps'. The proportion of experienced men varied greatly from unit to unit. Thus, the entire *203ʳᵈ Reserve Infantry Regiment* was composed of experienced reservists while some 33 per cent of the *211ᵗʰ Reserve Infantry Regiment* were inexperienced volunteers, and 18 per cent of the *201ˢᵗ Reserve Infantry Regiment* students, teachers or school leavers. Though casualty rates are far less precise in suggesting the actual percentage of inexperienced soldiers in a unit, just under 20 per cent of the dead of the *214ᵗʰ Reserve Infantry Regiment* were *kriegsfreiwillige* between 15 October and 31 December.

Compared to regular divisions, the reserve divisions had only nine field batteries instead of twelve, the artillery having a smaller percentage of trained men than the infantry units. Moreover, many batteries lacked telephones or modern guns. For those new to the army – 61 per cent had had no previous military training – training consisted of just fourteen days at a recruit depot followed by ten days' platoon training and a shorter period of company and battalion training. In the case of infantry and artillery, however, the percentage of trained men was higher than those to be found in the units of Kitchener's New Armies. There were, however, conflicting reports on how far these reserve corps were ready for war when committed to Ypres in October 1914. One corps commander who inspected some of the new formations in September and early October, General von Huene, believed that they were ready but another, General von Lowenfeld, felt the reserve officers lacking in tactical knowledge and the troops too ready to manoeuvre in mass without regard to their vulnerability to fire. In the event, those corps committed to the West were followed by a stream of impressed civilian carts carrying those who had become casualties of hard marches from soft feet in new boots.[18]

In fact, despite Lowenfeld's views about the dangers, the German infantry was trained generally to attack in thick waves, each about 500 yards apart, to create a shock effect, artillery and machine guns providing covering fire: the belief was that fire superiority was a precondition of a successful bayonet charge. The standard infantry weapon was the 7.9 mm calibre 1898 model Mauser magazine rifle sighted to 2000 yards. There had been something of a reversion to close order tactics after 1888 in the belief that troops in open order would be too difficult to control on the battlefield and that potentially heavier casualties were acceptable in order to ensure adequate control. Consequently, the 1888 Drill Regulations were slightly modified in 1906 whereby close order might be broken up into groups if the enemy's fire had not been suppressed by artillery support, but with the expectation of still reforming a single line within 400 or 500 yards of the enemy from which a charge could be executed once close range rifle fire had neutralised the defenders. In many respects, however, there was no particular consensus among German officers as to the best methods to be utilised. Indeed, the lessons of the German Wars of Unification and subsequent conflicts such as the Russo-Turkish War of 1877–8, the South African War and the Russo-Japanese War were bitterly contested in the German army, traditionally minded officers often being able to influence doctrine in all arms of the service. Particularly once casualties began to mount, some units adopted dispersed skirmish lines but many still clung to close order tactics. Commanded and trained by older officers, indeed, and in their short period of training – some five weeks at most – the reserve corps had been taught only the rudiments of attacking in broad and deep columns.[19]

The expectation in France was that between 5 and 13 per cent of men would not appear upon mobilisation. In the event only 1.5 per cent were absentees. A three-year term of military service had been introduced in 1913, two years having been the norm since 1905. Thus, the 1911–13 cohorts (those born from 1891 to 1893) were serving when the war broke out. The French called up the 1896–1910 cohorts in August 1914 and the 1914 cohort in September 1914. By the end of 1914 they had called up the 1892–5 cohorts (those born between 1872 and 1875) as well as the 1915 cohort. Indeed, some 80 per cent of all French males between the ages of 18 and 46 had been called up by the spring of 1915 and France eventually mobilised about

45 per cent of its male population, a greater proportion than any other of the major belligerents. It was also the case that, in peacetime, the French had increasingly reduced the grounds for exemption from military service and called up a much higher proportion of those eligible for conscription than did Germany, approximating to 82 per cent of those eligible in the last decade before the war, compared to only 59 per cent in the case of Germany though this was offset by the German manpower pool being larger. The initial French field strength was just over a million men, which, with the addition of Territorials and other reservists, made up about 4.4 million men on mobilisation compared to Germany's 5.2 million men on mobilisation.

At the completion of the term of service, the conscript would pass to the active reserve, then to the French Territorials until the age of 40, at which point service obligation ceased though, technically, they were still members of the territorial reserve. Like the active army, the active reserve was organised in twenty military regions and would rejoin regular units on mobilisation. By contrast, the French Territorials, who also included some men previously judged unfit for conscription, had an entirely separate organisation within each region, the assumption being that they would have a supporting rather than a combat role.[20]

French infantry carried the 1889 or 1893 model .32 Lebel magazine rifle. Each infantry regiment – mostly each comprising three battalions – normally possessed two .32 Puteaux machine guns though those regiments attached to corps on the frontier had had three machine guns. The excellent 75 mm field gun used by both field and horse batteries was capable of twelve to sixteen shells per minute, the army as a whole deploying some 618 field and twenty horse batteries, each of four guns, with twenty-one 6-inch howitzer batteries and fifteen mountain batteries.

Like other European armies, the French were trained primarily for offensive action. Indeed, the recognition of the potential effects of modern firepower on morale upon an extended battlefield, on which command and control might be problematic, had led to a decided reaction among French officers against new infantry regulations introduced in 1904. Drawing upon the British experience in South Africa, these abandoned the close formations prescribed in those of 1894, which had specified advancing 'elbow to elbow in mass formation, to the sound of bugles and drums'. Thus, generals like Joffre and Foch invested the offensive with the power of renewing the spirit of the French nation itself. The author of new field service regulations for larger formations in October 1913, Colonel Louis de Grandmaison, who was to be killed in 1915, proclaimed that the army 'returning to its traditions, recognises no law save that of the offensive'. The renewed emphasis was now upon rapidity in attack rather than method. It is perhaps symptomatic of the obsession that French infantry continued to carry colours into action until 1916. The offensive spirit served a number of political purposes in offering perceived traditional values to the political right, moral rejuvenation to the political left and the revival of the army's prestige to those like Joffre concerned by the damage done to the army through past political interference. At the same time, however, it also reflected perceptions of weakness deriving from unresolved internal doctrinal confusion, from organisational defects and from material shortages.[21]

The Belgians also fielded a conscript army though one of only recent creation. Indeed, prior to 1909, the Belgian army had been primarily a professional one of long service volunteers, conscription only being applied to maintain a strength of some 40,000 men; substitution was also permitted. The Flemish Catholics who had dominated government for much of the period since 1870 had been both anti-militarist and also opposed to allowing Catholic youths to mix with Walloons, who might be tainted with socialism. Growing European tensions resulted in an increase in the size of the army in 1902 with the period of liability extended from eight to thirteen years. Then, consequent upon the First Moroccan Crisis in 1905, there was a significant change in attitudes. Thus, just a few days before his death, King Leopold II signed a new conscription law in 1909. Through its provisions, military training became compulsory for one son in each family, with the liability fixed at twelve years. Further legislation in 1913 extended the principle of conscription with provision for an available annual contingent of 67,000 men, of whom 49 per cent were to be drafted, with exemption for clerics and sons in families in which a son was already serving. Service would now begin at the age of 19 with a liability of eight years with the colours and five in the reserve though the actual period of service would only be between fifteen months and two years depending upon arm of service. The annual training period thereafter would vary from three to eight weeks, again depending on arm of service. One year volunteers were permitted, limited to about 2000 in all, these being those regarded as suitable for commissioning.

The intention was to raise the strength of the army progressively to about 100,000 men in peacetime with a field army upon mobilisation of 150,000 and a garrison army for the key fortresses of Antwerp, Liége and Namur of

130,000, and an available reserve of 60,000 men. In the event, the Belgian field army in August 1914 comprised 117,000 men in six infantry divisions and a cavalry division and some 130,000 garrison troops, the army as a whole reflecting the 1909 rather than the 1913 arrangements, with a large percentage of long-service regulars but few trained reserves. The Belgian first line infantry were armed with the 7.65 mm calibre Mauser magazine rifle, but many of the reserves carried the 11 mm calibre Comblain rifle. The basic artillery piece was the 1905 model Krupp 7.5 cm gun.

The uncertain state of relations with France as well as Germany and the failure of negotiations even with Britain also resulted in the army's divisions being widely scattered immediately before the German invasion. Thus, in August 1914, despite the representations of the army's Chief of Staff, one division watched the coast from Ghent, another was at Antwerp, a third and fourth facing Germany at Liège and Namur, a fifth facing the French frontier from Mons, and the last covering Brussels. Technically, Belgium was not an ally of Britain and France but still nominally a neutral and, indeed, Belgians officially referred to the British and French forces as armies of the guaranteeing powers.[22]

The opening campaign of the war in the West was an instructive one for all four armies as pre-war plans largely fell apart. The German plan for the opening offensive, popularly known as the Schlieffen Plan, had foundered with the decision to retreat from the Marne on 6 September while the initial French offensive into the lost provinces of Alsace and Lorraine – Plan XVII – had collapsed by 28 August, Joffre dismissing an army commander, three corps commanders and thirty-six divisional commanders. The BEF's experience from the encounter battle at Mons on 23 August, through the subsequent 'great retreat', the advance from the Marne on 6 September and the first signs of deadlock on the Aisne from 12 September had been equally bruising.

Losses had been especially heavy and unexpected. The French had suffered 385,000 casualties in the first six weeks, a figure rising to 995,000 by the end of the first five months. The Germans were to lose 750,000 casualties in the West in the same period. Pre-war British estimates of wastage had been approximately 40 per cent for the first six months and 65–75 per cent for the first twelve months. The actual British casualty rate in the first three months was to run to 63 per cent and by 4 October the BEF had suffered 31,709 casualties. Most British units had been brought back to something approaching establishment by the last available drafts of reservists but it was particularly difficult to replace experienced officers. Indeed, to give one example, only 485 officers had joined the BEF between August and the beginning of October 1914.[23]

Lessons, however, had been learned. On the Aisne, the British had noted the superiority of German heavy guns and of their artillery observation. As a result, Haig's able Chief of Staff, Brigadier General Johnnie Gough VC, younger brother of Hubert Gough, advocated digging trenches on reverse slopes even if the field of fire was restricted in order to neutralise the effectiveness of the German artillery. Gough also felt it necessary to revert to the lessons learned in South Africa of dispersed 'loose and irregular elastic formations' adapting to the ground. Smith-Dorrien, too, had noted the need to conceal guns, to acquire heavier guns and more ammunition and that digging was now as important as shooting for infantry.[24] Having seen the enclosed nature of the Flanders countryside, Foch also increasingly grasped the realities. He issued an order while visiting the IX Corps on 28 October that, since deep formations were having little effect, initiative must be used rather than units blindly following such unproductive means in the hope of results.[25]

Of the Flanders landscape that the armies were to contest in 1914, there is an almost inescapable popular impression of a ravaged and almost featureless moonscape. This is so much so that it is hard for the modern visitor familiar only with the images of 1917 to reconcile the image with the reality of Flanders today. To see the Flanders of today, however, is to see it very much as it was in the autumn of 1914 before war had reduced its villages and farms to rubble and its woods to mere stumps. In many cases, indeed, not only do the modern woods follow the contours of the old, but also buildings were often reconstructed exactly as they had once been.

Flanders had long been an avenue of conflict, being generally a level plain broken only by a line of undulations rising to slight, almost imperceptible, hills which ran first west to east from Cassel to Mount Kemmel then, as gentle ridges, east to north-east through Wytschaete, Gheluvelt and Passchendaele, finally curving north to Dixmude. Technically, the plain was mostly heavy marine clay known as Ypres clay, the hills of Ypresian and Paniselian sand sediments overlying the clay.[26]

The hill line stood at about 400 feet at Kemmel, but not much more than 100 or 150 feet at Wytschaete and Gheluvelt and only 70 feet at Passchendaele. From Kemmel it was possible to see the whole countryside from Lille to Menin and Dixmude. Various spurs extended from the ridge line, as at Messines, the whole being covered in medium-sized woods of various mixed species, most with dense undergrowth. Typically, they were a mixture of ash, chestnut and oak, with hazel and maple undergrowth. They were also full of pheasants. Indeed, at one point in November, 'Ma' Jeffreys noted that one of his men had killed four pheasants and seven Germans 'all running across a ride he was watching' from his trench in Klein Zillebeke woods: 'He picked up the pheasants after dark and we (Battalion Headquarters) had one for dinner.'[27] Yet, given the low-lying nature of much of the plain, these gentle slopes took on the appearance of dominant features, a saucer-like rim appearing to the observer from Ypres lying at the centre of the plain. Gradients were gentle nearly everywhere, varying from 1 in 33 at Zandvoorde to 1 in 60 at Hooge.[28]

The partially canalised River Lys bisected the area, running west then south-west from Ghent to Armentières via Menin some 15–20 yards wide and 5–6 feet deep and passable only by bridges.[29] There was also a network of other canals originally constructed both for communication and defence, while numerous streams like the Steenbeek, Stroombeek and Kornebeek, and willow-lined dykes intersected the plain, fed by springs at the junction of the permeable sands and the impermeable clay. The Yser Canal connected to the Lys at Comines.

Apart from the lack of higher ground for purposes of observation, Flanders was also rendered difficult for mobile operations by the many villages and hamlets, the ramshackle barns and sheds, and small fields surrounded by wooded hedgerows. Paul Maze, Hubert Gough's French interpreter, recalled the smell of peat and the 'mellow lights of isolated farms' while Foch, climbing the tower of the Cloth Hall at Ypres at one point recalled 'a sea of green, with little white islands marking the location of the rich villages, with their fine churches and graceful steeples. To see open country in any direction was impossible.'[30]

Indeed, much of Flanders was highly cultivated, tobacco and beetroot in particular being staple crops. Many British soldiers were struck by the sickly stench of beetroot being kept for winter fodder, while manure heaps were also commonplace. At least the tobacco sheds, in which the leaves were hung to dry in the autumn, were to prove useful cover for observers, but generally clear fields of fire were few and far between and, therefore, all the more valuable. Equally, it was easy to conceal large numbers of men as well as guns. Captain Valentine Fleming MP of the 1/1st Queen's Own Oxfordshire Hussars remembered mounted patrol work 'as simply bumping along roads until you got shot at out of a house, you can't get off the roads because of the wire and the dykes and you can't search all the farms and cottages, because there are too many of them'. Accordingly, it was a case of 'buggering along and trusting to luck'.[31]

Both sides were to deploy aircraft for reconnaissance. Thus, Scott-Tucker of the 1st Kings (Liverpool) recorded that 'great care had to be taken to make ourselves look like cabbages when they [German aircraft] were near' while on 15 October, Cavalry Corps HQ was informed directly by an airman who 'descended' that the Zonnebeke-Roulers-Menin area was clear of Germans. Direction to artillery was also attempted. On 22 October, for example, C. Simpson from the 7th Divisional Ammunition Column recorded being called out of action by an aircraft dropping a smoke bomb.[32]

In the case of the Royal Flying Corps, Nos. 2 and 4 Squadrons at St Omer were to support I and II Corps, Nos. 3 and 5 Squadrons also at St Omer (but each with a detached flight respectively at Hinges and Bailleul) supported the Indian Corps, III Corps and the Cavalry Corps, each squadron being expected to carry out tactical reconnaissance up to 20 miles beyond the front line. No. 6 Squadron at Poperinghe served GHQ and was responsible for strategic reconnaissance.[33] Wireless equipped machines were in short supply, but, in any case, the weather was frequently too poor for clear visibility, while it became apparent that the tobacco hung out to dry under the lean-to shelters often looked like bivouacs from the air and the piles of beats and turnips covered by earth looked like trenches. Moreover, flying over troops was still a decidedly dangerous enterprise at this stage of the war. On 26 October, for example, though one account had it that it was a German aircraft with British markings and another a British aircraft 'in charge of German officers', a RFC machine from No. 4 Squadron was brought down in flames by men from the 1st Black Watch while on an artillery reconnaissance at about 1000 feet, the infantry taking its coloured light signals – it had no wireless – as proof of its hostility. The aircraft had a large Union Jack, which was considered visible at 1000 feet though it was pointed out by a French officer that at such a distance only the cross would really be visible, the incident hastening the adoption of French-style roundels. Lieutenant Cyril Hosking and Captain Theodore Crean, pilot and observer respectively, were both burned to death though, again, some accounts suggest they fell to their deaths and even that they were only wounded. Indeed, even the official history of the war in the air suggests they were only wounded but both men are commemorated on the Arras Flying Services Memorial.[34]

There were some small factories producing sugar or alcohol from the beets, which provided some tall chimneys, but mostly church towers or the occasional windmill were the best observation platforms available. Otherwise the abundance of trees and hedges obscured direct observation for artillery work. Churches thus became a target to be destroyed in order to deny their use by the enemy. At Poelcappelle on 23 October, for example, 2nd Division's artillery demolished the church steeple though the CRA hesitated to actually order its destruction.[35]

At the centre of the plain lay Ypres, a once populous town in the Middle Ages now down to under 17,000 inhabitants in 1914, who were principally engaged in the manufacture of flax, lace, ribbons, cotton and soap. There was a modest tourist trade in Ypres, its medieval Cloth Hall, the first stone of which was laid in 1201 by Baldwin IX, Count of Flanders and Emperor of Constantinople, being the largest non-religious Gothic building in Europe. The Cloth Hall, completed in 1304, was also noted for its frescoes, first begun by Ferdinand Pauwels in 1861 and continued by Louis Delbeke in 1883, though the project was still not complete at the time of Delbeke's death eight years later. St Martin's Church dated mostly from the thirteenth and fourteenth centuries, St Peter's from 1073 and St Jacques from 1139. There was also a cavalry riding school and a barracks. What was to become famous as the Menin Gate was at the time merely a gap in the town ramparts, which had been widened in 1862, leading to a simple causeway across the moat, the famous pair of stone lions standing on pedestals either side of the road.

The earthen ramparts of Ypres were originally laid down by the great French military engineer Vauban, after the French capture of the city in 1678, but they had been largely demilitarised in the 1850s. Faced with brick, the surviving ramparts looked out towards the hill line between 4000 and 7000 yards to the south-east. Ironically, the most famous siege in the town's past had been that in 1383 when an English army led by the Bishop of Norwich failed to take Ypres and retired after two months upon the approach of a relieving army led by King Charles VI of France. Marching into Ypres, 'Ma' Jeffreys found it a 'nice old town, with narrow, cobbled-stoned streets and some fine buildings' though he noted the seemingly large number of priests and nuns. Similarly, Captain James Jack of the 2nd Scottish Rifles (Cameronians), serving as Staff Captain to 19th Brigade, found Ypres 'a gem of a town with its lovely old-world gabled houses, red-tiled roofs, and no factories visible to spoil the charm'. To J.L. Mowbray, later brigade major for 2nd Division's artillery, it was simply a 'big old fashioned town with wealthy inhabitants'.[36]

Towards the south, Béthune and Lens were coal mining areas with terraces of miners' cottages, and pit heads and slag heaps a plenty, the latter being used for artillery observation. To the east, Lille, Tourcoing and Roubaix were also industrialised and heavily urbanised areas. Lille in particular was a significant nodal point where five railway lines intersected. For the most part, however, there were only small villages. Langemarck was comparatively large with some 7400 inhabitants. Wytschaete had some 3500 inhabitants, a lime works, a drainpipe factory and various tobacco sheds. Messines with its lime works and mill had only about 1400 inhabitants and appeared especially dreary, though Maze found it 'a clean little town' with charming old houses with polished brass door handles and poplar trees facing out on to the little square at its centre. Here and there were some small breweries, the 2nd Seaforth Highlanders locating their battalion headquarters in one at Frélinghien and enjoying the barrels of malt beer they found abandoned in it until the Germans rather unsportingly demolished it with trench mortars.[37]

As was to become all too apparent in the later campaign around Ypres in 1917, the water table was high everywhere with surface water collecting easily in both natural depressions and also in man-made excavations. Consequently, the ground could quickly turn to mud, especially in autumn, making many of the rough and badly paved roads slippery and all but impassable. Only the main routes were paved, primarily that between Ypres and Wieltje, that between Zandvoorde and Passchendaele, and that between Messines and Wytschaete. Some roads were slightly elevated above the surrounding countryside such as the roads from Langemarck to Zonnebeke, and from Zonnebeke to Becelaere. Even the pavé, however, was unsuitable for any large volume of traffic since only the crown could be realistically used for vehicles and two could rarely be accommodated side by side. Wheels which slipped on to the unmetalled clay edges of the road could easily become stuck and, at the best of times, progress would be slow if there was any volume of traffic whether men, horses, wagons or motor vehicles. It made it exceptionally difficult to supply the front to the east of Ypres. West of the town, the only substantial road back to Poperinghe, in the words of a French general, Dubois of IX Corps, was notorious for traffic jams 'which could stop all movement for an hour or even longer'. The lack of suitable roads was to make medical evacuation and even the siting of aid posts difficult. The high water table also added to the difficulties the artillery had with observation, Reeve of 16th Battery, 4th Brigade RFA noting on 30 October that, having moved from one favourable position, they had to obtain planks from a cowshed when they hit water at only 5 feet when trying to dig in the guns.[38]

General Palat, who wrote under the pseudonym, Charles Lehautcourt, memorably described Flanders as being a monotonous countryside with an air of melancholic sadness melting almost imperceptibly into the grey waters of the North Sea, its rain a kind of 'liquid spleen' barely less tenacious than the fogs. Based on records made at Lille, in the twenty years between 1897 and 1916, however, the autumn months of September to November were dry or very dry on thirteen occasions with two regarded as normal and only five years wet or very wet. In 1914, the rainfall amounted to just 31 mm (1.2 inches) in October and 39 mm (1.5 inches) in November. Though mornings were often misty or foggy and the days remained dull, only drizzle on 20 October inconvenienced troops during the first phase of the battle and from 31 October to 2 November it was actually fine and unseasonably warm. Rain fell heavily on 4 and 11 November and then from 12 to 14 November with the first real frost only on 18 November, and snowfalls on 19 and 20 November, some flurries having been encountered on 15 November. By this time, however, the battle was effectively over.[39]

Notes and references

1 Ian F.W. Beckett (1985), 'The Nation in Arms, 1914–18' in Ian F.W. Beckett and Keith Simpson (eds.), *A Nation in Arms: A Social Study of the British Army in the First World War*, Manchester: Manchester University Press, pp. 6, 10; Edward Spiers, 'The Regular Army' in ibid., pp. 39–41, 44–6; Ian F.W. Beckett (1988), 'The British Army', in J.M. Turner (ed.), *The First World War*, London: Unwin Hyman, p. 102.

2 Ian Beckett, 'The Territorial Force' in Beckett and Simpson, *Nation in Arms*, pp. 128–30; ibid., 'The Territorial Force in the Great War' in Peter Liddle (ed.), *Home Fires and Foreign Fields*, pp. 21–2; ibid. (1991), *The Amateur Military Tradition, 1558–1945*, Manchester: Manchester University Press, pp. 217–22.

3 Peter Simkins (1981), 'Kitchener and the Expansion of the Army' in Ian F.W. Beckett and John Gooch (eds.), *Politicians and Defence*, Manchester: Manchester University Press, pp. 96–7.

4 Beckett, 'Territorial Force', pp. 130–1; ibid., *Amateur Military Tradition*, pp. 226–8; Simkins, 'Kitchener and the expansion of the army', pp. 87–90, 97–100; ibid. (1988) *Kitchener's Army: The Raising of the New Armies, 1914–16*, Manchester: Manchester University Press, pp. 31–46.

5 Beckett, *Amateur Military Tradition*, pp. 228–31; ibid., 'Territorial Force', pp. 131–7; F.W. Perry (1988), *The Commonwealth Armies: Manpower and Organisation in Two World Wars*, Manchester: Manchester University Press, pp. 9–10.

6 Beckett, 'Nation in Arms', pp. 7–8; Simkins, *Kitchener's Army*, pp. 49–75, 83–4; Clive Hughes, 'The New Armies' in Beckett and Simpson, *Nation in Arms*, pp. 100–7.

7 Beckett, 'Nation in Arms', pp. 8–9; Simkins, *Kitchener's Army*, pp. 104–33.

8 David Ascoli (1981), *The Mons Star*, London: Harrap, p. 8.

9 Keith Simpson (1981), *The Old Contemptibles*, London: Allen & Unwin, p. 25.

10 Atkinson, *Seventh Division*, pp. 2–4; King's College, Liddell Hart Centre for Military Archives (hereafter LHCMA), Edmonds Mss, 6/2, '7th Division, October 1914', Montgomery to Edmonds, 4 February 1921.

11 OFH, p. 16 n. 1 and 164 n. 1.

12 Simpson, *Old Contemptibles*, p. 31; Edward Spiers (1981), 'Reforming the Infantry of the Line, 1902–14', *Journal of the Society for Army Historical Research* 59, pp. 82–94; Martin Samuels (1995), *Command or Control?: Command, Training and Tactics in the British and German Armies, 1888–1918*, London: Frank Cass, pp. 98–103; M.A. Ramsay (2002), *Command and Cohesion: The Citizen Soldier and Minor Tactics in the British Army, 1870–1918*, Westport: Praeger, pp. 91–108.

13 Stephen Badsey (1991), 'Mounted Cavalry in the Second Boer War', *Sandhurst Journal of Military Studies* 2, pp. 11–28; Brian Bond (1965), 'Doctrine and Training in the British Cavalry, 1870–1914' in Michael Howard (ed.), *The Theory and Practice of War*, London: Cassell, pp. 97–125; Edward Spiers (1984), 'The British Cavalry, 1902–14', *Journal of the Society for Army Historical Research* 57, pp. 71–9.

14 Jeffrey Greenhut (1983), 'The Imperial Reserve: The Indian Corps on the Western Front, 1914–15', *Journal of Imperial and Commonwealth History* 12 (1), pp. 54–73; ibid. (1981), 'Race, Sex and War: The Impact of Race and Sex on Morale and Health Services for the Indian Corps on the Western Front', *Military Affairs* 45 (2), pp. 71–4. See also David Omissi (1994), *The Sepoy and the Raj: The Indian Army, 1860–1914*, London: Macmillan, and Gordon Corrigan (1999), *Sepoys in the Trenches: The Indian Corps on the Western Front, 1914–15*, Staplehurst: Spellmount.

15 Thomas Rohkrämer (1994), 'August 1914: Kriegsmentalität und ihre Voraussetzungen' in Wolfgang Michalka (ed.), *Der Erste Weltkrieg: Wirkung, Wahrnehmung, Analyse*, Munich: Seehamer Verlag, pp. 759–77; Eric Leed (1979), *No Man's Land: Combat and Identity in World War I*, Cambridge: Cambridge University Press, p. 40; Robert Wohl (1979), *The Generation of 1914* (Cambridge MA: Harvard University Press), p. 208; Roger Chickering (1998), *Imperial Germany and the Great War, 1914–1918*, Cambridge: Cambridge University Press, pp. 178, 195; Holger Herwig (1997), *The First World War: Germany and Austria-Hungary, 1914–18*, London: Arnold, pp. 33, 119, 248, 293,

325, 344, 397, 425; Wilhelm Deist (1997), 'The German Army, the Authoritarian Nation-state and Total War' in John Horne (ed.), *State, Society and Mobilisation in Europe during the First World War*, Cambridge: Cambridge University Press, pp. 160–72.

16 Harold C. Deutsch (1980), 'Training, Organisation and Leadership in the German Reserve System: The Eve of World War I' in *German and Allied Army Reserves in 1914*, Dunn Loring: Historical Evaluation and Research Organisation, pp. 5–27.

17 Karl Unruh (1986), *Langemarck: Legende und Wirklichkeit*, Koblenz: Bernhard & Graefe Verlag, pp. 15–16, 19–35, 43–59; Falkenhayn, *German General Staff*, p. 35; Theodor Fuchs, 'The Readiness and Performance of German Army Reserves in 1914 with particular reference to the combat of the XXV German Reserve Corps at Lodz' in *German and Allied Army Reserves*, pp. 28–64.

18 OFH, pp. 123–4; *Der Weltkrieg*, V, pp. 273–4; Unruh, *Langemarck*, pp. 37–41, 61–8; Bruce Gudmundsson (1995), *Stormtroop Tactics: Innovation in the German Army, 1914–18*, Westport: Praeger, p. 5.

19 Gudmundsson, *Stormtroop Tactics*, pp. 7–13, 17–25; Eric Dorn Brose (2001), *The Kaiser's Army: The Politics of Military Technology in Germany during the Machine Age, 1870–1914*, Oxford: Oxford University Press, passim; Samuels, *Command or Control*, pp. 71–8.

20 Marc Ferro (1973), *The Great War, 1914–18*, London: Routledge, p. 8; Douglas Porch (1988), 'The French Army in the First World War' in Allan Millett and Williamson Murray (eds.), *Military Effectiveness: The First World War*, London: Unwin Hyman, pp. 198–9; Adrian Gregory (1997), 'Lost Generations: The Impact of Military Casualties on Paris, London, and Berlin' in Jay Winter and Jean-Louis Robert (eds.), *Capital Cities at War: London, Paris, Berlin, 1914–19*, Cambridge: Cambridge University Press, p. 67; C. Curtiss Johnson, 'The French Reserves, 1872–1914' in *German and Allied Reserves*, pp. 65–110.

21 Michael Howard (1986), 'Men against Fire: the Doctrine of the Offensive in 1914' in Peter Paret (ed.), *Makers of Modern Strategy*, 2nd edn., Oxford: Oxford University Press, pp. 510–26; Douglas Porch (1981), *The March to the Marne: The French Army, 1871–1914*, Cambridge: Cambridge University Press, pp. 213–32; ibid. (1975), 'The French Army and the Spirit of the Offensive, 1900–14' in Brian Bond and Ian Roy (eds.), *War and Society; A Yearbook of Military History*, London: Croom Helm, pp. 117–43; Jack Snyder (1984), *The Ideology of the Offensive: Military Decision-making and the Disaster of 1914*, Ithaca: Cornell University Press, pp. 41–106.

22 G.H. Allen and H.C. Whitehead (1916), *The Great War: The Mobilisation of the Moral and Physical Forces*, Philadelphia: George Barrie's Sons, pp. 353–60.

23 Porch, *March to Marne*, p. 213; Herwig, *First World War*, p. 120; David French (1982), *British Economic and Strategic Planning, 1905–15*, London: Allen & Unwin, p. 26; Nikolas Gardner (2003), *Trial by Fire: Command and the British Expeditionary Force in 1914*, Westport: Praeger, p. 115.

24 PRO, WO95/588, Gough Memorandum, 27 September 1914; ibid., WO79/63, Smith-Dorrien to Douglas, 4 October 1914; Andy Simpson (1995), *The Evolution of Victory*, London: Tom Donovan, pp. 20–1.

25 *Armées Françaises* I, Pt. IV, p. 342.

26 Peter Doyle (1998), *Geology of the Western Front, 1914–1918*, London: Geologists' Association, pp. 11–14, 29–32.

27 Craster, *Fifteen Rounds*, p. 133.

28 John Hussey (1997), 'The Flanders Battleground and the Weather in 1917' in Peter Liddle (ed.), *Passchendaele in Perspective: The Third Battle of Ypres*, London: Leo Cooper, pp. 140–58.

29 PRO, WO95/668, 'Notes on the River Lys'.

30 Paul Maze (1934), *A Frenchman in Khaki*, London: Heinemann, p. 74; Foch, *Memoirs*, pp. 150–1.

31 IWM, Fleming Mss, 90/28/1, Fleming to 'Randolfo', 6 December 1914.

32 IWM, Scott-Tucker Mss, 90/7/1, diary, 23 October 1914; ibid., Simpson Mss, 89/7/1, diary, 22 October 1914; PRO, WO157/224, Intelligence Summary, 15 October 1914.

33 PRO, WO95/1, Report by Henderson on RFC, 15 November 1914.

34 IWM, Mowbray Mss, 82/16/1, account, 26 October 1914; ibid., Reeve Mss, 90/21/1, diary, 26 October 1914; ibid., Garwood Mss, 91/23/1, diary, 26 October 1914; LUBLLC, Green Mss, GS0657, diary, 26 October 1914; PRO, CAB45/142, Report on RFC at First Ypres, no date; Hopper (1985), 'Diary of Old Contemptible, p. 16; *Stand To* **13**, p. 48; Craster, *Fifteen Rounds*, p. 118, in which Jeffreys erroneously records the incident as taking place on the following day; Walter Raleigh (1922), *The War in the Air I*, London: HMSO, pp. 348–9.

35 IWM, Mowbray Mss, 82/16/1, account, 23 October 1914.

36 Craster, *Fifteen Rounds*, p. 108; John Terraine (ed.) (1964), *General Jack's Diary, 1914–18*, London: Eyre & Spottiswoode, p. 65; IWM, Mowbray Mss, 82/16/1, account, 20 October 1914.

37 Maze, *Frenchman in Khaki*, pp. 80–1; General Sir Aylmer Haldane (1948), *A Soldier's Saga*, Edinburgh: Blackwood & Sons, p. 290.

38 A. Dubois (1920), *Deux Ans de Commandement sur Le Front de France, 1914–1916*, II, Paris: Charles-Lavauzelle, p. 15; IWM, Smallman Mss, 97/4/1, diary, 27 October 1914; ibid., Reeve Mss, 90/21/1, diary, 30 October 1914.

39 General Palat (1922), *La Ruée vers Calais*, Paris: Librarie Chapelot, p. 23; John Hussey (1994), 'A Hard Day at First Ypres: The Allied Generals and their Problems, 31 October 1914', *British Army Review* **107**, pp. 75–89; Hussey, 'Flanders Battleground', pp. 140–58 quoting Philip Griffiths, 'The Effects of Weather Conditions on The Third Battle of Ypres, 1917', University of Birmingham: School of Geography, Working Paper No. 51 (1989).

chapter 3

Advance to contact

On 6 October Joffre and French had agreed that the BEF should be concentrated around Doullens, Arras and St Pol rather than closer to Lille, moving to the left of the French Tenth Army under General Maud'huy behind the cover provided by the French XXI Corps and I and II Cavalry Corps. The two cavalry corps were commanded respectively by Generals Conneau and de Mitry, the latter an intelligent 57-year-old and a passionate horseman from Lorraine whose conservative religious and political views had held him back from earlier promotion.[1] The BEF was tasked to support the French advance, Smith-Dorrien being ordered to begin an advance towards the Béthune-Lillers line on 9 October to connect with de Maud'huy.

Smith-Dorrien himself, now 56 years old, had a good reputation as an innovative trainer of troops but had a notoriously foul temper. He was close to Kitchener, but was disliked by French for the changes he had made to cavalry training at Aldershot. Indeed, French had specifically asked for Herbert Plumer to command II Corps when the originally designated commander, Grierson, died of a heart attack on his way to the front in August 1914, only for Kitchener to appoint Smith-Dorrien. Smith-Dorrien was senior to Haig, who harboured some jealousy towards him, not making co-operation between them easy. It was also unfortunate that the respective Chiefs of Staff of I and II Corps, Brigadier Generals Johnnie Gough VC and George Forestier-Walker, had their own feud dating back to an incident in Somaliland in 1903. It was symptomatic of the relationship between the two staffs that all contact had been lost between I and II Corps from 26 August to 1 September 1914 during the retreat from Mons.

On 8 October, there was a meeting between French and Foch, at which it was resolved to continue to push north-eastwards. French believed that Foch's appointment was intended to prevent him developing a separate campaign in conjunction with the Belgians but knew Foch of old and was happy to co-operate with him. Foch, indeed, was junior to both French and Albert. Sir John, however, declined to put his cavalry on the French left as he wished to employ them in a wide sweep along the coast as he had originally planned.[2] Though Foch had been directed by Joffre to concentrate on breaking the German lines south of Arras on 14 October, Joffre had also accepted Foch's plan four days earlier to advance eastwards from the Ypres-Nieuport line towards the Roulers-Thourout line, driving a wedge between Beseler and the remainder of the German army in Flanders. Having isolated Beseler, Foch would then force the Lys and take the German forces on the flank, an advance that could bring decisive results if linked to another proposed French offensive further south between Brimont and Craonne.

The meeting of French and Foch was a cordial one, Foch taking care to turn out a guard of honour and offer French 'a kind of tea and champagne party' though the Frenchmen present were apparently astonished that the British preferred cream pastries to dry cake. Foch played on French's emotions, pledging never to retreat himself and reminding French that 'the British army has never drawn back in its history'. Foch's optimism was infectious, what Basil Liddell Hart later called the 'Fochian serum' continuing for some time to bolster French's own offensive inclinations in the face of increasing evidence of a heavy German concentration of force opposite the BEF.[3]

Essentially, linking with de Maud'huy's forces at Vermelles just south of the La Bassée, II Corps would press towards La Bassée and III Corps towards Armentiéres, the two corps separated by the cavalry of Conneau and de Mitry. Operating on Pulteney's left, Allenby's Cavalry Corps would move on the Messines and Wytschaete ridges south of Ypres, while Rawlinson's IV Corps would secure Ypres, connecting in turn with French and Belgian forces on the Yser. There was still ignorance as to German intentions and the advance would be in the nature almost of a large-scale reconnaissance.[4] At the same time, however, German forces were also being deployed to the north. Three German cavalry corps were now operating in Flanders, the *IV Cavalry Corps* having entered Ypres on 7 October but fallen back, while the *XIV Reserve*, *XIX (Saxon)* and elements of the *XIII (Württemberg) Corps*, all part of Crown Prince Rupprecht of Bavaria's German *Sixth Army*, were all beginning to arrive behind the cavalry screen. These were formations withdrawn from Alsace-Lorraine and Champagne. Ruprecht himself was still only 45 and the eldest son of King Louis III of Bavaria. As already mentioned, on the night of 11/12 October, the Germans took Lille and, on the following morning, pushed the French out of Vermelles. The German cavalry extended from Menin to Armentières to link with the *14th Infantry Division* operating around Lille. In order to keep in touch with de Maud'huy, Smith-Dorrien at once turned the direction of his advance eastwards rather than north-eastwards, with 13th Brigade of 5th Division to the south of the canal, the original intention having been to keep all II Corps north of the canal.

Once the early morning fog had dissipated, II Corps made good progress on another gloriously sunny day in a series of skirmish-type actions across the difficult low-lying and largely sodden ground, intersected by various watercourses and divided by hedgerows. As yet few leaves had fallen, and the foliage added to the problems of observation. In addition, the many farmhouses and outbuildings provided ready means for defensive strong points, neither side having enough artillery shells available to use against such structures. German artillery and snipers had held up the advance here and there, but opposition from the German cavalry and its attendant *Jäger* was light. The village of Givenchy was reached by the evening of 12 October, but much greater German resistance was encountered on the following day. As directed by GHQ, the British advanced over a front of some 7 miles, in itself forcing Smith-Dorrien to commit reserves at an early stage. Units moving forward in extended line, this 'South African' formation being difficult in such close country. Similarly, due to the difficulties of observation, it took place without much in the way of artillery support.[5]

In the afternoon, there was a determined counter-attack by a composite brigade of German *XIV Corps*, the *3rd Guard Cavalry Brigade* and elements of other *Guard Jäger* and *Kürassier* on Givenchy amid misty conditions turning subsequently to heavy rain. It fell primarily on Brigadier General Count Edward Gleichen's 15th Brigade, which had 'a terrible day'. The 1st Bedfordshire Regiment was pushed out of the village, isolating the 1st Dorset Regiment at Pont Fixe, and compelling the surrender of many of the 1st Cheshire Regiment at Chapelle St Roche. Both the latter's new commanding officer and second in command were caught while out on a scouting party, suggesting the difficulty of inexperienced officers. In all, 15th Brigade suffered 579 casualties. Smith-Dorrien heard that a German company had pretended to surrender and the Dorsets had stopped firing only to be rushed by others, but he did not feel this was likely. Lieutenant Colonel

Bols of the Dorsets had been wounded and captured but managed to evade his captors and crawl back to the British trenches after dusk. A section of 11th Battery, RFA in Givenchy was also unable to get its two guns away when every man was hit except George Boscawen, the son of Lord Falmouth.[6] That evening, Captain Phillips, an NCO and Private H.W. Jackson of the 21st Field Ambulance crawled out to bring in an officer who had been badly wounded during the course of the day, shot through the right lung by a sniper. The ground was wet but they managed to get the young subaltern on a ladder they had found, dragging him back with some difficulty. The young subaltern was Lieutenant Bernard Law Montgomery of the 1st Royal Warwickshires, later Field Marshal Lord Montgomery of Alamein.[7]

On 14 October II Corps suffered a particularly serious blow when Major General Hubert Hamilton of 3rd Division was killed. Hamilton had been visiting the 2nd Royal Scots and, despite warnings, had walked down the Richebourg Road, which was being swept by German shells. A fragment struck him in the head while one of the company commanders accompanying Hamilton was first knocked unconscious and then severely wounded by another shell. The 'terrible loss' had a profound impact upon Smith-Dorrien, who wrote to his wife that he had 'lost my right arm, for in my Army Corps he was that to me'. Indeed, Smith-Dorrien left a poignant account of Hamilton's funeral at Lacouture that evening: 'It was a very dark night, and at about 8.30 as many officers as could be collected from the fighting line, all his staff, and several of mine assembled and marched in procession to the churchyard. All the time a determined night attack was being made by the Germans all along our line and just in front of the Church was very heavy indeed, so much so that the rattle of machine guns, musketry and artillery fire made it very difficult to hear the Chaplain, the Revd Macpherson, read the service. Quite unmoved by the heavy fire, much of it over our heads at the time, the Chaplain read the funeral service beautifully. It was quite the most impressive funeral I have ever seen or am likely to see – and quite the most appropriate to the gallant soldier and fine leader we were laying in his last resting place. I fancy all were much moved by the scene – as I was myself.' Command passed to Colin Mackenzie.[8]

During the afternoon of 14 October, Smith-Dorrien had met French at Béthune. Though French had pronounced his 'implicit belief' in Smith-Dorrien only three days earlier, the relationship between the two was fast deteriorating, Smith-Dorrien having already queried the details of the action at Le Cateau (26 August) given in French's official dispatch back on 7 September.

Though acknowledging the difficulties in operating among mining villages, pit heads and slag heaps, French subsequently claimed that Smith-Dorrien had been deeply depressed and 'needlessly pessimistic', saying that II Corps had never recovered from Le Cateau and that he had no confidence in its fighting spirit when its units were increasingly led by inexperienced and untrained replacement officers. In part, this does reflect French's contemporary perception of Smith-Dorrien's comments as recorded in his diary. French, however, also later contrasted the performance of II Corps with III Corps, claiming Smith-Dorrien should have made more progress. Indeed, French later claimed that he had begged Smith-Dorrien to hasten his operations back on 10 October, pointedly contrasting Smith-Dorrien with Pulteney, whom French characterised as imperturbable and ready to do anything asked of him. As Smith-Dorrien also later pointed out, II Corps had taken 1000 casualties on each of the two previous days, he was holding a front of 8 miles with no reserves, his left flank was in the air, and he had just learned of Hamilton's death. Nonetheless, as George Forestier-Walker confirmed, Smith-Dorrien was not depressed.[9]

German pressure continued through 14 and 15 October, the Germans disputing 'every hedge, dyke and village' though 3rd Division used its artillery, including anti-aircraft guns, up with the infantry in the firing line to drive the Germans out of loopholed villages, the infantry using planks to cross dykes. It had taken four days, however, to get just 3 miles and at the cost of 2000 casualties including ninety officers since, in such conditions, they had to take a significant lead.[10] It was arranged for 13th Brigade to be reunited with 5th Division north of the canal. It appeared, however, that the German cavalry was being withdrawn, suggesting to Smith-Dorrien the possibility of resuming his advance towards the north-east to connect with III Corps though, in the event, there were not sufficient French troops available to take over any positions that would be vacated. In any case, though anxious for Smith-Dorrien to resume the intended general direction of advance, Sir John French also wanted La Bassée taken and this fitted reasonably well with Smith-Dorrien's new proposal to shift the focus to the south-east to outflank those German forces still opposing the French. Givenchy was retaken on 16 October. Ninth Brigade managed to secure a foothold on the Aubers ridge on the following day, and 15th Brigade reached a bridge over the canal just east of Givenchy on 18 October.

On that same day, Sir Charles Fergusson of 5th Division went home, ostensibly because he was being promoted to Lieutenant General, his place being taken by Major General T.L.N. Morland. In reality, French had wanted Fergusson removed, feeling he did not have sufficient 'determination of character' to command a division though he had done so successfully since August. Lieutenant Colonel Lord Loch, indeed, acting as liaison officer between GHQ and II Corps, believed Fergusson was not to blame for the deficiencies of his division when it was spread over 5½ miles with no reserves: 'a man might be excused if he hesitated to attack in these circumstances even with the best troops, but with shaken half-trained men and half-trained officers, it is very natural to hesitate'. Smith-Dorrien, therefore, had lost both his original divisional commanders. Moreover, the commander of 13th Brigade, Brigadier General W.B. Hickie, who had only taken over at the start of the month, had gone sick with kidney trouble on 13 October and now another key staff officer broke his collarbone when his horse rolled on him.[11] Ironically, Fergusson was brought back to command II Corps when Smith-Dorrien was elevated to command Second Army in December 1914 though subsequently removed again in 1916.

As Smith-Dorrien's Corps struggled towards La Bassée, Pulteney and Allenby were advancing on the Armentiéres-Wytschaete line. Pulteney had been slow to start, as buses the French were supposed to provide had not materialised until 12 October and, due to the fighting at La Bassée, II Corps was not to close up with III Corps as originally intended. Pulteney has also been criticised for staying at his headquarters to oversee the transport arrangements rather than going forward to observe the ground, thereby missing the opportunity to outflank the German cavalry lining the Meterenbecque stream by moving more quickly on Mont des Cats. Elements of the German *IV Cavalry Corps* were found to occupy the hill line from Mont des Cats to Kemmel and, on the evening of 12 October, 3rd Cavalry Brigade took the position, with its prominent monastery, in a dismounted action. Among the captured Germans was a mortally wounded Prince Max of Hesse. With Allenby's cavalry moving to secure more of the hill line on 13 October, Pulteney's two divisions carried out what the Official History described as 'the first formal British attack of the war' on a 5-mile front opposite the village of Meteren, situated on a ridge running down from the hill line.[12]

On a dank and misty afternoon, the attack made slow progress through the surrounding cultivated fields, many of them hopfields, the German cavalry and *Jäger* having also dug in among the houses and walls of the village. Again, however, both Pulteney and Major General H.F.M. 'Fatty' Wilson of 4th Division have been criticised for not pressing the advantage gained by 10th Brigade of 4th Division in reaching the outskirts of Meteren by mid-morning, believing earlier reports of a substantial German presence rather than that of the brigade commander, Aylmer Haldane, who was aware that the Germans had been withdrawing. Wilson, not to be confused with the BEF's Sub Chief of Staff, Major General Henry Wilson, was new to 4th Division. His able predecessor, Thomas D'Oyly Snow, had suffered a bad fall from his horse on 9 September, fracturing his pelvis, and had been forced to relinquish command, initially to Rawlinson, on 23 September though he actually remained in France until 18 October.[13] By the time the attack was reorganised, the Germans had pulled out. Nonetheless, in the event, Pulteney's caution was arguably justified by the arrival of the fresh German corps in Flanders, of which French was only belatedly convinced. Reports from the RFC had revealed that the German *XIX Corps* had occupied Lille that same day and Pulteney resolved to continue his advance before the German cavalry opposite him could be reinforced.

The following morning dawned wet and misty with air observation impossible for some hours. Moreover, Pulteney awaited a decision by French as to whether he should send one of his divisions to help out II Corps. French had suggested it on the previous evening but Pulteney had countered that his own advance should ease pressure on Smith-Dorrien. As it happened, however, Rupprecht's *VII*, *XIII* and *XIX Corps* and the *IV Cavalry Corps* had been ordered to remain on the defensive on 14 October until the 50-year-old Duke Albrecht of Württemberg's newly constituted *Fourth Army* was brought up to Flanders. A zealous if humourless soldier, Albrecht had commanded an earlier incarnation of *Fourth Army* in Belgium and Luxembourg in August. In the absence of significant opposition, therefore, de Lisle's 1st Cavalry Division was able to link up with Byng's 3rd Cavalry Division south of Ypres, and Allenby reached both Kemmel and the Messines-Wytschaete line. The progress made by III Corps was slightly slower but they reached Bailleul on 14 October. The character of the advance was illustrated at one point when a platoon of the 1st Royal Fusiliers was ordered forward rapidly to rescue the car of the 6th Division's commander, Major General J.L. Keir, which was under fire though Keir himself was not present. French had not wanted Allenby to outstrip the infantry but Allenby persuaded Sir John that the cavalry might make Lille if given their head.[14] After conferring with Foch, therefore, French met both Pulteney and Allenby and ordered III Corps to push on to the Lys and Armentières with a view towards a further advance north of Lille. It had also been agreed by

Foch and French that de Maud'huy would launch a major offensive to take the pressure off II Corps at La Bassée.

French now anticipated that an opportunity beckoned for a more general advance eastwards by both III Corps and IV Corps, Allenby's cavalry securing the crossings over the Lys. Indeed, French's orders issued on 15 October stated that it was his intention 'to advance eastwards, attacking the enemy wherever met'.[15] With another foggy morning reducing the chance of aerial reconnaissance on 16 October, and the country again difficult, progress remained slow despite the relative lack of opposition. Indeed, at one point, Sergeant William Edgington of D Battery, Royal Horse Artillery, and his colleagues attached to 3rd Cavalry Brigade were being 'supplied with hot soup & coffee' by villagers in exchange for spent shell cases and, since the German artillery seemed inactive, 'between whiles we ran races etc. to enliven things up a bit'.[16]

The 16th Lancers from Gough's 2nd Cavalry Division fought a sharp little action in Warneton, bringing up a horse artillery gun to provide covering fire as they rushed a barricade in the fading light under the glare of German Verey lights, the first anyone had encountered.[17] Pulteney, however, was reluctant to exploit the crossings secured over the Lys until he was sure the far bank had been cleared, resolving to hold back the 4th Division until the 6th Division had accomplished this task. In fact, Armentières was abandoned by the Germans, who retired on 17 October to the slight Pèrenchies ridge to the east of the town, which represented the highest ground on the road to Lille a matter of just 3 miles beyond. For 18 October French intended III Corps to move down the Lys in the direction of Menin to assist Allenby's cavalry, which had not been able to make progress on Pulteney's left. Rawlinson's IV Corps would advance eastwards from Ypres to Menin.[18] Pulteney, however, felt it necessary to clear the ridge before he could safely cross in front of it. Accordingly, Keir's 6th Division was to probe the German positions on the ridge and force them back. If resistance proved stronger than anticipated then Wilson's 4th Division would support Keir. With initial opposition indeed weak, Pulteney pushed both divisions forward, but greater resistance was encountered as the day wore on.

While III Corps made a degree of progress, however, Rawlinson's IV Corps had not taken Menin as French had intended. Rawlinson's Assistant Chief of Staff later claimed somewhat improbably that Rawlinson had wanted to advance towards Ostend rather than Messines but, in part, Rawlinson's caution was due to the loose wording of the operational order issued by the BEF's Chief of Staff, Lieutenant General Sir Archie Murray, at 1910 hours on 17 October. Thus IV Corps was directed only 'to move' on Menin whereas II Corps was ordered to attack La Bassée, though in the context of an earlier paragraph which indicated French's intention 'to carry out a vigorous attack' in conjunction with the French forces on both flanks of the BEF. Henry Wilson's reaction was, 'How that could be construed into doing nothing I can't imagine.'[19] As a result, Capper's 7th Division, whom Rawlinson found 'still green' and lacking in fitness and discipline, merely wheeled forward to face south-east, Brigadier General H.W. Watts's 21st Brigade on the far left of the wheeling movement advancing about 4000 yards.

About noon, however, it became clear to GHQ that Rawlinson was not pressing ahead and, following the appearance of the GHQ liaison officer with IV Corps, L.A.E. Price-Davies, at his headquarters to assess progress, new orders were telephoned to him at 1345 hours to do so. Indeed, a somewhat unseemly argument had broken out between Price-Davies, and Rawlinson's operations staff, ultimately also involving Rawlinson himself as to the precise interpretation of the earlier orders issued to IV Corps. Price-Davies blamed himself for moving on to see Capper rather than doing more to inform GHQ at once. Haig, whose attitude towards the ambitious Rawlinson was somewhat hostile, had been lunching with Rawlinson. Noting that Rawlinson 'may have many faults as an officer, but his bright joviality is of great value to an Army when on active service', Haig was also amused by the makeshift nature of Rawlinson's staff, which included only two regulars, others including Rawlinson's brother, Toby, Leo Amery from *The Times*, the Duke of Westminster and two or three others 'who in peace time were connected with motors or polo ponies'.

A large number of German units were now reported at Courtrai some 7 miles beyond Menin and Rawlinson decided to postpone any attack until the following day though de Mitry's cavalry did reach Roulers. Indeed, it was fortuitous that Rawlinson had been cautious. While he did later acknowledge that Rawlinson's caution may have been justified, at the time French was in no mood to forgive. French had expressed his 'disappointment' and Rawlinson variously recorded that when they met on 25 October, Sir John was 'very cold to me, and evidently still angry about Menin' and that he got 'a whigging'. Henry Wilson certainly thought that an opportunity had been missed and the French were also very critical of Rawlinson's delay as well as what they regarded as British slowness and indecision generally. It had not helped, however, that, as in so many other cases in the BEF, there was an existing tension between Rawlinson and French, in this case dating back at least to 1904.[20]

That same day further reports were received of large numbers of Germans detraining near Brussels and considerable rail activity at Courtrai. With the capture of Antwerp, Falkenhayn had given *Fourth Army* the task of making a decisive attempt to break through north of Menin to the Channel ports before the British and French had completed the concentration of their own forces in Flanders. Falkenhayn had concluded that, while the German commander on the Eastern Front, Paul von Hindenburg, and the Austro-Hungarian Supreme Command, Armee-Oberkommando (AOK), had requested more reinforcements, the available reserve formations would be insufficient to force a decision on the Eastern Front. They might do so in the West, however, despite their relative inexperience. Falkenhayn would thus regain the initiative and could either further exploit any success achieved in the West or, subsequently, still shift the strategic focus to the East. There was a risk in withdrawing trained formations from elsewhere and, indeed, of rationing artillery shells elsewhere, while there was also obviously a risk in using poorly trained reserves. Accordingly, Albrecht was given four of the new reserve corps – the *XXII*, *XXIII*, *XXVI* and *XXVII Reserve Corps* – with Beseler's *III Reserve Corps* also coming under his command.

As already indicated, until *Fourth Army* was ready to advance, *Sixth Army* would remain on the defensive along the La Bassée-Armentières-Menin line to screen its arrival. With its entraining commencing on 10 October, the army had arrived in the vicinity of Brussels three days later. It completed its movement into line between *Sixth Army* and *III Reserve Corps* on 17 October. As the new corps came up, Beseler was able to open his attack on the Belgians on the Yser on 18 October, *Fourth Army* reaching the Courtrai-Thourout line, between 10 and 17 miles from the British and French. Indeed, had Rawlinson pushed Capper's division forward to Menin, the new German corps might soon have cut it off. In the memorable phrase of Joseph Galliéni, during the 'race to the sea', the British and French were 'always twenty-four hours and an army corps behind' the Germans.[21]

On 19 October, it was still not apparent that the situation had changed that much. Indeed, French intended the advance to continue, notably that of IV Corps on Menin, the order for the day from GHQ specifically directing Rawlinson to carry out the previous order, the emphasis now being placed firmly on the earlier paragraph about a vigorous attack. According to Henry Wilson, however, who was increasingly critical of French, Sir John was already wavering in his views: 'He began by cursing the French as usual for not pushing on his right. Then he sent a wire to Smith D. [to] tell him to stop pushing. . . . The man is a fool.'[22] His right flank protected by two armoured trains and Hubert Gough's cavalry and the left flank equally covered by Byng's cavalrymen, Capper brought all three of his brigades into the front line for the assault on Menin, beginning his move forward at 0630 hours. The morning was a dull one and aerial reconnaissance was proving problematic but at about 1030, Rawlinson received reports of strong German columns approaching Menin and Roulers.

Rawlinson at once ordered the attack abandoned, though by the time the order reached Brigadier General S.T.B. Lawford's 22nd Brigade in advance of 7th Division, it was already being heavily engaged and was extracted with some difficulty. Byng's cavalry was also forced back and Rawlinson established a defensive position on the Zandvoorde-Kruiseecke line. The German *Fourth Army* had advanced some 6 to 9 miles, the *233rd*, *234th* and *235th Reserve Infantry Regiments* of *XXVI Reserve Corps* taking Roulers from the French in the face of barricades, machine guns fired 'from holes in the roofs and windows, and concealed mines exploded among the advancing troops'.[23]

The BEF as a whole was now strung over some 25 miles, but French felt it necessary to maintain the link with the Belgians to the north and, therefore, directed Haig's I Corps, which had now detrained, to move north of Ypres where French still felt few German troops were likely to be encountered. A dour and inarticulate Scot, the 53-year-old Haig aspired to replace French, using his connections to undermine French's standing in London. Together with his fellow corps commander, Smith-Dorrien, Haig was the only man apart from French to have commanded a corps – that at Aldershot – albeit in peacetime. Something of a hypochondriac who dabbled in spiritualism, Haig was a curious mixture of the progressive and the reactionary. Though he had studied his profession with some seriousness, Haig had developed somewhat rigid concepts of the immutability of battle and of his own prescience for decision-making. Generally, however, he was more astute with regard to his own prospect of advancement and burnishing his own reputation than as a tactician or strategist. Fortunately, his Chief of Staff, the 43-year-old Johnnie Gough, was somewhat different from the usual obsequious mediocrities with whom Haig normally surrounded himself and did not hesitate to stand up to Haig. Gough, however, had not fully recovered from a serious illness in May 1914.[24]

In ordering Haig's advance, French chose to disbelieve new intelligence, derived from prisoners taken by III Corps, that there were now five and a half German corps rather than three and a half north of the Lys. Indeed, at about this time, there was a serious argument between French and Colonel George MacDonogh, GSO1 of GHQ's Intelligence Section. According to Charles Deedes, French asked what the situation was, only for MacDonogh to mention that he had identified fresh formations. Losing his temper and throwing down his pen, French exclaimed, 'How the devil do you expect me to conduct my business, when you keep bringing up these new corps?' MacDonogh himself gave a slightly different version with French exclaiming, 'How the Hell do you expect me to carry out my plan of campaign if you keep bringing up these blasted divisions?'. French simply could not believe in what he regarded as 'celestial' divisions, even when MacDonogh threatened to resign. The situation was not improved by Wilson and the GSO1 of the Operations Section, Colonel George 'Uncle' Harper, trying to persuade MacDonogh to give French only the information that suited their own preconceived views and only through them. French, however, also believed what he wanted to, Murray largely conforming to his superior's mentality. An additional problem for the taciturn and intellectual MacDonogh was that he had converted to Catholicism and his refusal to back the Goughs and their allies over the Curragh had made him something of a marked man. MacDonogh, who subsequently believed his intelligence assessments had been fairly accurate, 'made rows' about the interference of the Operations Section on both 10 October and 6 November, the latter having the desired effect of putting arrangements on what he regarded as a proper footing.[25]

Generally, field intelligence was coming in from a variety of sources including information from 'reliable agents', Belgian civilians, 'old fashioned' but effective German POWs, captured documents, patrols, radio intercepts, and aerial reconnaissance. To give but one example, IV Corps Intelligence Summary on 16 October listed information derived from an armoured car patrol, villagers, an agent at Staden, a workman at Poelcappelle, an air reconnaissance, and a paper found in Hooge Chateau signed by an officer of the 13th *Jäger zu Pferde* and dated 8 October. An agent network was in the process of establishment, Major Walter Kirke having begun to try to organise one behind German lines in late August although it was only on 16 October that a man and a woman were passed through the Belgian lines at Nieuport and only really by the end of November that Captain A.C. Cameron had established a network embracing agents at the rail junctions of Thielt, Thourot and Coutrai. These, therefore, were ultimately of more use in establishing the eventual shift of German forces from the West to the Eastern Front after the ultimate failure of the Ypres offensive. Of most significance was the interception of radio messages, the British and French picking up over fifty messages transmitted in plain language from German units between September and November 1914. Indeed, radio interception was to provide warning of six full-scale German attacks during the battle for Ypres. The use of ciphers was as yet in its infancy due to the cumbersome process but some German ciphers, too, were being broken on the Western Front in October and November 1914.[26]

The dispute over intelligence was sadly characteristic of much that was wrong about the staff arrangements at GHQ. Unfortunately, French, who lacked staff training himself, tended to be poor at choosing his personal staff. Archie Murray, though a man of considerable staff experience, was too ready to defer to French and, in any case, in very poor physical condition. In turn, Murray's position was being none too subtly undermined by Henry Wilson, who had earned a reputation as an intriguer even before his role in the Curragh affair. Wilson was to grow increasingly critical of French and Murray, urging his own candidacy to replace Murray on a number of occasions, not least during the Ypres campaign, and welcoming the apparent French support for his even greater elevation to command the BEF itself.[27]

Elements of all the German Reserve Corps had indeed been identified by 20 October but there was also a tendency by both the British and the French to regard them as largely untrained and ineffective. Consequently, on the evening of 19 October, French directed Haig to advance through Thourout to Bruges and Ghent though he also had discretion once through Ypres to attack towards Courtrai with a portion of his corps. Henry Wilson, who was beginning to grasp the difficulties of advancing further, noted sarcastically that 'Bruges for all practical purposes is as far as Berlin'.[28] Equally, II and III Corps were to continue their advances. The move of I Corps would be covered by IV Corps, which would also again attempt to take Menin if this did not threaten to interfere with the advance of I Corps.

Thus far, losses had been relatively light, the BEF suffering just over 4500 casualties between 9 and 18 October. French, therefore, may well have believed that his advance was a last effort to make progress before German reinforcements arrived and even something of a defensive movement to control as much of the coast as possible. Joffre later criticised what he saw as the slowness of the British in these first few weeks of fleeting opportunity. Interestingly, Archie Murray, visiting London later in October, remarked to Kitchener in a precursor of Galliéni's later view already quoted, that Joffre was always two days too late with always two divisions too few.[29] The situation was to change decisively, however, on 20 October for German *Fourth* and *Sixth Armies* were now both to be committed to a simultaneous offensive north and south of Ypres to attempt to envelop the BEF.

Notes and references

1 Ratinaud, Jean, *La Course* (1967), la Mer, Paris: Fayard, p. 222.

2 Gilbert, *Churchill Companion*, pp. 218–19; IWM, French Mss, PP/MCR/C32, diary, 7 and 9 October 1914; French, *1914*, pp. 199–205.

3 Holmes, *Little Field Marshal*, pp. 243–4; Liddell Hart, *Foch*, pp. 127, 139; Ratinaud, *Course*, pp. 212–14; Michael Neiberg (2003), *Foch*, Washington: Brassey's, p. 34.

4 *Armées Françaises*, I, Pt. IV, pp. 310–11.

5 PRO, WO 95/630, II Corps Operational Report for 11 October to 18 November 1914; ibid., CAB45/141, Stracke to Edmonds, 31 December 1923.

6 IWM, Smith-Dorrien Mss, 87/47/7, II Corps Operational Report, 13 October 1914; ibid., 87/47/2, war diary, 13 October 1914; Smith-Dorrien, *Forty-Eight Years*, pp. 444–5; Count Edward Gleichen (1917), *The Doings of the Fifteenth Infantry Brigade, August 1914 to March 1915*, London: Blackwood, pp. 160–5; Gardner, *Trial by Fire*, pp. 118–20.

7 IWM, Jackson Mss, 78/59/1, account of rescue of Montgomery; Nigel Hamilton (1981), *Monty*, New York: McGraw-Hill, pp. 87–8.

8 Lord Ernest Hamilton (1916), *The First Seven Divisions*, London: Hurst and Blackett, p. 151; Royal Archives (hereafter RA), Geo V Q.832/335, Smith-Dorrien to Wigram, 17 October 1914; IWM, Smith-Dorrien Mss, 87/47/2, war diary, 14 October 1914; ibid., 87/47/10, diary, 14 October 1914; Smith-Dorrien, *Forty-Eight Years*, p. 446.

9 IWM, Smith-Dorrien Mss, 87/47/5, Smith-Dorrien to wife, 11 October 1914; ibid., French Mss, PP/MCR/C32, diary, 14 October 1914; Ian F.W. Beckett (1993), *The Judgement of History: Sir Horace Smith-Dorrien, Lord French and 1914*, London: Tom Donovan, pp. 44, 57–60; French, *1914*, pp. 206, 209–10, 214–15.

10 IWM, Smith-Dorrien Mss, 87/47/7, II Corps Operational Report, 15 October 1914; Smith-Dorrien, *Forty-Eight Years*, p. 448.

11 IWM, French Mss, 75/46/6, French to Military Secretary, 13 October 1914; ibid., Smith-Dorrien Mss, 87/47/2, war diary, 18 October 1914; ibid., 87/47/5, Smith-Dorrien to wife, 27 October 1914; ibid., Loch Mss, 71/12/2, diary, 15 October 1914; Smith-Dorrien, *Forty-Eight Years*, pp. 445, 450–1.

12 Farrar-Hockley, *Ypres 1914*, p. 59; OFH, p. 96.

13 Farrar-Hockley, *Ypres 1914*, pp. 59–62; IWM, Snow Mss, 76/79/1, Snow to wife, 10 September, 23 September and 18 October 1914.

14 T.O. Marsden (1920), *A Short History of the 6th Division, 1914–19*, London: Hugh Rees, p. 7; Anthony Farrar-Hockley (1973), *Goughie*, London: Hart-Davis, MacGibbon, pp. 135–6.

15 OFH p. 507; SHAT 18N 134, Murray to BEF, 15 October 1914.

16 IWM, Edgington Mss, 88/52/1, diary, 16 October 1914.

17 Gough, *Fifth Army*, p. 59.

18 IWM, Wilson Mss, HHW 3/8/8, notes of meeting with Foch, 17 October 1914.

19 OFH, pp. 508–9; PRO, CAB45/141, Kerr Montgomery to Edmonds, 3 June 1923; ibid., WO95/1, GHQ Operations Section War Diary, 18 October 1914; Atkinson, *Seventh Division*, pp. 22–4; NAM, Rawlinson Mss, 5201-33-25, diary, 18 and 19 October 1914; IWM, Wilson Mss, DS/MISC/80, diary, 18 October 1914.

20 Robin Prior and Trevor Wilson (1992), *Command on the Western Front*, Oxford: Blackwell, p. 13; Atkinson, *Seventh Division*, pp. 25–30; PRO, WO95/706, IV Corps Operations Section War Diary, 18 October 1914; ibid., Kitchener Mss, PRO30/57/51, WB4, Rawlinson to Kitchener, 17 October 1914; IWM, French Mss, 75/46/6, French to Kitchener, 20 October 1914; ibid., PP/MCR/C32, diary, 19 October 1914; ibid., Price-Davies Mss, 77/78/4, Price-Davies to wife, 18 October 1914; NAM, Rawlinson Mss, 5201-33-25, diary, 25 October 1914; ibid., 5201-33-17, Rawlinson to Kitchener, 17 October 1914; NLS, Haig Mss, Acc 3155/99, diary, 18 October 1914; French, *1914*, p. 225; SHAT 18N 134, Huguet to Foch, 19 October 1914; *Armées Françaises* I Pt. IV Annexes Vol. III, pp. 730–1, 778–9, Huguet to Foch, 19 October and 20 October 1914; ibid., Annexes IV, pp. 893–6, Foch to Joffre, 13 November 1914; Holmes, *Little Field Marshal*, p. 127.

21 *Ypres, 1914: An Official Account published by Order of the German General Staff*, London: Constable, 1919, trans. by G.C. W[ynne], pp. 6–8; Joseph Galliéni (1920), *Mémoires du Général Galliéni*, Paris: Payot, p. 197.

22 OFH, pp. 510–11; IWM, Wilson Mss, DS/MISC/80, diary, 19 October 1914.

23 PRO, WO95/706, Capper to Rawlinson, 19 Oct. 1914; *Ypres, 1914*, p. 24.

24 Beckett, *Johnnie Gough*, p. 181.

25 Deedes, 'View from GHQ', p. 31; PRO, CAB45/141, MacDonogh to Edmonds, 14 and 22 November 1922 and undated; ibid., Radcliffe to Edmonds,

23 November 1923 and 21 January 1924; Michael Occleshaw (1989),
Armour against Fate: British Military Intelligence in the First World War,
London: Columbus Books, p. 28.

26 PRO, CAB45/141, MacDonogh to Edmonds, no date; ibid., WO95/706,
Intelligence Summaries; David French (1984), 'Sir John French's Secret Service
on the Western Front, 1914–15', *Journal of Strategic Studies* 7, pp. 423–40;
John Ferris (1988), 'The British Army and Signals Intelligence in the Field
during the First World War', *Intelligence and National Security* 3/4, pp. 23–48.
See also John Ferris (1992), *The British Army and Signals Intelligence during the
First World War*, Stroud: Sutton for Army Records Society.

27 IWM, Wilson Mss, DS/MISC/80, diary, 7, 8, 24, 29 October 1914.

28 NLS, Haig Mss, Acc 3155/99, diary, 19 October 1914; IWM, Wilson Mss,
DS/MISC/80, diary, 20 October 1914; French, *1914*, p. 230.

29 Philpott, *Anglo-French Relations*, p. 48; Brock and Brock, *Asquith*, pp. 287–8.

chapter 4

Kindermord

Two actions in particular on 20 October – at Le Pilly and Ennetières – were to typify much of what was to happen frequently thereafter. On II Corps' front, the 2ⁿᵈ Royal Irish Rifles of 8ᵗʰ Brigade in 3ʳᵈ Division were cut off in the village of Le Pilly and the survivors compelled to surrender. In the course of its doomed defence, a battalion, which had mustered 578 all ranks, lost 257 dead, including its commanding officer, Major E.H. Daniell, and 290 taken prisoner. The battalion had received the latest draft of six officers and 353 men only five days earlier, the seventh draft since the retreat from Mons. Mackenzie of 3ʳᵈ Division had realised the battalion was too far forward and it had been intended to pull it back that very night.[1] Smith-Dorrien's Corps, especially 5ᵗʰ Division, was becoming increasingly exhausted, and on 20 October the attempt to take La Bassée was abandoned, the intention being to look for opportunities on the front of I Corps, by now arriving at Ypres. A more extensive German counter-attack than that which had trapped the Royal Irish Rifles developed on 21 October, 3ʳᵈ Division being pulled back to a more defensive line that evening. There was then a general withdrawal of about a mile to 2¹⁄₂ miles to a hastily prepared reserve line on 22/23 October, Smith-Dorrien having received French's permission at 0200 hours.

During 22 October, both the Cheshires and the Dorsets had been forced back from Violaines. Smith-Dorrien concluded they 'did not put up a resolute resistance, and it was apparent to me that the spirit of other Battalions of the Fifth Division, who were not closely engaged today, is by no means what it should be if they are to repel successfully the resolute attacks which the enemy have been making during the last two days, and appear likely to continue to make'. Yet, the Cheshires, of course, had already suffered severely on 13 October, and their new commanding officer had pleaded with Morland to allow them to remain in an exposed forward. Morland had consented against his own better judgement. The 1st Duke of Cornwall's Light Infantry had been tasked with restoring the line but was itself in an exhausted state with not much more than 300 men remaining. The retirement was covered by the arrival of the advance units of the Lahore Division of the Indian Corps, though Smith-Dorrien was only authorised to call upon them if absolutely necessary.

Smith-Dorrien claimed he had not realised 'how little reliance can now be placed on several battalions' in 5th Division until he had seen Morland that afternoon. However, it seems that it was the intervention of Forestier-Walker and Lord Loch that forced Smith-Dorrien to bring the state of the division to the attention of French. According to Loch, 'Smith-Dorrien would not tell the C-in-C, so I gathered, so I made up my mind to report it myself. I luckily did not find Smith-Dorrien at the HQ so I left a message with Forestier-Walker as to what I was going to say – F. Walker agreed with me and said he would do his best to get Smith-Dorrien to own up. I reported to the C-in-C and did not hide anything.'[2]

The Indians had landed at Marseilles on 26 September and detrained at Hazebrouck on 20 October under the command of the 57-year-old Lieutenant General Sir James Willcocks, a British officer who had seen much of his service in West Africa. The Sirhind Brigade of the Lahore Division had been temporarily left in Egypt to help in the defence of the Suez Canal until Territorial formations could get there from Britain. Meeting French in the company of Pulteney and the 54-year-old Major General H.B.B. Watkis of the Lahore Division at Estaires on 23 October – division and brigade commanders in the Indian Corps were far older than their British counterparts – to discuss the positioning of the Indians, Smith-Dorrien was struck by the incongruity of the honour guard of French Spahis from North Africa thoughtfully provided by Conneau: 'The scene was more suited to an Eastern pageant than to a town which had been partly destroyed by shell fire a few days before, and which was still the headquarters of the French Cavalry General, whose guns could be heard at the moment engaged with the enemy not very far distant.'[3]

In the case of III Corps, German pressure was particularly exerted around the villages of Escobeques, Englos and Capingham. Pulteney had ordered his divisions to try and keep sufficient numbers of men in reserve for local counter-attacks but it had not been possible to do so given the continuing German activity. Moreover, the positions in which III Corps found itself at nightfall on 19 October were by no means continuous, with, in many cases, isolated platoons thinly spread across a wide frontage. Subsequently, Pulteney was to emphasise the need to entrench ground gained but to straighten the lines and make them continuous as soon as practicable, with local reserves kept in hand and potential 'supporting points' in the rear identified.[4]

Occupying some French trenches at Fromelles, officers of the 2nd Royal Welch Fusiliers of 19th Brigade were suspicious that the trench seemed very shallow and the parapet remarkably high; poking a stick into the parapet they found it was simply hay revetted with ladders and with only a loose covering of earth. Generally, the Royal Welch stood in their trenches shoulder to shoulder with little room to spare, one particularly bad-tempered company commander who had recently joined from the 1st Battalion drawing his revolver and threatening to shoot men getting in his way as he attempted to squeeze past them. With one of the platoon commanders adopting similar methods, the two were soon nicknamed Buffalo Bill and Deadwood Dick.[5]

At Ennetières, the 2nd Sherwood Foresters of Brigadier General Walter Congreve VC's 18th Brigade, 6th Division was assaulted in the afternoon of 20 October by the German *26th Division* of *XIII Corps* then, in the gathering dusk of early evening, by *25th Reserve Division*. In exposed trenches, unable to see sufficiently clearly to fire at long range and after two nights without rest, the Foresters were overwhelmed in a running battle back towards La Vallée. There the survivors found themselves intercepted by yet more Germans. Indeed, in the confusion, these Germans were initially assumed to be British reinforcements. Virtually the entire battalion had been killed or captured and the brigade as a whole took 1119 casualties. Further north, 17th Brigade was forced back from Prémesques. Here, two officers of the 2nd, The Prince of Wales's Leinster Regiment, Captains F.E. Whitton and R.A. Orpen-Palmer were captured, Whitton unable to walk and Orpen-Palmer losing one eye and temporarily blinded in the other. Somehow, they managed to escape, Orpen-Palmer carrying and following Whitton's directions until they stumbled across the 1st Royal Fusiliers.[6]

Like Smith-Dorrien, Pulteney ordered a withdrawal, in places of up to 2 miles to a shorter and more defensible line. To complete the increasingly difficult situation, some 24,000 Germans also forced the 9000 men of

Allenby's Cavalry Corps back to the St Yves-Messines-Hollebeke line. In the case of Gough's 2nd Cavalry Division on the eastern slopes of the Messines-Wytschaete ridge, of the eighteen 13-pounder guns available, many had now become all but useless as the buffer springs broke from constant use. Short of wire and shovels, Gough had instructed his staff officer, 'Moses' Beddington, to impress the local inhabitants to help dig trenches around Wytschaete: 'It all went well until a few shells whizzed over their heads, when they immediately dispersed, leaving me with a very few.'[7] Meanwhile, IV Corps had pushed towards Menin once more but had come under heavy artillery fire and had also fallen back to the Zandvoorde-Langemarck line. Covered to some extent by IV Corps, Haig had deployed 2nd Division behind Byng's 3rd Cavalry Division and 1st Division behind 2nd Division on the Elverdinghe-Poperinghe line.

The point had arrived when, to quote the historian of the Royal Scots Greys, the cavalry had 'gradually congealed' from 'a fluid line of mounted men occasionally dismounting to use their rifles' to 'a rigid line of dismounted men occasionally using their horses to move from one part of the battlefield to another'.[8] Directing Smith-Dorrien, Rawlinson and Allenby to entrench and hold their positions, French now anticipated that Haig could make good progress against the supposedly ill-trained German reserve formations. At most French seemed to believe there were only a few *Landwehr* divisions and 'nothing of any quantity or consequence'.[9] In reality, German strength was increasing all the time and II, III and the Cavalry Corps were all hard pressed throughout 21 October. Pulteney, for example, was holding a 12-mile frontage against two German corps, Brigadier General Aylmer Hunter-Weston's 11th Brigade being broken up so that its four battalions could be thrown in as stop gaps elsewhere. Hunter-Weston took something of a paternalistic view of his brigade somewhat out of character with his later reputation as a thrusting corps commander indifferent to losses. At the same time, however, he believed his duty done once an engagement had commenced, leaving the conduct to his subordinates, happily going off game shooting on 28 October, for example, while his brigade was in action. In the case of 19th Brigade, it was holding 2 miles with effectively a single line of men, with no supports, with only a few strands of wire some 25 yards to the front of its positions and a field of fire rarely more than 400 yards at most amid the trees, buildings and haystacks. In the Cameronians, Captain Ritchie noted that his men seemed almost to enjoy the shelling: 'The men are quite calm although the shells are nasty. Five men on the right flank bow down gracefully together, ducking from a shell. I laugh and they laugh, amused at being caught at it.'[10]

In the late afternoon of 21 October the 2nd Inniskilling Fusiliers of 12th Brigade were forced temporarily out of Le Gheer, the situation being restored by the commitment of the 1st Somerset Light Infantry and two companies of the 1st East Lancashire Regiment from Hunter-Weston's brigade and a single company of the 2nd Essex Regiment, though it took until dusk to regain all the lost ground. Lieutenant Colonel R.S. Fox's 38th Brigade, RFA also did sterling work in winning time for a counter-attack to be organised. Hunter-Weston reported that 'the enemy were mown down and completely bewildered and ran in all directions'. Captain F.S. Bradshaw of the 1st Somerset Light Infantry similarly recorded, 'Did not have to go out last night, but early this morning went out and took the village of Le Gheer. . . . Stayed there all day, had a deuce of a fight, killed a lot of Huns and took about 60 prisoners.' In fact, some 130 Germans were captured.[11] It was noticeable that some Germans were learning from the failure of massed attack in column and were now advancing in continuous swarms of small groups. Similarly, a gap that opened in 19th Brigade's line around Le Maisnil was only closed at midnight by a partial withdrawal.

The initial loss of Le Gheer had endangered the flank of de Lisle's 1st Cavalry Division but it was able to hold out on the Messines ridge despite the thinning ranks of individual regiments. By contrast, 3rd Cavalry Brigade of Hubert Gough's 2nd Cavalry Division was shelled out of the trenches at Kortewilde. The line was withdrawn to Hollebeke Chateau but, mistaking Gough's directions as to a possible further line of retreat if necessity compelled it for an actual order to retreat, the brigade evacuated the chateau grounds. Gough at once ordered the ground retaken, 6th Cavalry Brigade and Capper's 7th Division both moving to cover the gap.[12]

In the event, the German cavalry which had been advancing on Hollebeke proved remarkably passive and most of the ground was re-occupied at small loss. Significantly, the overall commander of the German cavalry, Lieutenant General von Hollen, formerly commanding German *IV Cavalry Corps*, who had been given direction of all three German cavalry corps in the Ypres section only on 20 October, was promptly superseded on the evening of 21 October by General von Marwitz. In turn, Capper's 7th Division had come under great pressure, its difficulties increased by holding some 5$\frac{1}{2}$ miles of frontage with the division bent almost at a right angle around Kruiseecke and with entrenching tools in very short supply. Efforts to find agricultural implements in the surrounding farms and villages proved largely fruitless. Moreover, given the earlier failure to reach Menin, Capper's men were dug in where they could easily be seen by German artillery observers on the ridge around Passchendaele and Becelaere. In part, this was a result of the inexperience of the division compared to those who had been on the Aisne and who had learned that partial concealment and a short field of fire was preferable to being under such observation.[13]

The Germans broke through Capper's line at Poezelhoek at the junction between the positions of 20th and 21st Brigades. A single company of the 2nd Royal Scots Fusiliers, however, managed to hold on in the grounds of Polderhoek. As I Corps began to advance to the left of IV Corps, moreover, some of the pressure eased hence Capper's ability to cover the gap at Hollebeke uncovered by the retreat of 3rd Cavalry Brigade. Indeed, during the course of the day, there was only a minor withdrawal by 22nd Brigade around Zonnebeke Chateau.

Haig meanwhile was endeavouring to advance towards Thourout in accordance with French's intentions to maintain an offensive since Sir John still chose to believe that only one German corps was in the vicinity. The opposition actually encountered appears to have given Haig and Johnnie Gough an increasingly poor opinion of French's judgement.[14] It was intended that no advance should begin until 1st Division had come up level with 2nd Division, the assumption being that this would be by about 0700 on 21 October. In the event, 1st Division was delayed over the roads and the Yser bridges by the number of civilian refugees and the movements by French Territorials, who were holding Langemarck. Notwithstanding the problems presented I Corps by French troops, the French found the British movements 'eccentric' but Sir John chose not to change the direction of Haig's advance towards Courtrai as Foch wished.[15] Consequently, the advance only began at 0850, the first objective being the Passchendaele-Poelcappelle line. The enclosed nature of the country intersected by streams and high hedgerows greatly impeded progress as did the lack of clear lines of visibility among the cottages and many small copses.

The nature of the problem can perhaps be illustrated by the experience of the 2nd Oxford and Bucks Light Infantry of 5th Brigade as it advanced towards Poelcappelle. Just short of the Haanixbeek stream, a hedge was encountered, interwoven with barbed wire. There was a gateway in the hedge, however, but when officers and men tried to pass through it they came under machine-gun fire. According to one popular account, five officers were killed and five wounded before the gateway was successfully forced and other gaps made in the hedgerow but, in reality, as the regimental chronicle recorded, few if any of these officers were hit at this point, though the battalion did suffer thirty casualties getting through the hedgerow. Most, indeed, of the battalion's 220 casualties that day including its officer losses occurred later when the battalion came up against German trenches between the Haanixbeek and Stroombeek streams near Langemarck. Captain Harry 'Rabbit' Dillon, who found himself commanding men from the 2nd Highland Light Infantry as well as an assorted group from various Oxford and Bucks companies, recorded that 'high explosives, shrapnel, machine-guns, and rifles blended into one unending roar' and he was almost completely deaf by nightfall.[16]

At one point, the 1st Irish Guards from 4th (Guards) Brigade were also detached to assist 7th Division at Zonnebeke. Trefusis, the adjutant of the Irish Guards, accompanied his CO to the headquarters of 22nd Brigade and found the staff 'in a very nervous state. There were a certain amount of bullets flying about in the town, but nothing unusual under the circumstances; but they seemed to fear almost immediate attack and decided to retire.' Trefusis borrowed a car and went to inform his own brigade, not getting back to his battalion until 0300 on the following day. Reports that reached Haig during the day that the 1st (Guards) Brigade had been forced back as a consequence of a withdrawal by 22nd Brigade proving happily false. Rawlinson, however, criticised Lawford of 22nd Brigade for taking unnecessary casualties 'due to the bad siting of trenches', though rifles and machine guns had also become clogged with the sand thrown up by German shells. Haig was also critical of Lawford, judging him inexperienced.[17]

German artillery fire continued to increase through the day so that 2nd Division was halted just beyond Zonnebeke having advanced between 1000 and 2000 yards. Men of the 2nd Grenadier Guards took the opportunity to milk the cows aimlessly wandering about whenever there was an interval in the German shelling. To the west 1st Division advanced about 1000 yards before also being halted. Patterson of the 1st South Wales Borderers noted that the larger German shells – 'coal-boxes' – had more of a psychological than a physical effect: 'We are shelled from every side and the big coal-boxes are almost more than flesh and blood can bear, though the damage they do is next to nothing unless one lucky shot happens to get in the middle of a mass of men.'[18] By the time 1st Division was halted, the French Cavalry Corps on its left had begun to withdraw to the Yser in the face of a strong German force from the *46ᵗʰ Reserve Division* of General von Kleist's *XXIII Reserve Corps* advancing from the direction of Houthulst forest. Fortunately, the commander of the French 7ᵗʰ Cavalry Division refused to obey the order until it was repeated, for which Haig was duly grateful. Indeed, generally I Corps benefited from the presence of the French as well as its own greater initial strength at the start of its Ypres operations compared to II Corps.[19] Even further to the north, the Belgians were also being heavily shelled. Haig was also mindful of the pressure being exerted on Rawlinson's corps to his right and resolved not to attempt to go beyond the original first objective.

As it happened French arrived at Haig's headquarters during the afternoon as did General de Mitry. Rawlinson and the commander of the French Territorials, Bidon, were also present. French, who was aware that Joffre was moving up more troops, approved of Haig's decision and impressed on de Mitry the need to protect Haig's left flank, against which the Germans were now advancing in the absence of the French cavalry. Sir John, indeed, suggested he might be forced to pull back if the French did not assist, Haig noting that, 'Sir J's French is most amusing but the French generals kept their countenance wonderfully & seemed much upset.'[20] The only available reserve – 2ⁿᵈ Brigade – had to be committed, forming a distinct salient in Haig's line.

Aerial reconnaissance had been all but impossible during the course of 21 October due to low cloud, but information received from German prisoners and the sheer weight of opposition had now clearly confirmed that there were large German forces opposite the BEF. *German Fourth Army* had elements of von Carlowitz's *XXVII Reserve Corps* opposite IV Corps and elements of its *XXIII* and *XXVI Reserve Corps* opposite I Corps. The French and Belgians were confronted by more elements of the *XXIII Corps* together with elements of *III* and *XXII Reserve Corps*. To the south of Ypres, German *Sixth Army* had elements of its *VII Corps* opposite II Corps and elements of *XIII Corps* and *XIX (Saxon) Corps* opposite III Corps and Conneau's French Cavalry Corps, with units from the *I, IV* and *V Cavalry Corps* confronting Allenby's Cavalry Corps. As the Official History later put it, 'seven and one third British divisions and five Allied cavalry divisions, reduced by fighting, were holding a front of some thirty-five to thirty-six miles against eleven German divisions, eight of which were fresh, and eight cavalry divisions'.[21]

Finally accepting the impossibility of continuing his projected advance, a disillusioned French directed the BEF to entrench and hold its ground. In

I Corps Haig's CRA, Brigadier General Henry Horne, who was later to command First Army, feared the worst: 'We are now digging trenches and it looks rather as though this may also degenerate into the same sort of stalemate which existed on the Aisne.'[22] At least the Lahore Division was now becoming available while, on a visit to GHQ, Joffre also promised to send the French IX Corps from the Champagne region to Ypres. As the meeting wore on, however, Joffre was considerably alarmed when French asked him for assistance in forming an entrenched camp at Boulogne large enough for the entire BEF. According to Henry Wilson, 'Joffre's face instantly became quite square and he replied that such a thing could not be allowed for a moment.' French had spoken of fortifying Calais or Boulogne as early as 5 October, reiterating his request to Kitchener five days later, and had then raised the same possibility with Foch on 10 October. Foch had suggested as an alternative a line of defence along the St Omer-Bethune Canal. In fact, French's initial concept of a fortified base had been partly suggested to him by Wilson, though the latter had merely envisaged holding Boulogne with Territorials. Alarmed at French and Murray contemplating actual withdrawal, Wilson had therefore contacted Foch on 14 October, prompting a visit from Foch on the following day.[23] Inwardly seething, Joffre maintained his customary outward calm, pointing out that measures had been taken to inundate the approaches to Dunkirk if necessary and to establish a reserve line of defence. Joffre then passed on the Belgian headquarters at Furnes where he was cheered by the arrival of the French 42nd Division, which he reviewed in the company of King Albert. On 28 October, however, Joffre was to authorise Foch to create a fortified zone to cover the Channel ports in the rear of Tenth Army. In the meantime, mercurial as ever, French telegraphed Kitchener a few minutes after midnight to predict that 'the enemy are vigorously playing their last card and I am confident that they will fail'.[24]

The Germans did not concentrate their resources on any one sector but continued to operate along the whole front from Armentières in the south to the Yser in the north. They do not appear to have realised the weakness of the BEF's overstretched line and such had been the British resistance that they believed they faced strongly entrenched positions. They themselves had to improvise trenches with anything that came to hand in the general absence of entrenching tools. The semi-official history of the Ypres campaign published in 1917, indeed, suggested they faced a 'well planned maze of trenches behind broad wire entanglements' held by picked troops. The reality was that the British trenches were invariably short disconnected sections of trench not much more than 3 feet in depth and without wire or dugouts: the first consignment of two million sandbags ordered since the beginning of the war arrived in France only on 28 October.[25] Rarely was there any second position prepared while the forward positions were themselves often separated by anything between 200 and 400 yards. In most cases, therefore, small groups of British soldiers, whether infantrymen or dismounted cavalrymen, fought separate actions. By day the gaps could be covered to some extent by artillery and by crossfire from other British positions, the available artillery batteries being dug in where possible on reverse slopes and reserves for counter-attack held under cover of the woods. It was generally not possible to improve the positions until nightfall, when supplies were also moved up to the front. At the same time, however, gaps in the line were highly vulnerable to penetration once the light began to fade.

It was on 22 October that the German legend of Langemarck was born although it was not until 11 November that a communiqué was issued by OHL referring to young regiments 'west of Langemarck' singing 'Deutschland, Deutschland über Alles' as they 'broke forward against the front line of the enemy's positions'.[26] Apart from selecting the more Germanic name of Langemarck over the more accurate Bixschoote, the patriotic and nationalist notion of singing the national anthem, and the emotive but inaccurate reference to young regiments, the language was studiously vague on the actual result of this offensive though it was claimed that 2000 French and six machine guns had been captured. Adolf Hitler, who served with the *16th (Bavarian) Reserve Infantry Regiment* of the *6th Bavarian Reserve Division* in *XIV Reserve Corps*, later described his apparent impressions in *Mein Kampf*: 'And from the distance the strains of a song reached our ears, coming closer and closer, leaping from company to company, and just as Death plunged a busy hand into our ranks, the song reached us too and we passed it along: Deutschland, Deutschland über Alles, über Alles in der Welt.' It has been suggested quite plausibly that Hitler's brief allusion to one specific aspect of Langemarck indicates that it was of more significance to the Nazi movement than to Hitler himself and that he merely paid lip service to the myth because it was opportune to do so. Moreover, according to the regimental history, the song was 'Die Wacht am Rhein' and it was sung primarily to identify the unit in the mist as they wore *Landsturm* caps rather than pickelhaubes and had been mistaken for English troops as a result.

Other German regimental accounts concur that German troops attacking 1st Division sang as a recognition signal on 22 or 23 October, the *206th*

Reserve Infantry Regiment singing 'Deutschland über Alles', and the *204th Reserve Infantry Regiment* singing both 'Deutschland über Alles' and, then when that failed to stop them being shelled by their own artillery, breaking into 'Die Wacht am Rhein' though this was on the evening of 25 October. It is also said that men of *XXII Corps* sang while attacking Dixmude on 21 October, while some German regimental histories also refer to singing while attacking French positions on 10 November again at Dixmude. Similarly, the *17th (Bavarian) Reserve Infantry Regiment* sang patriotic songs as a recognition signal when fired on by the *21st Reserve Regiment* by mistake at Wytschaete on 31 October. The regimental history of the *205th Infantry Regiment* also mentions its men finding a piano in a ruined house at Bixschoote on 10 November and playing 'Deutschland über Alles'. One German veteran, Rudolf Binding, who did much to give a specific nationalist meaning to the event, recalled in his memoirs in 1929 that a neighbouring division – he was serving with the cavalry – sang as they pressed home their attack. Another veteran, Ludwig Renn, however, suggested that it would have been physically impossible to sing while undertaking a bayonet charge.[27]

British accounts certainly mention the Germans shouting and singing, though the latter was often mentioned at second hand. Captain R.M. Glazebrook of 1st Gloucestershire Regiment in 3rd Brigade wrote in 1922, for example, of those Germans from the *46th Reserve Division* attacking 1st Brigade as singing 'patriotic songs'. Hubert Gough recalled the attack on his 2nd Cavalry Division at Wytschaete on 31st October being accompanied by the Germans singing 'Die Wacht am Rhein' while his French interpreter, Paul Maze, sent into the village at about 2100 hours that night also heard a German band playing their men into battle with the same song. On the other hand, Haig's CRA, Henry Horne, recorded the Germans attacking 'in dense formation and singing "The Watch on the Rhine"' on the evening of 23 October. Horne had heard that some were only 16 or 17 and was 'sad to think of all this waste of young life'. Henry Wilson, who could not have been an eyewitness, also recorded the singing of 'Die Wacht am Rhein' in his diary for 24 October. Similarly, Archibald Home of 1st Cavalry Division, though actually spending 25 October shooting pheasants behind the lines, also heard later that day of the Germans singing 'Die Wacht am Rhein', noting 'they are fine *men* these Germans and fine fighters. . . . As a nation they have a fine patriotism to drive them on in this way.'[28]

The British also readily acknowledged, as G.C. Wynne made clear in his notes on the semi-official German account of the battle, that the Germans had attacked with great courage, 'officers carrying regimental colours ran on ahead of the men and planted the colours in the ground to give their men a point to make for, a mounted officer rode forward, exposing himself recklessly, to encourage his soldiers, but the musketry of the British infantry was too much for the Germans . . .' Similarly, Rawlinson wrote that the German infantry 'has astonished me by the steady advance they make in extended lines one after the other just as one sees at manoeuvres'.[29]

Whatever the truth, the reserve corps came on with considerable courage and died in large numbers. The German semi-official account, which also proclaimed the troops had sung 'Deutschland über Alles', indicates some German regiments had been reduced by half, necessitating the commitment of the army's 'last reserves', the *37th Landwehr Brigade* and *2nd Ersatz Brigade*. The *205th Reserve Infantry Regiment* had 977 casualties between 19 and 31 October, the *234th* some 681 between 21 and 24 October and the three battalions of the *240th* a total of 1155 between 20 and 31 October. Some may have lost up to 70 per cent of their effectives, in many respects sacrificed 'with no overview of the strategic situation, no clear knowledge of the terrain, the strength and positions of the enemy, or of the appropriate fighting tactics'. Binding felt the inexperienced troops were 'too helpless, particularly when the officers have been killed'.[30] Certainly, it was a harsh experience. One Bavarian, General Karl von Fasbender, spoke of the battles among the villages being 'truly terrible. . . . We have to conquer the houses one by one, drag the enemy out of cellars and storage sheds, or kill them by throwing hand-grenades down at them. The casualties are always high.' Subsequently, Fasbender wrote, 'All churches, including their steeples, are destroyed, all roofs torn off, walls caved in, entire houses bared to the elements; human beings and animals lie about, the barns are empty, cows roam about lowering, horses stand stupidly in the middle of roads; none are fed, watered, or milked because no one has remained in the villages.'[31]

Faced with the German assault, Sir John French had resolved to stand on the defensive. By contrast, the newly designated French commander in the north, the 56-year-old Victor d'Urbal, whom French was delighted to find was a cavalryman like himself – he likened him to a 'Murat kind of beau sabreur' – ordered a counter-attack against units of the German *XXIII Reserve Corps* moving towards the French positions around Dixmude. D'Urbal, however, did so without informing the BEF of his intentions and, while French apparently regarded d'Urbal as a man of courage and tenacity, the Frenchman was a domineering character prone to rudeness and quite prepared to lay down an artillery barrage behind his own infantry to prevent them from retreating. Haig variously described d'Urbal on one occasion as 'a big smart looking polite man' and, on another, as a 'tall suave elderly gentleman – rather an actor, or the type of man seen on the stage in the part of the respectable uncle and very polite'.[32] On 22 October D'Urbal had been given the direction of IX Corps, the two Territorial divisions, 42nd Division, de Mitry's cavalry corps, and the marine fusilier brigade, the whole now confusingly designated the Belgian Army Detachment, subsequently becoming the French Eighth Army in mid-November.[33]

The French expected that I Corps would support them. Haig became aware of the impending French attack only at 2300 hours on 21 October. Johnnie Gough hastened to GHQ at 0230 to try to get the attack postponed, accompanied by Rawlinson's Chief of Staff, Archie Montgomery. The GSO1 of I Corps' Operational Section, Colonel Hugh Jeudwine, was also dispatched to find de Mitry while Lieutenant Colonel Neill Malcolm, Jeudwine's GSO2, went on a similar mission to find d'Urbal. These efforts were not successful.[34] In the event, elements of the French 87th Territorial Division passed behind the British line at Bixschoote during the morning of 22 October in order to attack the Germans but were then driven back through the line held by Haig's 1st Division between Langemarck and Steenstraat in the early afternoon. For most of the morning, 1st Division had observed large numbers of Germans, who were from *XXIII Reserve Corps*, about a mile distant, and had been under heavy shellfire.

Captain James Patterson of 1st South Wales Borderers watched the shells destroy Langemarck: 'The Germans went for the church spire until the whole church was in flames and falling to pieces, and then they turned their attention to the rest of the town and simply blew it to pieces.' Patterson, who was to be mortally wounded on 29 October, could understand that the Germans would want to prevent the church spire being used for artillery observation but felt the bombardment of the town went far beyond any military reason. The church continued to burn into the night, the inhabitants being evacuated later that night though, as Patterson also recorded, 'the poor cows and pigs suffered a lot'. Serving as a company commander with 2nd Welch Regiment in the same brigade, H.C. Rees also watched the destruction of Langemarck, largely by 8-inch howitzers: 'It was really a splendid spectacle. A number of field guns were also employed. I saw a field gun shell strike the spire of the church just below the cross and send the cross some twenty yards into the air.' The CO, Lieutenant Colonel C.B. Morland, passed Rees at one point: 'He had had two houses blown down over his head in succession in the village and as he remarked, it was safer in the front line.'[35]

On the heels of the retreating French Territorials, an attack then developed on the centre of the line with the Germans pushing into gaps between the British trenches towards dusk. In 5th Brigade of 2nd Division, Captain Harry Dillon of the 2nd Oxford and Bucks Light Infantry looked over the parapet of his trench: 'The firing stopped, and I had been straining my eyes so for a moment I could not believe them, but, fortunately, I did not hesitate long. A great grey mass of humanity was charging, running for all God would let them straight on to us not 50 yards off – about as far as the summer-house to the coach-house. Everybody's nerves were pretty well on edge as I had warned them what to expect and as I fired my rifle the rest all went off almost simultaneously.' Dillon had 'never shot so much in such a short time', his right hand being left as 'one huge bruise from banging the bolt up and down'. Under the weight of fire, the Germans veered off to the left and the attack died away. From the darkness, all that could be heard was 'a great moan'. In Dillon's graphic account, there were men 'with their arms and legs off trying to crawl away; others, who could not move gasping out their last moments with the cold night wind biting into their broken bodies and the lurid red glare of a farmhouse showing up some clumps of grey devils killed by the men on my left further down. A weird awful scene!' Now the only captain left in the battalion and acting second in command, Dillon was moved to record his outrage: 'The whole of this beautiful country is devastated – broken houses, broken bodies, blood, filth, and ruin everywhere!' In the same brigade, Private H.J. Milton of the 2nd Highland Light Infantry had witnessed the same attack. The farm as far as he could make out had been set alight by the Germans because they thought it would help them direct their fire, but 50 yards from the HLI trenches they 'were simply running into death, they gave great yells after they started but very few got back. The screams were terrible.'[36]

Haig moved up his available reserves and put together an ad hoc assault force, drawing battalions from three separate brigades as well as the reserve. He directed Brigadier General E.S. Bulfin of 2nd Brigade to restore the position in a dawn attack with five battalions since it was deemed too difficult to operate after dark whereas the Germans routinely used the darkness to mount attacks. Assisted by morning mist, Bulfin's counter-attack was mounted at 0400 hours on 23 October and retook the lost ground, releasing some men of the 1st Cameron Highlanders who had been captured the night before and taking almost 800 German prisoners. Almost 500 Germans had also been killed for a British loss of just forty-seven dead and 184 wounded. Lieutenant J.G.W. Hyndson of the 1st Loyals recorded 'the glorious sight of masses of grey-coated men standing up to surrender'. One German in a wind-mill continued to fire even when the windmill was set on fire, ultimately dying in the flames.[37]

To the right of 1st Division, 2nd Division was also heavily shelled between Zonnebeke and Langemarck but no real attack developed during the course of 22 October with the exception of an attempted rush on the line held by 5th Brigade at dusk. To the right of 2nd Division, Capper's 7th Division similarly came under shellfire but though large columns were detected by aerial reconnaissance approaching Becelaere and a German order to attack it was intercepted, no serious effort was made in this sector. Around Reutel, a more serious attack by German *XXVII Reserve Corps* developed against 21st Brigade, only for the Germans to be shot down in very large numbers, the German semi-official account compiled in 1917 referring to the British as having 'reaped a great harvest'.[38] It was also the case that, with the arrival of French reinforcements, the balance of forces between the Germans and the allies had been largely equalised around Ypres, the German losses increasingly convincing them that a breakthrough in the immediate future was now unlikely.

Further French reinforcement had now been received in the form of Grossetti's 42nd Division, which had joined the Belgians at Nieuport, and the 17th and 18th Divisions of the French IX Corps of General Dubois, which was arriving west and south of Ypres. In response to a request from Henry Wilson, Foch and d'Urbal agreed on making an effort to relieve pressure on I Corps by launching a general offensive. The Belgians and 42nd Division would advance east of Nieuport with the support of British naval gunfire, the Dixmude garrison towards Thourout and General Guignabaudet's 17th Division with two of de Mitry's cavalry divisions towards Roulers in the expec-tation of reaching the Becelaere-Passchendaele line. D'Urbal in particular was highly optimistic and scornful of German capabilities, but an interview with King Albert on 22 October apparently ended 'rather abruptly' when Albert expressed his astonishment that, in the circumstances described by d'Urbal, the allies 'not yet had reached the Rhine'.[39]

Foch also requested that I Corps itself push towards Houthulst Forest but copies of the orders to the French units to attack at 0900 hours on

23 October only reached GHQ and I Corps around 0200 and Foch's written request for co-operation even later. Haig did not feel that any attack could be practically mounted at such short notice and French concurred, suggesting that Haig merely cover the flank of any advance by the French 17th Division if it actually materialised. Indeed, it would have been exceptionally difficult to make the arrangements for the French to pass through the British lines and to be supported by British artillery. In the event, the 17th Division was held up by congestion on the roads and did not reach the front line until early afternoon. Visiting General Moussy on 23 October to help arrange the passage of the French through the British line, 'Ma' Jeffreys of the 2nd Grenadiers found the Frenchman on the Wieltze road with two of his staff officers. As his men moved forward, Moussy walked among them encouraging them to advance but each time 'he had turned to go to another group they dropped down again. In between he kept explaining to me that he had lost many officers and had nothing but sous-officiers and promoted sous-officiers, and that these were no good.' It seemed to Jeffreys that Moussy was acting as a regimental commander rather than as a divisional commander.[40]

By this time, 1st, 2nd and 7th Divisions had again come under heavy pressure, 1st Division having suffered 1006 casualties between 22 and 24 October as operations continued. Private Samuel Knight, a former copy boy with the *Cambria Daily Reader*, was serving with the 2nd Welch Regiment in 3rd Brigade when they came under artillery fire on 23 October. Feeling a barn, in which some of his colleagues were sheltering, unsafe, Knight found the top of a rabbit hutch and an old field rake and improvised a roof for a dugout, covering it with clay: 'The shrapnel is shrieking through the lane. I can hear the groans of our wounded. One man drops helplessly into our dug-out. He extends an arm battered beyond description. We bandage it. His groans are terrible. A shell bursts very near us. The shrapnel pieces fall through our roof. A piece strikes me on the shoulder. Luckily its force is spent. I am all right.' Unfortunately for Knight's comrades, however, a shell hit the barn, killing several, the fire then setting off the ammunition in the men's pouches. By the following day, Knight's nerves were taut, the constant shelling causing him a slight concussion, as he automatically tended to hold his breath each time there was an explosion.[41] In the case of the 1st Cameron Highlanders, E. Craig Brown led a section back to reoccupy a trench from which one of his platoons had been reportedly forced back one night at this time. Finding the trench full of men with bayonets fixed, Craig Brown started to fire at the nearest man with his revolver and wounded him before he realised they were his own men still in possession.[42]

Haig took some pride in noting that the men of two half companies of the 1st Gloucesters in 3rd Brigade (1st Division) had reportedly fired an average of 500 rounds per man to repulse one attack on its trenches along the Langemarck-Koekuit road. German cavalry had first appeared but had ridden off to the right of the Gloucesters while German infantry had then approached from dead ground and worked down a ditch alongside the road under cover of cattle and smoke from a burning farmhouse. According to one private, the fire from the Germans at one point was so intense that many of the Gloucesters' bayonets were broken by the bullets, causing several wounds from flying fragments. A slightly surreal atmosphere also derived from pieces of mangold, which had been incorporated in the parapet of the trench, also showering the defenders.[43] That same day, Drummer Kelly of the 2nd Gordons, serving with 20th Brigade (7th Division), won the VC rescuing wounded men on five different occasions.

Dubois concluded that it was better initially to reinforce the line and, during the night, Guignabaudet's Division took over the positions held by 2nd Division, which moved to the east of Ypres to reinforce 7th Division. Some French Territorial units, however, declined to go into the trenches. In one case, the British CO told the reluctant commander of the French 72nd Territorial Regiment that he was a representative of Lord Kitchener and the BEF would pull out of France unless the relief went ahead. After seven hours, the Frenchmen finally moved into the trenches being vacated.[44]

For 24 October, however, both Foch and d'Urbal intended to resume the attempt at an advance. Like Sir John French before him, d'Urbal assumed the Germans were 'newly-raised corps without great value' and that an advance could be pushed without regard to what was happening on either flank.[45] At the same time, the French would also relieve 1st Division so the whole of I Corps could be reconcentrated for its own offensive. Though the French were advancing across some of the more open ground in the vicinity, but over which the Germans had good observation, they made reasonable progress between Zonnebeke and Langemarck. The French were supported by 2nd Division, which had also arrived in time to relieve the left of 7th Division, whose trenches had come under a great weight of shellfire as the Germans tried to push into Polygon Wood.

At one point the 2nd Wiltshires of 21st Brigade at Reutel on the eastern side of Polygon Wood were left isolated by not being aware of the retirement of other units and the battalion was overwhelmed by three German battalions. Of over 450 men, only the Quartermaster, the Sergeant Major, six sergeants and 200 men survived death or capture. Hugo Montgomery subsequently suggested that they 'were probably all asleep, as they got no rest from the shelling'. Capper was forced to commit his only reserve, the squadron of the Northumberland Hussars, which thus became the first unit of the Territorial Force to see serious action: it suffered almost 300 casualties with its commanding officer killed. Capper's own headquarters staff supplemented with a few cyclists, clerks, cooks and officers' servants also hastily prepared for a last stand. Communications were also severely disrupted, the cables laid out from divisional headquarters to the 7th Signal Company's three cable wagons – one with each brigade – being continually cut by shells.[46]

At this moment, help arrived from 2nd Division, the 2nd Highland Light Infantry and 2nd Worcesters of 5th Brigade advancing into the wood and engaging in hand-to-hand combat with bayonets to push the Germans back, the inexperienced German formations having largely come to a halt once they had got into the wood without realising that they had opened a critical gap in the British line. Major E.B. Hankey, who was to lead the famous attack by the Worcesters at Gheluvelt on 31 October, considered this earlier attack a 'finer show'. This was because of its difficulty and the need for good discipline though it was only against 'disorganised elements' and a 'mop up fight' in the sense that 'we were actually beating back and mopping unsuccessful but bewildered enemy groups in woods'. Of the precise sequence of events during these counter-attacks, however, the 7th Division historian recorded that they seemed 'to defy all efforts at elucidation'. Capper's right had also come under attack around Gheluvelt, only one company remaining in reserve at the height of the action. Indeed, by the end of the day, 7th Division's losses in just three days had reached a total of 2820 officers and men. Yet, in the words of the divisional historian, 'The majority of its officers and men had to remain in the positions they had already been defending for nearly a week, weary, unwashed, unshaven, short of sleep and sometimes of food, but grimly resolute.'[47]

The Germans, too, had taken heavy losses and on 23 October Falkenhayn told Albrecht and Rupprecht that their conduct of operations would be reviewed unless more success was forthcoming, the gains at such cost having been purely tactical. Rupprecht's Chief of Staff, Krafft von Delmensingen, proposed reducing the frontage of *Sixth Army*. Albrecht prompted by his Chief of Staff, Ilse, concluded that, while opportunities should still be taken to seize significant ground, the offensive in front of Ypres should be halted, with the effort now directed further north against the Belgians and French. Both German army commanders were aware that losses among trained officers and NCOs were still further reducing the effectiveness of the reserve formations. Accordingly, *Fourth Army* made a major assault on Dixmude on the evening of 24 October using 350 mm and 420 mm siege guns to bombard the defences, manned by Ronarc'h's sailors and marines. The French held on, however, repulsing some fifteen separate attacks over a period of 5 hours. Ronarc'h doubted if his men could hold on for much more than 24 hours given his losses and the fatigue of his men. The Belgians, too, were at the limit of their moral and physical resistance and there were no reserves available.[48]

Another effort was being made further north by Beseler against the Belgians on the Yser. The *III Reserve Corps* had been attempting to cross the Yser since 18 October. A relatively narrow and sluggish stream, the Yser had only low banks, though that on the western side was higher than that on the eastern bank and there were only eight places where it was bridged. The German effort was hampered by fire from Royal Navy monitors, which persuaded Beseler that it was not possible to cross the river at Nieuport. Elements of *XXII Reserve Corps* had therefore been brought up to assist Beseler at Dixmude. On 24 October, however, having previously been restricted to operating at Nieuport, Grossetti's French 42nd Division reinforced the Belgians, with instructions from d'Urbal to hold 'with or without the Belgian army'. Beseler was checked, though not before he had got across the Yser. On the following day, however, the *43rd Reserve Division* broke into Dixmude in a flurry of street fighting, some twenty to thirty shells a minute falling on the defenders. According to one Belgian account curiously reproduced in the German semi-official history, the Germans had attacked 'with the howls of wild beasts; lusting to massacre, they tread the wounded under foot and stumble over the dead: and, though shot down in hundreds, they keep coming on. Then follow isolated fights with bayonets and the butts of rifles: some are impaled, others strangled or have their skulls bashed in.' In fact, there were a number of documented atrocities with at least 161 Belgian civilians slaughtered out of hand in Dixmude, the episode reminiscent of the many earlier atrocities committed during the original invasion of Belgium.[49]

The ground, itself impeded by wide dykes and thick hedges, was generally below sea level and extremely swampy, hindering the German attempt to bring up ammunition and supplies and they were driven out of Dixmude. The Belgians, however, had taken heavy losses and the Dixmude-Nieuport railway embankment was now seen as the last possible position that could be held. As a result, preparations were made to break the locks and allow the sea to flood the approaches to Nieuport, where no less than six canals and watercourses met. Foch later claimed that he had suggested the line of the embankment and also that he had prevented the Belgians from retreating even further but Albert countered that such a retirement had never received his agreement.[50]

There are various versions of the origins of the inundation policy. Foch was one who claimed the initiative, supposedly raising it with the Belgians on 25 October and seeking Joffre's authorisation on the following evening. Foch had also previously raised the possibility of flooding the area in front of Dunkirk, orders for which were suspended when the Belgians objected and it was felt too difficult to evacuate civilians. The chief lock keeper in Nieuport, G. Dingens, however, had apparently raised the possibility on 19 October and a young Belgian officer, Commandant Delarmoy, was also credited with suggesting the scheme earlier. Albert's military adviser, Major Emile Galet, credited the idea to Captain Nuyten of the Belgian General Staff, who had also selected the railway embankment as a suitable last line of defence, while Wielemans had certainly been shown papers by a magistrate in Furnes, Emeric Feys, on the flooding of the area in the 1794 campaign during the French Revolutionary Wars. There seemed little alternative for, on 26 October, Albert, accompanied by Galet, visited GHQ to ask for some British reinforcements. French displayed what the Belgians characterised as 'phlegmatic solidarity' but had none to give.[51]

Supervision of the inundation was undertaken by Karel (sometimes rendered as Charles-Louis) Kogge, another lock keeper on the Furnes Canal, who agreed to do so only if he received a decoration; a veteran waterman, Hendrik Geeraert, who knew where the lock cranks to the weir gates were hidden; and Captain Femand Umé. The first attempt by Kogge to open the sluices of an abandoned canal at Nieuport on the night of 27–28 October was not successful as the tides were too low. A second attempt by Geeraert and Umé on the night of 29–30 October succeeded in opening eight weir gates at Noovdvaart under the very noses of the Germans, beginning to flood the area between the Yser and the railway embankment. This coincided with expected higher tide levels and Geeraert repeated the operation on the next three nights. The waters gradually continued to rise, 'a silent conqueror at first scarcely visible'. The flood reached between Pervyse and Dixmude by 28 October, reaching Pervyse on 31 October. The German forces in front of the Belgians were already suffering shortages of supplies. A diary found on the body of an officer from the *202nd Reserve Regiment* on 27 October had recorded three days earlier: 'For several days we have had no hot food. The bread, etc., is hardly sufficient. The emergency rations are exhausted. The water is very bad, quite green, but it is drunk, as no other is obtainable. Man is reduced to the state of a beast.' Indeed, the officer in question, describing himself as in a 'shocking plight', was relying on what little could be shared with his men. Initially, the Germans seem to have attributed the rising water to recent rainfall and not realised what the Belgians had done. Eventually, the flooded area was rendered into a lagoon between 18 and 21 miles long, between $1^3/4$ and $2^1/2$ miles wide, and 3 to 4 feet deep.[52]

Beseler attempted to continue his offensive, briefly taking Ramscappelle south of Nieuport on 30 October, until it became apparent that the water might actually cut off the leading divisions of *III Reserve Corps*: 'On the morning of the 30th the advancing troops had been up to their ankles in water; then it had gradually risen until they were now wading up to their knees, and they could scarcely drag their feet out of the clayey soil.' Indeed, when the Germans looked behind them, 'the green meadows were covered with dirty, yellow water, and the general line of the roads was only indicated by the houses and the rows of partly covered trees'. Effectively, the German effort on the Yser ceased on 30 October, having cost the Belgians some 18,000 casualties and the Germans at least 9500 casualties from five regiments.[53] It secured the allied left but, equally, rendered the German right secure and they were able to deploy their forces further south.

With the repulse of the German attacks all along the line from Ypres to the sea, Sir John French became optimistic once more, now reporting to Kitchener that the battle was 'practically won'.[54] Ammunition for the guns, however, was fast becoming a significant problem with limits having to be placed on expenditure. Indeed, French had raised the issue with the Master General of the Ordnance back on 26 September and on 10 October French had reported that he had only six rounds a day for his 18-pounders, nine for the 60-pounders and eleven for the 4.5-inch howitzers.[55] On 24 October French similarly reported to Kitchener that there were only about 150 rounds per gun in the theatre of operations which had not been already issued to the ammunition parks, and that only seven rounds per gun per day were being received from Britain. Even earlier, on the Aisne, French had warned that the rate of expenditure was double that of supply. Compared to the average expenditure of fourteen rounds per day per 18-pounder on the Aisne, moreover, it had reached seventy-six rounds a day over the last three days. By 1 November French reported only an average of 180 rounds left for each 4.5-inch howitzer and 320 rounds for each 18-pounder.

In view of what French regarded as a 'deplorable state of affairs', an order had to be issued on 24 October to restrict expenditure to thirty rounds a day for 18-pounders and fifteen rounds a day for 4.5-inch howitzers. In the case of II Corps, Smith-Dorrien directed that the 18-pounders and 4.5-inch howitzers should only be used against infantry attacks or vulnerable targets such as hostile batteries on the move, unlimbered batteries in the open or mass infantry formations accurately located. They could not be used to search for enemy batteries under cover but the 60-pounders and siege howitzers could be so used, provided their average expenditure of ammunition did not exceed twelve rounds a day. On 25 October, however, II Corps was authorised to increase expenditure of 60-pounder shells to an average of twenty a day and, on 26 October, all limits for 60-pounders, 4.7-inch guns and siege howitzers were lifted and the expenditure for 18-pounders increased to fifty rounds a day though 4.5-inch howitzers remained restricted to fifteen rounds with all targeting restrictions also still in place.

Responding to French's entreaties, Kitchener noted that he had already dispatched 16,000 rounds of 18-pounder ammunition between 20 and 21 October and between 23 and 30 October another 34,840 rounds for the 18-pounders together with 3000 for the 4.7-inch guns, 5000 for the 60-pounders, 8000 for the 13-pounders, and 10,490 for the 4.5-inch howitzers. Moreover, in some respects, the shortages were also a result of the strain on the BEF's logistic system, the Quartermaster General, Major General Sir William Robertson, having had to request the Inspector General of Communications, Major General F.S. Robb, to slow down deliveries on 16 October due to the BEF's move to the north. Serious difficulties were then encountered with railway delays in the Boulogne area, compounded by the mixing of national contingents across each other's supply lines.[56]

Pre-war assumptions had made allowance for a rate of artillery expenditure based on that in the South African War, the lesson drawn from the subsequent Russo-Japanese War being the need to ensure fire economy rather than increasing the supply available. The Mowatt Committee of 1904 had therefore concluded that the need was to have in hand at the outbreak of any war some 57,000 rounds of 13-pounder ammunition, 486,000 rounds of 18-pounder ammunition, 129,600 rounds of 4.5-inch howitzer shells, and 24,000 shells for 60-pounders. It also laid down the proviso of having an additional 400–500 rounds per gun manufactured within the first six months of any war. The Murray Committee in 1907 had also concluded that government ordnance factories could be cut back since the private sector would be perfectly capable of meeting these modest requirements. Thus, each of the army's standard 18-pounder field guns was allocated 1000 rounds for active service with a further 500 rounds held in reserve in Britain and a further 500 rounds to be manufactured within the first six months of any war. This represented a stock in hand two and half time greater than that in 1899 but, in practice, if the 18-pounder ammunition was fired at the preferred Rate 4 – four rounds a minute – the entire stock envisaged for each gun for the first six months of operations for each gun would have been exhausted in under seven hours of continuous action.[57]

The allowance had actually been worked out as an average expenditure of ten rounds a day, when fifty rounds a day was the reality at Ypres with the average rising to eighty rounds a day at critical with some individual batteries recorded as firing 1200 rounds within 24 hours. It made the limits placed on expenditure all but meaningless and, indeed, a quarter of the divisional guns had to be withdrawn altogether at the end of October while those batteries under fire were rarely able to reply with more than one round per half-hour. In addition, brigade ammunition columns were generally withdrawn and concentrated for divisional use, but initially were kept too far back, involving a round journey of 18 rather than the regulation 2 miles for each replenishment cycle in the case of 2nd Division, with consequent extra exhaustion of its horses. Between 21 October and 22 November, for example, I Corps expended 54 per cent of all the 18-pounder shells, 53 per cent of all the 4.5-inch howitzer shells, and 57 per cent of all the 60-pounder shells it would fire between August 1914 and November 1918. Not perhaps surprisingly, matters did not improve rapidly given this rate of ammunition expenditure, Robertson reporting on 16 November that the stock of 18-pounder shells was still very small indeed, the stock of 4.5-inch shells 'hopeless' and the supply of 9.2-inch howitzer shells decreasing by the day.[58]

It was not just shells that were in increasingly short supply, for trained officers and manpower reserves were similarly scarce. As early as 14 October French had drawn to Kitchener's attention the failure of counter-attacks 'because ignorant and untrained company officers failed to make any attempt to rally men'. Of the drafts, even the Official History later commented that they were 'dregs of the depot' and 'old worn drunken wasters'.[59] For the drafts making their way up to the front, the experience was often disquieting. W.A. Quinton, who joined the 2nd Bedfordshires sometime in October, recalled marching up in almost complete darkness with no moonlight: 'It was difficult to see the forms of the men immediately in front of us, and only our training regards speed and length of pace prevented us from treading on each other's heels. The blinding flashes from a battery of our own long-range guns would light the column up for a brief moment, only to make it seem darker than ever afterwards. Whereas when we had started the road had been hard and firm, underfoot was now soft and spongy, and so uneven that occasionally one or the other would stumble badly. In the darkness of the night we were more like a ghost-army than anything: no smoking, no conversation, just a muttered ejaculation here and there as some fellow would step in a hole and stagger about badly until he regained his balance.'[60]

The French, too, were to expend enormous quantities of shells. Already on the Aisne, the French 75 mm guns had been down to 400 rounds a piece, the reserve depots having only 45 rounds per gun and the manufacturing capacity still being only a maximum of 10,000 rounds a day. Consequently, Joffre had been forced to reduce the allowance to just 200 rounds a gun to try and create some kind of larger reserve. Between 15 October and 14 November, d'Urbal's Belgian Army Detachment fired over 344,000 shells and the Tenth Army over 167,000, this representing over 55 per cent of the shells fired by the entire French army in that period. The French IX Corps apparently never had more than 10,000 shells on any day during its engagement at Ypres. After just six days of the fight for the Yser line, the Belgian 75 mm and 150 mm guns had been reduced to less than 130 rounds per gun per division, the Belgian Second Division having only sixty rounds per gun left by 30 October. The French, therefore, agreed to try and provide up to 2000 rounds a day.[61]

The Germans had entered the war with larger stocks of shells, having some four million field artillery shells in August 1914 sufficient for 987 shells for every field artillery piece and 973 for every howitzer. This fell short, however, of pre-war demands by the General Staff and production schedules envisaged a need to increase these to only 1029 and 1044 shells respectively and by September 1914 shell supplies had been reduced to less than 500,000. Thus, the German advantage in terms of the numbers of heavy howitzers over the British and the French was increasingly nullified.[62]

Despite the ammunition shortages, French and d'Urbal agreed on the afternoon of 25 October to advance, d'Urbal instructing Dubois to continue towards Roulers though de Mitry was to hold his existing front. On the British side, I, IV and the Cavalry Corps were all also to advance, though each formation in turn would wait for that to its left to make progress before commencing its own operations. In the event, slow progress by Dubois's IX Corps delayed the intended advance by Haig's 2nd Division from 1100 hours to 1500 hours. Notwithstanding the late start and the stiff German resistance – General von Meyer of the *2nd Ersatz Brigade* was killed during the day's fighting – 4th Brigade led by the 1st Royal Berkshires from 6th Brigade actually crested the top of the Becelaere-Passchendaele ridge but heavy rain began to fall with nightfall and the men had to dig in for the night as best they could. Some German probes were made during the night but apparently only at patrol strength as recorded by Major Lord Bernard Gordon-Lennox of the 2nd Grenadiers, 'During the night we were attacked three times, about 9 p.m., 12 midnight and 3 a.m. (sounds like a prescription on a medicine bottle). Very heavy firing each time, but I don't think they really meant to come on.'[63] The Irish Guards, who had lost contact with the Grenadiers several times during the course of 25 October, also had a difficult night: 'The enemy got scouts all round us and sniped at us from every direction. They made attacks by fire on the left and right of our position, but never actually against us. We had practically no trenches except of the most meagre description, so it was altogether a most unpleasant night and we were all drenched through and none of us were in the least disappointed to see the arrival of the Coldstream batt at 5.30 a.m.'[64]

To the right of 2nd Division, 7th Division, which had had another trying day on 24 October, started even later and made little headway. Moreover, its 20th Brigade, which held the tip of the existing salient in the British line at Kruiseecke, itself came under attack from the German *54th (Württemberg) Reserve Division*, 200 men of the latter's *242nd Reserve Infantry Regiment* being captured. The British position, however, was precarious with no communication trenches and no wire, the German artillery fire having prevented any improvements to the position and most of the British occupying a forward slope of the hill around the village under German observation. Capper, indeed, favoured siting trenches on forward slopes with overhead cover, deriving the method from Japanese practice in the Russo-Japanese War, Rawlinson later pointedly writing in his operational report that the division's heavy losses 'may possibly in some small measure have been due to want of experience in the construction and location of trenches on the part of troops fresh from garrison stations abroad'.[65]

Covering the trenches with planks and earth, however, was actually more dangerous than open trenches when the Germans were firing high explosive shells rather than shrapnel. That night, the Germans rushed the 2nd Scots Guards, creating a gap of a quarter of a mile in the forward line. The line was retaken by a counter-attack and the brigade was reinforced by one of Capper's reserve battalions. Capper himself was reportedly 'too proud' to call for further help that day, saying, 'I will not squeal.'[66] The Hon. St Vincent Broke de Saumarez of the Scots Guards, meanwhile, had been tasked with looking for snipers in Kruiseecke: 'In searching the houses I came across an estaminet in the village which was full of wounded men. It was a terrible sight; every other man had expired. They had been there for days with nobody to look after them and amongst them I discovered Lieutenant Holbeach. Some of the wounded men were clean off their heads. Lieutenant Holbeach had been dragged into this terrible shambly which must originally have been an advanced dressing station, which I think it must have been, and was left.'[67]

Like Sir John French, Joffre was still very optimistic that an offensive could be successful, many of those Germans taken prisoner appearing young, unfit and lacking in morale.[68] The intention on 26 October, there-fore, was to continue the advance as before in echelon from left to right, but the French again made only slow progress since d'Urbal decided to widen the frontage of his attack to include both Poelcappelle and Passchendaele as objectives, causing Dubois to shift artillery to his left. The newly arrived French 31st Division was also committed to the attack on Poelcappelle. At the same time, some of his battalions drifted across the front of I Corps and pulling them back also caused delay in the French arrangements. Haig meanwhile hoped to recover Becelaere. In the event 2nd Division found the stiff resistance of the previous day repeated and Haig then halted his opera-tions temporarily when information was received from GHQ purporting to indicate that 2nd Division would be attacked by the whole of the German reserves. An intercepted message then suggested that, far from advancing to the attack, the German reserves were urgently needed to support XXVII Corps opposite the French. The advance was resumed but little progress could be made. To Élie Chamard, under German bombardment with his colleagues in the 77th Infantry Regiment (36th Brigade, IX Corps) at Zonnebeke, brick houses seemed to disappear in a great cloud of red dust, while farms and hayricks burned, and trees crashed down.[69]

In the meantime, the Germans also renewed their bombardment of Kruiseecke, heavy artillery shells completely destroying the trenches held by the forward companies of both the 2nd Scots Guards and 1st Grenadier Guards. Men were buried in the sandy soil and had to be dug out, while the sand also choked the mechanisms of rifles and machine guns. Among those affected was de Saumarez's platoon of the Scots Guards. His men had spent much of the day trying to improve their trenches, which were not much more than 4 feet deep and on a forward slope. His entire platoon was buried by one shell and de Saumarez and his sergeant desperately tried to dig as many men out as possible. Running to find out what was happening further to the right, de Saumarez dodged into a ruined cottage to avoid a shell but was knocked unconscious by the blast: 'When I came to my senses there was a badly wounded man lying on me and above this wounded man lay a dead one. In this position I was unable to move as a great many bricks had fallen in the ditch all round us and we could only just breathe through the debris.' De Saumarez remained in this position until dark when he heard German voices. A little later a man lying in the ditch managed to extricate de Saumarez and they crawled back to the village, eventually finding some gunners who told them the line had been withdrawn.[70]

The retirement had been caused by an attack by fifteen German battalions against 20th Brigade. Some Germans had got through the British line about 0900 into the wood behind the village and caused considerable confusion by calling out 'retire' in English when the main German attack began at 1000. Men of the 1st South Staffordshires began to withdraw and this enabled the Germans to break through behind the advanced Guards companies, nearly all of whom were captured. Small groups of men were making their way back over a 3-mile frontage. Brigadier General H.G. Ruggles-Brise of 20th Brigade managed to form a new line and Capper sent in all his available reserves. Over 1000 officers and men in 20th Brigade had by now become casualties, one wartime account characterising it as having 'fought till there were no more left to fight'. In the case of the 2nd Border Regiment, it was reckoned that two German shells had landed on their trenches every minute from dawn to dusk for three days from 24 to 26 October, their casualties averaging 150 a day. The divisional losses in the nine days since it had become engaged now amounted to 162 officers (43.6 per cent) and 4320 other ranks (37.2 per cent).[71]

Haig was alarmed at reports that Capper's division was giving way, it being reported that several units were passing back through his 1st Brigade in disorder. Haig himself rode out to Hooge Chateau at 1500 hours 'and was astonished at the terror-stricken men coming back' concluding the Division had been 'reduced to inefficiency through ignorance of their leaders, in having placed them in trenches in forward slopes when enemy could see & so effectively shell them'.[72] Haig had moved elements of 1st Division to Capper's support and it was intended to launch a counter-attack but aerial reconnaissance then suggested another German division approaching, causing the attack to be called off. Similarly, the Cavalry Corps had abandoned its own attempted advance when Kruiseecke had been lost, the Royal Horse Guards also being sent to support Capper. Byng's 3rd Cavalry Division had previously been withdrawn from Rawlinson on 25 October and given to Allenby and now French resolved to give 7th Division to Haig on 27 October.

Following the Menin affair, Rawlinson had again offended French on 25 October by telegraphing that IV Corps was 'only hanging on by our eyelids' and matters would only ease once 8th Division arrived from England. According to Archie Murray, this had given French a sleepless night and French's military secretary, Willy Lambton, was dispatched to demand an apology, telling Rawlinson, 'you will have to apologise and eat humble pie if you want to remain on in command'. It appears to have been Henry Wilson who suggested that, with no role, Rawlinson and his staff should now return to England to prepare 8th Division for its introduction to the front in due course. French agreed ostensibly in the belief that 7th Division was a drag on I Corps and had suffered heavily 'owing entirely to badly constructed and wrong sited trenches' and it was important that 8th Division not make the same mistakes.[73] Now 7th Division held the line from Zandvoorde to the Menin Road, 1st Division from the Menin Road to Reutel, and 2nd Division from Reutel to the Moorslede to Zonnebeke road.

French was still optimistic and Kitchener promised to send six Territorial battalions to France to replace the battalions that had so far had the largest losses. Accordingly, there were further attempts to press forward on both 27 and 28 October and the same method of echeloning the attack again meant delays in the British starting time when the French failed to progress. A notable casualty on 27 October was Lieutenant Prince Maurice of Battenberg, grandson of Queen Victoria, nephew of the First Sea Lord, Prince Louis, and cousin to King George V. Serving with the 1st King's Royal Rifle Corps, Prince Maurice was killed by shrapnel on the top of Passchendaele ridge, the battalion losing five officers and 115 men that day, trying to advance towards the Keiberg spur.

French remained optimistic and, indeed, on 28 October the British bases at St Nazaire and Nantes began to be transferred to Le Havre and Rouen, which had been hastily abandoned during the retreat from Mons. For some, however, there was something of a lull after earlier exertions. The 2nd Welch had been pulled out of Langemarck into reserve on 24 October, some of the men finding a punt and a gondola at Bellewarde and 'going for a row on the lake'. There was then a recall to the front to retake some lost trenches at what was to become Hill 60 on 26 October followed by another rest period in Veldhoek woods on 28 October. That evening Private Knight joined a small group humming and then singing a Welsh hymn: 'More comrades gather round. We are now about 200 in number. The air is filled with the old Celtic harmonies. Favourite hymns are called for. "Delyn Aur" and "Beth sydd imi yn y byd" are special favourites.' Passing officers stopped to listen and a chaplain 'bursts through and stops at the edge of the crowd, exclaiming, "Wonderful! Wonderful! The greatest incident I have witnessed during the whole of the campaign."'[74]

Aerial reports, however, began to suggest that there was an increasing concentration of vehicles between Roulers and Moorslede heading in the direction of Ypres. In part, these reports were interpreted as including refugees. In reality, the Germans were bringing forward a new army group between *Fourth* and *Sixth Armies* under cover of the cavalry holding their line between St Yves and Gheluvelt with the intention of breaking through south of Ypres and heading north-westwards towards the Messines-Zandvoorde line. General von Fabeck, formerly commanding *XIII Corps*, was given command of this newly designated *Army Group Fabeck* on 27 October, comprising *II Bavarian Corps* brought up from the *Second Army*, General von Deimling's *XV Corps* from the Aisne, *6th Bavarian Reserve Division* from *Fourth Army*, *26th Division* from *Sixth Army*, and *I Cavalry Corps*. These were not fresh formations, therefore, in the manner of those reservists and volunteers initially thrown into the Flanders battle, but the net effect was to increase the number of German divisions opposite the allied lines, defended by $11\frac{1}{2}$ divisions, from $17\frac{1}{2}$ to $23\frac{1}{2}$ divisions. Fabeck also received large amounts of heavy artillery amounting to 262 heavy howitzers and mortars, in addition to 484 guns of smaller calibre.

Issuing his directions on 27 October, Falkenhayn intended that *Army Group Fabeck, Fourth* and *Sixth Armies* would co-operate in a general attack on 30 October. Fabeck's concentration would be covered by a preliminary attack by *6th Bavarian Reserve Division, I Cavalry Corps* and *XXVII Corps*, now commanded by General von Schubert, against Gheluvelt on 29 October. The attacks by *Fourth* and *Sixth Armies* would help to draw in what were assumed to be only a few reserve units available to the allies and Fabeck would punch through, initially seizing the high ground of the Messines ridge. On the day Falkenhayn issued the orders for the offensive, French was reporting to Kitchener that the Germans were 'quite incapable of making any strong and sustained attack'.[75]

Notes and references

1 IWM, Smith-Dorrien Mss, 87/47/7, II Corps Operational Report, 20 October 1914; PRO, WO95/1416, Account of Le Pilly by M.C.C. Harrison, 1917; Myles Dungan (1995), *Irish Voices from the Great War*, Dublin: Irish Academic Press, p. 30; Smith-Dorrien, *Forty-Eight Years*, p. 453.

2 IWM, Smith-Dorrien Mss, 87/47/2, war diary, 22 October 1914; ibid., 87/47/10, diary, 20 and 21 October 1914; ibid., Loch Mss, 71/12/2, diary, 22 October 1914; PRO, WO95/629, Report by Smith-Dorrien, 22 October 1914 and Smith-Dorrien to Pulteney, 23 October 1914; ibid., CAB45/182, Headlam to Edmonds, 2 April 1923; LUBLLC, A.N. Acland Mss, GS0003, diary, 22 October 1914; Smith-Dorrien, *Forty-Eight Years*, p. 456.

3 Smith-Dorrien, *Forty-Eight Years*, p. 457.

4 PRO, WO95/668, Note by DuCane, 24 October 1914.

5 *War Infantry Knew*, p. 74; Frank Richards (1964), *Old Soldiers Never Die*, 2nd edn., London: Faber & Faber, p. 35.

6 PRO, WO95/668, Report by Congreve, 22 October 1914; ibid., CAB45/140, Account of Ennetières by Captain E.N. Drury-Lowe; Dungan, *Irish Voices*, p. 31.

7 Gough, *Fifth Army*, p. 61; Farrar-Hockley, *Goughie*, p. 138.

8 Anglesey, *History of Cavalry*, p. 209.

9 Farrar-Hockley, *Ypres 1914*, p. 89.

10 Terraine, *General Jack's Diary*, p. 70; LUBLLC, Ritchie Mss, GS1361, diary, 21 October 1914; British Library (hereafter BL), Hunter-Weston Mss, Add Mss 48363, diary, 28 October 1914; Gardner, *Trial by Fire*, p. 18.

11 NAM, Hunter-Weston Mss, 6503-39-20, Account of 11th Brigade at Le Gheer, 21 October 1914; PRO, WO95/668, Report by Lt. F. Gore Anley, 22 October 1914 with comments by Major-General Keir, 24 October 1914; LUBLLC, Bradshaw Mss, GS0184, diary, 21 October 1914.

12 Gough, *Fifth Army*, pp. 266–7; Farrar-Hockley, *Goughie*, pp. 140–1.

13 IWM, Thorne Mss, DS/MISC/11, Notes on First Ypres.

14 PRO, CAB45/141, MacDonogh to Edmonds, 11 October 1922.

15 *Armées Françaises* I Pt. IV, Annexes Vol. IV, pp. 8–9, Huguet to Foch, 22 October 1914.

16 Hamilton, *First Seven Divisions*, pp. 178–9; IWM, Dillon Mss, 82/25/1, letter, 22 October 1914; Mockler-Ferryman, *OBLI Chronicle*, pp. 177, 185; Wyrall, *Second Division*, p. 113.

17 IWM, Trefusis Mss, 82/30/1, diary, 21 October 1914; NAM, Rawlinson Mss, 5201-33-17, Confidential Narrative of 2nd Division, 21–22 October 1914; ibid., Rawlinson to Capper, 22 October 1914; NLS, Haig Mss, Acc 3155/99, diary, 22 October 1914; Atkinson, *Seventh Division*, pp. 34, 39.

18 Craster, *Fifteen Rounds*, p. 112; LUBLLC, Patterson Mss, GS1232, diary, 21 October 1914.

19 NLS, Haig Mss, Acc 3155/99, diary, 21 October 1914; Gardner, *Trial by Fire*, pp. 211–12.

20 Wyrall, *Second Division*, p. 115; NLS, Haig Mss, Acc 3155/99, diary, 21 October 1914.

21 OFH, pp. 167–8.

22 IWM, Horne Mss, Horne to wife, 22 October 1914.

23 IWM, Wilson Mss, DS/MISC/80, diary, 4, 5, 14, 15 and 21 October 1914; ibid., French Mss, 75/46/6, French to Kitchener, 5 and 10 October 1914; Brock and Brock, *Asquith*, pp. 277–8.

24 *Armées Françaises*, I, Pt. IV, p. 273; OFH, pp. 519–520, French to Kitchener, 22 October 1914.

25 *Ypres 1914*, p. 42; Farrar-Hockley, *Ypres 1914*, p. 113.

26 Unruh, *Langemarck*, p. 9.

27 Colin Fox (1995), 'The Myths of Langemarck', *Imperial War Museum Review* 10, pp. 13–25; Unruh, *Langemarck*, pp. 61–7, 151–63; Ypres, 1914, p. 79; Bernd Hüppauf (1988), 'Langemarck, Verdun and the Myth of a New Man in Germany after the First World War', *War and Society* 6 (2), pp. 70–103.

28 Gough, *Fifth Army*, p. 64; Maze, *Frenchman in Khaki*, p. 88; IWM, Horne Mss, Horne to wife, 24 October 1914; ibid., Wilson Mss, DS/MISC/80, diary, 24 October 1914; ibid., Home Mss, 82/18/1, diary, 25 October 1914; Wyrall, *Second Division*, p. 119.

29 Mockler-Ferryman, *OBLI Chronicle*, p. 181; PRO, WO95/1278; *Ypres, 1914*, pp. 37, n. 1; NAM, Rawlinson Mss, 5201-33-17, Rawlinson to Wigram, 24 October 1914.

30 Hüppauf, 'Langemarck, Verdun and Myth of New Man', pp. 70–103; Unruh, *Langemarck*, pp. 181–6; *Ypres, 1914*, pp. 39 and 43; Rudolf Binding (1929), *A Fatalist at War*, London: Allen & Unwin, p. 19.

31 Herwig, *First World War*, p. 115.

32 French, *1914*, p. 239; Hussey, 'Hard Day at First Ypres', pp. 70–89; NLS, Haig Mss, Acc 3155/99, diary, 23 October and 9 November 1914.

33 Joffre, *Memoirs*, I, p. 314; *Armées Françaises* I, Pt. IV Annexes Vol. IV, p. 6, Joffre to Foch, 22 October 1914.

34 Beckett, *Johnnie Gough*, p. 190; Johnnie Gough Mss (hereafter JEG), Papers concerning the proposed French attack on 22 October 1914; NLS, Haig Mss, Acc 3155/99, diary, 23 October 1914.

35 LUBLLC, Patterson Mss, GS1232, diary, 22 October 1914; IWM, Rees Mss, 77/179/1, 'A Personal Record of the First Seven Months of the War', 22 October 1914.

36 IWM, Dillon Mss, 82/25/1, letter, 24 October 1914; Mockler-Ferryman, *OBLI Chronicle*, pp. 186–8; IWM, Milton Mss, 81/1/1, diary, 22 October 1914.

37 PRO, CAB45/140, Bulfin diary, 23 October 1914; J.G.W. Hyndson (1933), *From Mons to the First Battle of Ypres*, London: Wyman, pp. 80–1.

38 *Ypres, 1914*, p. 42.

39 IWM, Wilson Mss, DS/MISC/80, diary, 22 October 1914; Cammaerts, *Albert of Belgium*, p. 194.

40 Craster, *Fifteen Rounds*, pp. 112–14.

41 IWM, Knight Mss, 77/64/1, account, 23 and 24 October 1914.

42 IWM, Craig Brown Mss, 92/23/2, diary, 26–28 October 1914.

43 NLS, Haig Mss, Acc 3155/99, diary, 25 October 1914; Farrar-Hockley, *Ypres 1914*, p. 106.

44 NLS, Haig Mss, Acc 3155/99, diary, 25 October 1914; PRO, CAB45/141, account of Captain Warde-Adam of 24 October 1914.

45 Dubois, *Deux Ans* II, p. 26.

46 LHCMA, Edmonds Mss, 6/2, Montgomery to Edmonds, 4 February 1921; IWM, Garwood Mss, 91/23/1, diary, 21 October 1914.

47 PRO, CAB45/140, Hankey account, 23 March 1924; Atkinson, *Seventh Division*, pp. 51, 56.

48 *Armées Françaises* I, Pt. IV, pp. 332–3.

49 Ratinaud, *Course*, p. 294; Pierre Dauzet (1917), *La Bataille des Flandres*, Paris: Charles-Larauzelle, p. 55; *Ypres, 1914*, pp. 47–8; John Horne and Alan Kramer (2001), *German Atrocities 1914: A History of Denial*, New Haven: Yale University Press, pp. 72–4.

50 Cammaerts, *Albert of Belgium*, p. 199; Foch, *Memoirs*, pp. 143–4; CinC, Belgian Army (1915), *The War of 1914: Military Operations of Belgium*, London: W.H. & L. Collingridge, p. 73.

51 Foch, *Memoirs*, p. 144; *Armées Françaises* I, Pt. IV, p. 337; ibid., Annexes Vol. IV, pp. 137–8, Foch to Joffre, 25 October 1914; Thielemans, *Albert*, p. 43; Thielemans and Vandewoude, *Roi Albert*, pp. 535–6; Palat, *Ruée vers Calais*, pp. 125–6; Capitaine Gabriel de Libert de Flemalle (1915), *Fighting with King Albert*, London: Hodder & Stoughton, pp. 297–8; Cammaerts, *Albert of Belgium*, pp. 196–7; Louis Madelin (1919), *La Mèlée des Flandres: L'Yser et Ypres*, Paris: Librarie Plon, p. 103.

52 Cammaerts, *Albert of Belgium*, p, 197; Essen, *Invasion and War in Belgium*, p. 336; Robert Cowley (1989), 'Albert and the Yser', *Military History Quarterly* 1 (4), pp. 106–17.

53 *Ypres, 1914*, p. 51; Goffre, *Dixmude*, pp. 94–6; Dauzet, *Bataille des Flandres*, pp. 84, 97.

54 OFH, p. 520, French to Kitchener, 24 October 1914.

55 French, *1914*, p. 165; David Lloyd George (1933), *War Memoirs*, I, London: Ivor Nicholson & Watson, pp. 141–3.

56 IWM, French Mss, 75/46/6, French to Kitchener, 24 October and 1 November 1914; ibid., 75/46/7, Kitchener to French, 24 and 31 October 1914; ibid., Wilson Mss, DS/MISC/80, diary, 25 and 26 October 1914; PRO, WO95/629, Memoranda by Forestier-Walker, 24, 25 and 26 October 1914; OFH, p. 360; Brown, *British Logistics*, pp. 63–4.

57 Jonathan Bailey (1996), 'British Artillery in the Great War' in Paddy Griffith (ed.), *British Fighting Methods in the Great War*, London: Frank Cass, pp. 2–49; ibid (1996), *The First World War and the Birth of the Modern Style of Warfare*, HMSO: Strategic & Combat Studies Institute, p. 9; OFH, pp. 12–14.

58 OFH, pp. 13, 165; IWM, Mowbray Mss, 82/16/1, account, 25 October 1914; Beckett, *Johnnie Gough*, p. 191; PRO, WO95/196, Note on Ammunition Expenditure; ibid., WO159/15, Robertson to Von Donop, 16 November 1914.

59 IWM, French Mss, 75/46/6, French to Kitchener, 14 October 1914; OFH, p. 449.

60 IWM, Quinton Mss, 79/35/1, memoir, pp. 12–13.

61 Joffre, *Memoirs*, I, pp. 283–4; *Armées Françaises*, I, Pt. IV, p. 556; ibid., Annexes IV, p. 266, Foch to Minister of War, 29 October 1914; Palat, *Ruée vers Calais*, p. 364; Dauzet, *Bataille des Flandres*, p. 56.

62 Brose, *Kaiser's Army*, pp. 150–1, 172, 211–12.

63 Craster, *Fifteen Rounds*, p. 117.

64 IWM, Trefusis Mss, 82/30/1, diary, 25 October 1914.

65 OFH, p. 248; PRO, WO95/706, IV Corps Operational Report, 14 November 1914; IWM, Garwood Mss, 91/23/1, diary, 29 October 1914.

66 IWM, Garwood Mss, 91/23/1, diary, 24 and 25 October 1914.

67 LUBLLC, Saumarez Mss, GS0454, reminiscences, 25 October 1914.

68 *Armées Françaises*, I, Pt. IV, p. 272.

69 Élie Chamard, 'Zonnebeke', *Revue des Deux Mondes*, 1935, pp. 103–41.

70 LUBLLC, de Saumarez Mss, GS0454, reminiscences, 25–26 October 1914.

71 Hamilton, *First Seven Divisions*, pp. 235–6; Atkinson, *Seventh Division*, p. 68.

72 NLS, Haig Mss, Acc 3155/99, diary, 26 October 1914.

73 Prior and Wilson, *Command*, pp. 13–14; IWM, French Mss, 75/46/6, French to Kitchener, 27 October 1914; NLS, Haig Mss, Acc 3155/99, diary, 27 October 1914; NAM, Rawlinson Mss, 5201–33–25, diary, 25 October 1914; CAC, Rawlinson Mss, RWLN 01/001, Lambton to Rawlinson, 25 October 1914.

74 IWM, Rees Mss, 77/179/1, 'Personal Record', 25–28 October 1914; ibid., Knight Mss, 77/64/1, account, 28 October 1914.

75 OFH, p. 252.

chapter 5

The South

Before dealing with the critical phase of the battle of Ypres, however, it is necessary to look further south to the concluding actions in what were regarded as the battles of La Bassée and Armentières. Due to the Germans not anticipating the withdrawal to the new position running from the La Bassée Canal to Fauquissart, to which it had retired on the previous night, II Corps had not come under attack on 23 October. In some respects, the sector covering the coalfields around Béthune was not as strategically vital as Ypres, which covered the approach to the Channel ports. Nonetheless, the Germans tried repeatedly to break through between Armentières and Arras until 29 October. The area was largely flat and waterlogged, with the result that the trenches were shallow and had to be supplemented by all too visible breastworks. As indicated earlier, sandbags were in short supply until later in October and the Royal Engineers also had to scour the countryside for fence posts and ordinary wire in lieu of barbed wire.

In the case of the 2nd Royal Welch Fusiliers at Fromelles, German snipers concealed in houses were a particular problem when any movement or work was needed: 'The want of communication trenches, which there had not been time to get on with, and the places where sections had not yet dug out far enough to join up, were the causes of many casualties.' The livestock still roaming the countryside was also a problem, a few strands of wire being put out principally to keep cattle and horses out of the trenches at night rather than to impede the Germans. One old soldier in the Royal Welch remarked that, 'the British Government must be terribly hard up, what with short rations, no rifle-oil, no shells, and now sending Engineers up to the front line to stretch one single bloody strand of barbed wire out, which he had no doubt was the only single bloody strand in the whole of France, and which a bloody giraffe could rise up and walk under'. The bloated corpses of cows, which had died from udder complications when they had not been milked, proved especially unpleasant though the battalion did manage to get one Friesian cow into an enlarged bay in a company trench from which they obtained fresh milk until 8 November when 'she met a full toss from a shell'. A nearby orchard enabled men to retrieve apples but the only pig found in a farm was soon consumed, its fat being saved to oil rifles, Vaseline being used for the same purpose in the absence of rifle oil.[1]

A particularly vivid description of the conditions in the Royal Welch at Fromelles has been left by Frank Richards, a reservist recalled to the colours in 1914: 'There was no such thing as cooked food or hot tea at this stage of the war, and rations were very scarce: we were lucky if we got our four biscuits a man daily, a pound tin of bully between two, a tin of jam between six, and the rum ration which was about a tablespoon and a half.' The jam in particular was of poor quality and tobacco, cigarettes and matches were also in short supply. Sanitary arrangements were also primitive: 'we used empty bully-beef tins for urinating in, throwing it over the back of the para- pet. If a man was taken short during the day he had to use the trench he was in and then throw it over the back of the trench and throw earth on it.' Night-time forays out of the trenches also netted German spiked hel- mets for latrine buckets, it taking several days to complete a communica- tion trench back to a square pit prepared as a more suitable latrine. The dead, too, were put on the back of the parapet until they could be removed under cover of darkness, anything useful such as boots being removed. Richards could only remember the battalion cooks preparing one 'dicksee' of cold tea during the whole period at Fromelles, the men also being 'as lousy as rooks' by the time they were finally relieved on 15 November.[2]

Probing attacks on 24 October were generally broken up by British artillery though not without anxieties. Lieutenant Colonel George Geddes of 42nd Brigade, RFA, wrote to his wife, 'Messages kept coming in every few minutes artillery fire was required here there & everywhere. Things looked so black that baggage wagons & mess wagons were all sent to a village some miles back. Shell & rifle fire going fast & furious. This was one of the occasions when it is hopeless to imagine the worst though preparations for it have to be made. Horses harnessed up ready for a sudden retreat. All these pre- cautions had the desired effect like unfurling one's umbrella to stop the rain.' Geddes heard later in the day the 4th Division had successfully blown a bridge while German troops were on it, then pouring machine-gun fire on those who had survived: 'I am told it was a ghastly sight but an agreeable one from our point of view! What blood thirsty ruffians we are all becoming!! But naturally we want to exterminate those who are trying to exterminate us!!'[3]

Despite the efforts of the artillery, the Germans did force their way into a gap between the 1st Gordons of 8th Brigade (3rd Division) and the 15th Sikhs of the Jullundur Brigade, the Lahore Division having now concentrated at Neuve Chapelle and having been allocated to II Corps. Both battalions lost heavily, being almost equally inexperienced. Visiting the front line, indeed, Smith-Dorrien found the Indians walking about in total disregard to the shellfire, notably the so-called portmanteau effect of German heavy howitzers, likened to someone throwing a portmanteau in the air. He had to suggest to Major General Philip Carnegy of the Jullundur Brigade that this was not a very good idea. Despite their difficulties, however, Smith-Dorrien still also concluded that the Gordons had 'disgraced themselves', largely by not having sufficient covering parties forward of the trenches to give warning of dawn attacks.[4]

The Sikhs, of course, had only just arrived and battalion strength was generally low in the Lahore Division while the Ferozepore Brigade had been detached in support of Allenby's Cavalry Corps, and, as previously related, the Sirhind Brigade had remained in Egypt. The Gordons had suffered grievously back at Le Cateau in August to the extent that the battalion bore no resemblance to the original, having lost some 80 per cent of its men as casualties and all but two or three officers, being kept going mostly on drafts of special reservists and young officers. The position was restored, however, by a counter-attack by the 4th Middlesex of 8th Brigade. Matters were quieter on 25 October although heavy shelling forced some units to withdraw from their trenches temporarily, returning at dusk.

Smith-Dorrien believed the Germans would probably not make a major effort against him in the immediate future but he was sufficiently concerned by the scale of losses and the continuing exhaustion of his men to ask French for further support. Writing to his wife, he noted, 'I have been having a pretty trying time of it. My poor troops are simply worn out – & their losses are tremendous. Day & night without cessation they are in close touch with the Enemy fighting hard – This was bound to be for we who are out here first must have the hardest fighting.' Smith-Dorrien had seen Gleichen of 13th Brigade, Brigadier General Stanley Maude of 14th Brigade, who had taken over when S.P. Rolt had recently broken down, and the acting commander of 13th Brigade, Lieutenant Colonel Martyn. They all painted a gloomy picture. As previously indicated, Smith-Dorrien had also concluded some days earlier that some battalions and even brigades in 5th Division were no longer reliable. Accordingly, Smith-Dorrien visited de Maud'huy then motored on to see French on the evening of 25 October. Smith-Dorrien's own contemporary account merely suggests that he realised that any retreat by II Corps would probably prove fatal to French's plans and makes no particular comment on the fact that French visited him next morning and also spoke to both Mackenzie and Morland. According to Henry Wilson, however, French was 'rather short' with Smith-Dorrien, believing that the II Corps commander was exaggerating.[5] The incident once more poisoned the relationship between the two men.

It has been suggested that Smith-Dorrien was perhaps unduly influenced by the gloomy predictions of his divisional commanders. It is clear, however, that II Corps was in a parlous state and, given Smith-Dorrien's reluctance to inform French of the state of his men on 22 October, presumably only real necessity now persuaded him to do so. In response, despite his attitude towards Smith-Dorrien, French, who had again been made aware of the position by Loch, did promise to make more men available. Accordingly, Allenby sent one of his cavalry brigades to support 3rd Division; two batteries of 4.7-inch guns being kept in reserve at Hazebrouck due to the lack of shells and a naval armoured train were also moved up. As previously indicated, French also authorised Smith-Dorrien to exceed the limits on the daily expenditure of shells for his 18-pounders. Clearly, however, French certainly believed he had more evidence of Smith-Dorrien's potential to become discouraged.[6]

De Maud'huy also moved up units, the French taking over the defence of Givenchy, enabling 5th Division to muster three battalions as a reserve, de Maud'huy feeling that its loss 'will mean the first step in the separation between the two armies'. In all, de Maud'huy sent four battalions and three batteries to the north of the La Bassée canal. He also placed at Smith-Dorrien's disposal from Conneau's Cavalry Corps a total of 300 men from a chasseur battalion, a battalion of dismounted cavalry of between 600 and 700 men, 4–5000 cyclists, and nine batteries, though he suggested that all these would be best employed east of Laventie as the ground around Givenchy was too marshy for cavalry and cyclists. Generally, indeed, the good relationship between Smith-Dorrien and his French counterparts such as de Maud'huy, Conneau and Maistre proved invaluable. Smith-Dorrien indeed was to write to de Maud'huy on 26 October expressing his deep appreci-ation of the French efforts. So anxious was Smith-Dorrien to ensure the good relationship continued that 3rd Division was admonished for refusing one offer of help from Conneau's horse artillery.[7]

There had been a tendency on the Aisne for mutual recriminations but, under heavy German pressure, the past was largely forgotten. Indeed, French and British units, especially artillery, now frequently came under the orders of the others' commanders. Brigadier General Headlam of 5th Divi-sion's artillery, for example, had several conferences with his counterpart in XXI Corps, General Maistre, on their respective artillery methods. Maistre seems to have greatly appreciated the accuracy of the British artillery com-pared to that of the French, who would usually cease fire when the infantry started to move forward whereas the British would continue to fire in support of an attack.

Unequivocal support from de Maud'huy proved timely as, notwithstanding Smith-Dorrien's belief that the main German effort opposite him had ceased, a heavy attack developed on the junction between the 3rd and 5th Divisions at Neuve Chapelle on 26 October. Indeed, the Germans broke into the village through the positions of the 2nd Royal Irish Rifles, a unit reduced to barely twenty officers and men, some of whom had been dug out of col-lapsed trenches at least twice already. Corporal John Lucy, a 20-year-old serv-ing with the battalion, wrote an extraordinary vivid account of the ordeal of the battalion which 'perished here [Neuve Chapelle] almost completely'. The Germans had brought up the heavy howitzers they had used against the Belgian frontier forts in August 1914: 'It was the loudest shell we had heard in transit to date. . . . Would it never come down? It took an un-believably long time. Then every man in the front line ducked as the thing shrieked raspingly louder and louder down on us. There was a terrific thump which shook the ground, and quite a pause, then a rending crash so shat-teringly loud that each of us believed it to be in his own section of trench. A perceptible wall of air set up by a giant explosion struck our faces. The monster shell had burst well behind us in amongst the houses of the village.' As the bombardment intensified Lucy and his comrades had 'crouched wretchedly, shaken by the blastings, under a lasting hail of metal and displaced earth and sods, half-blinded and half-choked by poisonous vapours, waiting for the enemy infantry, while our overworked stretcher-bearers busied themselves with new dead and wounded'. By day movement was all but impossible and constant shelling of the rear prevented supplies reaching the front trenches. After three days of this, the men 'were by now all very tired, cold, dirty, and ill-nourished. We were living on our nerves. Men detailed to rest gasped and grunted in broken sleep and jumped awake nervously when touched on the shoulder to be detailed for look-out.'[8]

Four guns were also lost.[9] Fortunately, the battalions on either side held and the eighty men left in the reserve company of the 1st Wiltshires managed to plug the gap. A counter-attack by five companies gathered from three different battalions was then organised in fading light and it managed to restore most of the line, though the Germans remained at the northern end of the village. Visiting Smith-Dorrien that night, French demanded vigorous local attacks to recover the lost forward trenches and clear the village. In trying to mount such an attack, however, the remainder of the Royal Irish was again driven back with heavy casualties during the morning of 27 October. The only senior officer on the spot, Colonel N.R. McMahon of the 4th Royal Fusiliers, gathered together elements from eight different units including French cyclists and chasseurs sent by Conneau for a counter-attack at 1330 hours. It got no further than the northern outskirts of the village, the men already exhausted by the exertions of the past 24 hours and under heavy fire from machine guns and from snipers concealed in cottages. At the very moment that McMahon was trying to push north of the village, however, a new German attack developed to its east sweeping through the remnants of the 1st Wiltshires and all but surrounding the 1st Queen's Own Royal West Kents, which had only two young subalterns left. It was stopped with difficulty by the commitment of the last reserves available to 14th Brigade, namely the 20th and 21st Companies, Sappers and Miners from the Lahore Division, plus the 9th Bhopal Infantry, and the reserve battalion from the neighbouring 15th Brigade. It was not possible, however, to regain the whole of the village and the line was pulled back around and behind it. Lieutenant Billy Congreve, Hubert Hamilton's former ADC in 3rd Division, was not surprised by the day's events, 7th Brigade in particular being 'nearly done for' with 'hardly any officers left, and the men are few and rather nerve-broken'.[10]

Some twenty-four German battalions were now opposite 3rd Division, and the entire *14th Division* of *VII Corps* had been used in the attack. Nonetheless, having believed 26 October the worst day he had experienced since Le Cateau, Smith-Dorrien was noticeably more optimistic on 27 October, believing the Germans nearing the end of their resources and cheered by the news from the Eastern Front of Russian success. Indeed, his thoughts began to turn to domesticity: 'I honestly do not see how the war can be a very long one – & still believe I shall be walking round the garden with my Dear, looking at the borders & hoping the pet one will really come out all blue, before the Daffodils have ceased to flower.'[11]

When French met with Smith-Dorrien and the commander of the Indian Corps, Willcocks, however, he decided that II Corps should be withdrawn for a few days' rest, being replaced by the Indian Corps. Smith-Dorrien cautioned that the Indians would become fatigued if required to hold the whole line for long. French, however, chose to disregard Smith-Dorrien's suggestion that the Indians hold only half the line.[12] In the meantime, however, Smith-Dorrien decided to mount a counter-attack on Neuve Chapelle with 3rd Division, while every other man was used to prepare a second line of defence. The attack on 28 October was entrusted to Brigadier General F.W.N. McCracken of 7th Brigade, assisted by 14th Brigade and Richard 'Gobby Chops' Mullens's 2nd Cavalry Brigade to his right and Indian troops, French cyclists and chasseurs, and a battalion lent by 6th Division on his left. Morning fog prevented an early start and it was not until 1100 hours that a preliminary artillery bombardment was laid down with the intention that the infantry should move forward at 1130. In most cases, however, the men were exhausted, staff officers found it difficult to co-ordinate the hotchpotch of units, and the support was not forthcoming from either left or right. Indeed, only two companies of the 47th Sikhs and the 20th and 21st Companies of the Sappers and Miners advanced on the village itself. Amazingly, they reached the village and drove the Germans back in hand-to-hand fighting. The inevitable German riposte, which developed into a wider attack, swept the Indians back, the Sikhs losing all but sixty-eight out of 289 men committed to the attack and the Sappers and Miners losing all their officers and a third of the men.

Smith-Dorrien had never intended that valuable technical troops such as the Sappers and Miners should have been used for the attack. Indeed, the Sappers and Miners should have been returned to Carnegy of the Jullundur Brigade on 27 October but, through some misunderstanding, Mackenzie of 3rd Division retained them and instead three squadrons of the 15th Lancers were dispatched to Carnegy. Smith-Dorrien nonetheless chiefly blamed McCracken for the affair. From the beginning, Geddes of the 42nd Brigade, RFA, had doubted McCracken's capacity for commanding such a mixed force, noting that the cavalrymen were particularly critical of the lack of information they had received from 7th Brigade's staff.[13]

The wider German attack, however, was held and the Germans evacuated Neuve Chapelle on 29 October, having taken about 6000 casualties in the actions around the village. The 2/8th Gurkhas from the Bareilly Brigade lost nine of its British officers. The day's diary entry of Second Lieutenant Douglas McDougall of the 2nd Royal Scots, commissioned only in February 1914 and shot through the lower stomach during the course of the day, summarised his experience tersely: 'Woke up after dawn. Started to improve my trench. Machine Gun placed just behind it. Received parcel from home. Went out 2nd time to get a Sikh, picked off by sniper. Stayed in house for most of day, taken away at night to Field Ambulance. MO dressed my wound then went by wagon to dressing station.'[14]

On 31 October Willcocks formally took over command of the line from Smith-Dorrien, the Meerut Division having also been moved up, though Smith-Dorrien left most of his artillery to support the Indians. The Meerut Division had landed at Marseilles between 12 and 14 October, the voyage having been slowed by the poor speed of some of the sea transports, the need to issue the latest pattern rifle at Marseilles and further transport delays in France itself. On 31 October the first VC won by any native soldier since the Mutiny was awarded to a sepoy of the 129th Baluchis, Khudadad Khan, for continuing to man his machine gun at Hollebeke after his British officer had been wounded. The general feeling in II Corps, however, was that the Indians had been severely tried by their experience thus far and too many units of unknown quality had been chosen for overseas service without sufficient care being exercised.[15]

Smith-Dorrien had anticipated that his men would receive ten days' rest. In the event, battalions were detached to support both I and III Corps. Between 12 and 31 October II Corps had suffered heavily. The casualties of 3rd Division numbered 5835, with its four brigades all severely depleted: 8th and 9th Brigade together could barely muster a full brigade between them. On 31 October II Corps as a whole had only 14,000 infantry, down from an establishment of 24,000. Moreover, over 1400 of these remaining men had not been with their units a week, being new drafts. Smith-Dorrien had also lost another divisional commander. Mackenzie had never fully recovered from an appendicitis operation before coming out to succeed Hubert Hamilton and he was invalided home on 29 October, being replaced by Major General F.D.V. Wing. In 3rd Division, however, it was assumed that Mackenzie had been told by Smith-Dorrien that 'he looked seedy and had better try a change of air in England' after mishandling the counter-attack

Plate 1 Troops of the 6th Cavalry Brigade (3rd Cavalry Division) from Rawlinson's IV Corps entering Ypres, 13 October 1914 [IWM]

Plate 2 Belgian civilians fleeing towards Messines during shelling, October 1914 [IWM]

Plate 3 Machine gun detachments and troops from 2nd Cavalry Division at the entrance to the grounds of Hollebeke Château, 22 October 1914. A photograph taken by Hubert Gough's French interpreter, Paul Maze [IWM]

Plate 4 French cavalrymen resting close to the railway station in Ypres, October 1914. A photograph taken by Sergeant C. Pilkington of the 2nd Scots Guards [IWM]

Plate 5 German prisoners taken by the Belgians in the square at Furnes, October 1914 [IWM]

Plate 6 Transport of 7th Division in the congestion of Thielt market place, 12 October 1914, that of the 2nd Scots Guards in the centre. Another photograph taken by Pilkington [IWM]

Plate 7 Men of the 11th Hussars near Doullens on the march from the Aisne to Flanders, 9 October 1914. A photograph taken by Lieutenant Colonel Thomas Pitman [IWM]

Plate 8 The 2nd Royal Scots Fusiliers digging trenches at Terhand to the south east of Beselaere close to the limit of 7th Division's advance towards Menin, 19 October 1914 [IWM]

Plate 9 The memorial to the 2nd Worcesters at Gheluvelt, commemorating the famous charge on 31 October 1914

Plate 10 Armoured cars passing men of the Northumberland Hussars on the Zillebeke road, 15 October 1914

Plate 11 Brigadier General Charles Briggs (left) and his staff, including a French interpreter, on the canal bridge at St Michel-sur-Ternoise during the march to the north, 10 October 1914

Plate 12 French dead lying outside a ruined church in Pervyse, 1 November 1914

Plate 13 Major General Hubert Gough (left) reading despatches in the grounds of Hollebeke Château during October 1914. Another photograph by Paul Maze

Plate 14 The memorial to the 2nd South Wales Borderers at Gheluvelt, situated close to the line held by the battalion on 31 October 1914

Plate 15 The memorial to the 1/14th London Regiment (London Scottish) of the Territorial Force on the Wytschaete to Messines road, commemorating their action on 31 October 1914

to restore the line after the Gordons had given way on 25 October. Indeed, Smith-Dorrien confided to his wife that though but a few days earlier Mackenzie had appeared to know his work well, he had shown 'no power of decision'.[16]

With his battalions – 'mere skeletons' – being fed piecemeal into the battle further north, Smith-Dorrien found himself temporarily without troops and, somewhat bizarrely, spent a couple of days watching his staff shoot pheasants since they only had one gun between five of them. French, meanwhile, later claimed the state of II Corps had caused him particular worries on 2 November though, by then, it had been relieved. By contrast, Smith-Dorrien still believed French the best man to be CinC as 'he is so determined & full of courage in the face of very great difficulty' and on 8 November recorded French's attitude as 'ever more friendly each day'. Smith-Dorrien also expressed his confidence in French to the King's assistant private secretary, Clive Wigram.[17] Subsequently, Smith-Dorrien went back to England on 10 November at French's request to report to the King and Kitchener, returning to duty on 14 November, by which time fourteen of his battalions were fighting with I Corps.[18]

Once installed in the trenches of II Corps, the Indians came under heavy artillery bombardment and suffered some localised German attacks, taking unnecessarily heavy casualties from the tendency to remain in the trenches rather than withdrawing from them temporarily as British units had learned to do. By 3 November, the Indian Corps had already suffered 1989 casualties, including fifty-four British officers but only thirty-one Indian officers.[19]

On the previous day, Willcocks had reported his battalions unreliable in the trenches with an increased incidence of self-mutilation and, on the following day, declined to be responsible for the consequences unless he received support from a British division. Henry Wilson, too, had noted that same day that 65 per cent of all casualties in the Indian Corps had been self-inflicted. Yet, in fact, since such cases were not always punished by courts martial, the Deputy Judge Advocate General recorded just nine Indian troops convicted for self-mutilation over the whole period the Indian Corps was in France. As it happened, French could send Willcocks only four battalions from 14th Brigade, sent back up in motor buses though, apparently, French's first reaction to Willcocks's belief that his men might give way at any moment was to tell him 'that if they must go, they could go – into the sea, or to h-ll, & that he would not send more than 2 battalions'. Problems with the Indian Corps continued, the Indians eventually being withdrawn from France in November 1915.[20] The Germans, however, were winding down their effort between Arras and Armentières for on 27 October Falkenhayn had directed *Sixth Army* to send all its heavy artillery and all its heavy shells northwards to support a new effort to break through there.

To the north of II Corps, Pulteney's III Corps held the line between the British and French cavalry covering Smith-Dorrien's left to connect with more British cavalry north of Armentières. Like Smith-Dorrien his orders were to hold his line, but he was opposed by almost twice his strength, the Germans having *XIII, XIX* and *I Cavalry Corps* opposite him. Pulteney was apprehensive at the gap between Smith-Dorrien and himself when he had no reserves but, fortunately, he was not put under great pressure though artillery fire and snipers continued to test the men's endurance.[21] Indeed, it became the practice to remove men from the front line positions. Fourth Division was not seriously troubled at all though 6th Division was attacked on 22 and 23 October.

Ritchie of the Cameronians in 6th Division had been clearly excited by his experiences, recording on 22 October that 'It is all a splendidly exhilarating battle. A real battle, not one in which nothing happens.' On the following night, however, his mood darkened when on a night patrol he came across a dead German from whom he took a diary: 'He was fond of sketching, and it was interesting and sad. Poor man. There was a letter to his father, unposted, and another to a woman. . . . It makes me very sad and suddenly tired of it all. Until now, I think I have been nothing but intensely interested. I don't remember feeling frightened, but the shells make one have a rather go-down, suddenly-in-the lift feeling.' Compared to neighbouring battalions, Ritchie felt his men 'perfectly calm and unexcited, thinking only of sleep and food and their rum ration'. He felt the Germans, however, 'more soldierly' in terms of 'soldierly spirit', pushing their patrols up much further to get information than the British customarily did.[22]

The Germans did reach the British line around Le Quesne on 23 October before being expelled and 16th Brigade did pull back its line some 500 yards or so on the night of 25–26 October. The 1st Leicesters in 16th Brigade in particular were engaged in hand-to-hand fighting on 25 October in and around a barricade at a level crossing south of the railway station at La Houssoie, in which the battalion had its headquarters. As further north at Langemarck, according to Lance Corporal William Dalby, a well-known rugby player in Leicester, the Germans apparently advanced 'in thousands singing "Wacht am Rhein" and blowing penny trumpets and making as much noise as possible'. There are discrepancies between the contemporary Regimental War Diary, the later regimental history and the Official History on details and losses but the Leicesters took at least 188 casualties in dead, wounded and missing, many of the latter captured when a company was overrun.[23] Greater German efforts were made on both 28 and 29 October. The Germans, mostly from the *223rd* and *224th Regiments* of *XXIV Reserve Corps*, managed to occupy a portion of the line held by the 1st Middlesex only temporarily, the British communications having been interrupted by telephone cables being cut by shells.

Though Pulteney's corps suffered some 5779 casualties between 15 and 31 October, his line was not really imperilled though there was often anxiety, not least at night. This was fortunate when, as elsewhere, mud was clogging rifles and the shortage of rifle oil put more and more rifles out of service.[24] Therefore, with the heavy German attacks developing to the north, Sir John French directed Pulteney on the afternoon of 30 October to send 4th Division's reserves to reinforce Allenby while 6th Division's reserves covered the whole of III Corps's front. In the event, the retirement of Allenby's cavalry from Messines on 1 November did pose a more serious problem and French therefore sent some of Smith-Dorrien's battalions to reinforce III Corps while also lifting daily limits on III Corps' expenditure of shells, the existing forty rounds a day limit for the 18-pounders and 4.5-inch howitzers being doubled. Robertson's system had been to allocate most shells to those formations that needed to use most and, though he recognised the potential for waste, he considered that 'we must be lenient to some extent when fighting is taking place'.[25]

Allenby meanwhile had held the line between Pulteney and Haig's I Corps up to 1 November with great determination. Fortunately, they were only opposed by German cavalry, who lacked heavy artillery support and were not as well equipped as British cavalry for a dismounted role. More testing times were ahead for the British cavalry.

Notes and references

1 Richards, *Old Soldiers Never Die*, pp. 43–5, 49–50; *War the Infantry Knew*, pp. 79–80, 83–4.

2 Richards, *Old Soldiers Never Die*, pp. 42–4, 51.

3 IWM, Geddes Mss, 78/65/1, Geddes to wife, 24 October 1914.

4 IWM, Smith-Dorrien Mss, 87/47/2, war diary, 24 and 25 October 1914; ibid., 87/47/10, diary 25 October 1914; PRO, WO95/629, Note by Forestier-Walker, 25 October 1914; Smith-Dorrien, *Forty-Eight Years*, p. 458.

5 Smith-Dorrien, *Forty-Eight Years*, pp. 460–1; IWM, Smith-Dorrien Mss, 87/47/5, Smith-Dorrien to wife, 25 October 1914; ibid., Wilson Mss, DS/MISC/80, diary, 25 October; French, *1914*, p. 244.

6 Holmes, *Little Field Marshal*, p. 247; IWM, Loch Mss, 71/12/2, diary, 25 October 1914.

7 IWM, Smith-Dorrien Mss, 87/47/7, de Maud'huy to Smith-Dorrien, 26 October 1914 (also PRO, WO95/629); SHAT 18N 134, Smith-Dorrien to de Maud'huy, 26 October 1914 (also in *Armées Françaises*, I, Pt. IV, Annexes Vol. IV, p. 197); PRO, WO95/629, Forestier-Walker to 3rd Division, 26 October 1914; ibid., WO95/630, Forestier-Walker to de Maud'huy, 27 October 1914; ibid., File of Communications with French Commanders, especially Conneau to Smith-Dorrien, 16, 23 and 26 October 1914, de Maud'huy to Smith-Dorrien, 23 October 1914, and Maistre to Smith-Dorrien, 20 October 1914.

8 John Lucy (1938), *There's a Devil in the Drum*, London: Faber and Faber, pp. 211, 219–20, 230.

9 IWM, Geddes Mss, 78/65/1, Geddes to wife, 8–9 November 1914.

10 IWM, Smith-Dorrien Mss, 87/47/7, II Corps Operational Report, 26–27 October 1914; Pamela Fraser and L.H. Thornton (1930), *The Congreves: Father and Son*, London: John Murray, p. 238.

11 IWM, Smith-Dorrien Mss, 87/47/5, Smith-Dorrien to wife, 27 October 1914.

12 IWM, Smith-Dorrien Mss, 87/47/2, war diary, 28 October 1914; ibid., 87/47/10, diary, 28 October 1914.

13 Smith-Dorrien, *Forty-Eight Years*, p. 464; IWM, Geddes Mss, 78/65/1, Geddes to wife, 29 October 1914; ibid., Smith-Dorrien Mss, 87/47/7, II Corps Operational Report, 28 October 1914; PRO, WO95/629, Note on Sappers and Miners by Smith-Dorrien, 3 November 1914.

14 LUBLLC, McDougall Mss, GS1010, diary, 29 October 1914.

15 PRO, WO95/629, Milward diary, 28 and 31 October 1914.

16 IWM, Smith-Dorrien Mss, 87/47/2, war diary, 29 October 1914; ibid., 87/47/5, Smith-Dorrien to wife, 30 October 1914; ibid., St John Mss, 83/17/1, diary, 25 October 1914; RA, Geo V Q.832/338, Smith-Dorrien to Wigram, 6 November 1914.

17 IWM, Smith-Dorrien Mss, 87/47/2, war diary, 31 October 1914; ibid., 87/47/5, Smith-Dorrien to wife, 3, 4 and 8 November 1914; ibid., 87/47/10, diary, 31 October 1914; Smith-Dorrien, *Forty-Eight Years*, pp. 465, 467; Beckett, *Judgement of History*, p. 60; French, *1914*, p. 244; RA, Geo V Q.832/338 and 339, Smith-Dorrien to Wigram, 6 and 9 November 1914.

18 IWM, Smith-Dorrien Mss, 87/47/7, II Corps Operational Report, 14 November 1914.

19 Gardner, *Trial by Fire*, p. 193.

20 IWM, French Mss, 75/46/6, French to Kitchener, 2 and 3 November 1914; ibid., Smith-Dorrien Mss, 87/47/10, diary, 2 November 1914; ibid., Wilson Mss, DS/MISC/80, diary, 2 November 1914; LHCMA, Clive Mss, II/1, diary, 4 November 1914; Timothy Bowman (2003), *The Irish Regiments in the Great War: Discipline and Morale*, Manchester: Manchester University Press, p. 45.

21 PRO, WO95/668, Pulteney to Smith-Dorrien, 22 October 1914.

22 LUBLLC, Ritchie Mss, GS1361, diary, 22, 23, 24 and 25 October 1914.

23 Matthew Richardson (2004), 'Tigers at Bay?: The Leicestershire Regiment at Armentières', *Stand To* **69**, pp. 9–12.

24 *War Infantry Knew*, p. 84; Terraine, *General Jack's Diary*, p. 74.

25 Brown, *British Logistics*, p. 63; PRO, WO159/15, Robertson to von Donop, 4 November 1914.

chapter 6

Army Group Fabeck

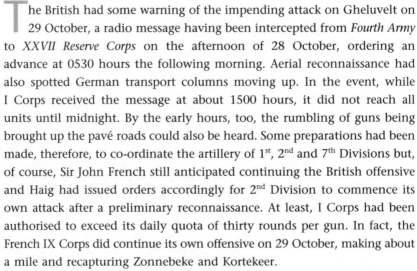

The British had some warning of the impending attack on Gheluvelt on 29 October, a radio message having been intercepted from *Fourth Army* to *XXVII Reserve Corps* on the afternoon of 28 October, ordering an advance at 0530 hours the following morning. Aerial reconnaissance had also spotted German transport columns moving up. In the event, while I Corps received the message at about 1500 hours, it did not reach all units until midnight. By the early hours, too, the rumbling of guns being brought up the pavé roads could also be heard. Some preparations had been made, therefore, to co-ordinate the artillery of 1st, 2nd and 7th Divisions but, of course, Sir John French still anticipated continuing the British offensive and Haig had issued orders accordingly for 2nd Division to commence its own attack after a preliminary reconnaissance. At least, I Corps had been authorised to exceed its daily quota of thirty rounds per gun. In fact, the French IX Corps did continue its own offensive on 29 October, making about a mile and recapturing Zonnebeke and Kortekeer.

It was expected that any German attack would come from the direction of Kruiseecke south of the road from Menin to Gheluvelt. In the event, the weight of the German attack would fall on the Gheluvelt crossroads where the Menin Road crossed that between Kruiseecke and Poezelhoek. The crossroads formed the junction between 1st and 7th Divisions, the flank of each being coincidentally held by a Guards battalion. The left flank of 7th Division south of the crossroads was held by 1st Grenadier Guards in 20th Brigade and 1st Coldstream Guards in 1st (Guards) Brigade held the right of 1st Division north of the crossroads, though the latter was weak in numbers. Brigadier General Charles Fitzclarence VC had moved up two companies of the 1st Black Watch and a platoon of the 1st Gloucesters from 3rd Brigade to assist the Coldstream.[1] Grandson of the Earl of Munster, the 48-year-old Fitzclarence had won his VC at Mafeking when attached to the Protectorate Regiment for three separate acts of gallantry between October and December 1899. He had transferred from the Royal Fusiliers to the new Irish Guards in October 1900, commanding its 1st Battalion from 1909 to 1913, before receiving command of 29th Brigade in August 1914. He had moved to command the 1st Guards Brigade in September.

Unfortunately, the trenches occupied by the British had originally been intended as support positions and were deep and narrow with overhead cover. They were by no means continuous, and there were neither communications trenches nor dugouts. The only wire was a single strand of ordinary wire with tins containing pebbles slung on it to act as a trip-wire warning signal if the Germans suddenly rushed the position. In most cases, observation from the trenches was limited in any case by buildings, gardens and orchards, which impeded artillery support when observers could not identify targets, and the lack of easy means of communication meant that one trench could easily be overcome with those on either flank unaware of the situation. Haig had hoped to further improve the trenches of 7th Division by preparing a second line to the rear, but there was no time to do so.[2]

Understandably, the strain could tell on men under fire by day and endeavouring to improve their positions by night, as recorded by a 22-year-old Huddersfield solicitor, Yorkshire county rugby player and Special Reserve officer, Lieutenant Rowland Owen of the 2nd Duke of Wellington's on 28 October: 'In the daytime you are shot at if you show a whisker (of which we have plenty just at present) outside the trench: so everything has to be done at night. The rations have to be fetched and issued, any reliefs made and additional trenches dug, and so on; so the night is fairly busy. Also, at intervals, some mooncalf goes and imagines he sees Germans "like millions of ants" advancing, and the Germans, terrified by the belief that *we* are advancing, pour a hail of lead at us. Then some other person on our side thinks the Germans really are advancing and sticks his head up (although he ought to know they couldn't fire and advance at the same time) and gets shot through the brain which he refused to use. Then the man next to him ferociously passes a message "that the Germans are advancing on the right", "look at the rifles flashes" (the French line being a continuation of ours only 50 yards in front) and the man on my left swings round and empties his piece at our easily excited ally (such a terrible breach of the Entente Cordiale) shooting right across my face, and knocks me with a whack on to my hindmost man on the back of the trench, so that I can only with difficulty find breath for uttering the oaths which are indispensable to the occasion. Thus you see the nights are fairly busy.' Subsequently, Owen was wounded on 7 November, a letter he sent to his rugby club while recuperating, together with a cartoon, being used to try and induce more rugby players to enlist. Owen returned to front line duties only in February 1915, being killed during the second battle for Ypres in April 1915.[3]

As predicted, the German bombardment began at 0530 on 29 October. Initially, the attack on the Coldstream and the Black Watch by the three battalions of *16th Bavarian Reserve Infantry Regiment* from *54th Reserve Division* of *XXVII Reserve Corps* was held. Problems arose, however, when two British machine guns placed close to the crossroads jammed and a large number of rifle cartridges proved too large for the rifles. Indeed, generally, there were reports that day of cartridges not fitting rifles and others that could not be easily extracted, the latter largely caused by difficulties in keeping rifles clean and oiled in muddy conditions and in continuous action. Indeed, no oil had been available for the last three days. Eventually, by about 0630 the Germans penetrated the line and captured most of the Black Watch and two of the Coldstream companies. It was a foggy morning with visibility no more than 40 yards and an error had also been made in directing the supporting artillery only to fire on German guns rather than on German infantry, given the fact that there were only nine shells per gun available.

The remaining two Coldstream companies held on and, learning what had occurred about 0700, Fitzclarence committed the rest of the Gloucesters, its commanding officer, Lieutenant Colonel A.C. Lovett, sending his companies forward independently in order that they came into action as soon as possible. Meanwhile, the Grenadiers were entirely unaware of what had happened to the north of the crossroads and Brigadier General Ruggles-Brise had actually sent his immediate reserves to the rear for breakfast in the belief no attack would now occur. Covered by the fog, large masses of Germans – some four battalions – attacked at about 0730 and though a breeze began to lift the fog and give the defenders visibility up to about 80 yards, they broke through almost at once in hand-to-hand fighting. By the end of the day the Grenadiers had lost 470 officers and men, only five officers and under 200 other ranks remaining. The reserves were hurriedly brought back and the German advance was halted south of the Menin Road.

The fog and poor communications contrived to prevent Capper learning of his line having been forced back until 1015 hours though Major General Samuel Lomax of 1st Division had received somewhat earlier notice of the attack on his line. As the British began to move up their reserves, so the Germans widened their effort to include most of the frontage held by I Corps, though as so often in the recent past they had not quite grasped the significance of the advantage that they had won. They also began to bombard the town of Ypres with artillery and aircraft, though at the time Ypres was virtually devoid of troops beyond the headquarters of General Dubois of the French IX Corps and rear elements of I Corps staff. Lomax committed three battalions from 3rd Brigade to restore the line previously held by the Coldstream and Capper sent in two battalions from his divisional reserve to support the Grenadiers. Before 3rd Brigade could reach the front, however, a fresh German attack overwhelmed the remaining companies of the Coldstream and the Black Watch, the former being able to muster just eighty men commanded by the battalion quartermaster, Lieutenant Boyd, by the end of the day. Subsequently, as losses continued to mount over the next few days despite drafts, Boyd was told by Fitzclarence to take the few survivors out of the line on 2 November 'so that the Battalion should not be wiped out altogether'.[4]

The 1st Scots Guards had been rushed from the rear about 1000, some men not firing as they had been told previously that the Black Watch would be coming that way. C.E. Green, a 21-year-old serving in the 1st Scots Guards, was among those captured, remaining in German hands for the remainder of the war. He was marched off with some 200 other POWs: 'I shall never forget that march and the ensuing few hours afterwards. The now-gallant Huns made us go on knees, & proceeded to take our money, tobacco, cigarettes etc, from us and make away with them. As luck would have it, the searcher gave me back my tobacco-pipes. Some fellows, who had previously obtained German money from dead Huns, were very roughly handled.' After about an hour of being compelled to march with hands above heads, they were halted for a rest and those wounded were attended in a nearby farmhouse. Proceeding further, 'we passed many German soldiers, who made signs as if they would like to cut our throats'. Arriving at a German headquarters some 4 or 5 miles behind the front, a German officer attempted to question two captured officers while Green and the others were kept in a church. At about 1600 all were put on transport for Courtrai, where they were then 'packed into cattle trucks very tightly' for the journey to a POW camp.[5]

Somewhat belatedly in view of the early successes by *16th Bavarian Reserve Regiment*, the German *XXVII Reserve Corps* began advancing around Poezelhoek Chateau at about 1130. To support the newly promoted Major General Herman Landon's 1st Brigade, Brigadier General Lord Cavan of 4th Brigade put in his own reserve to help out and Haig then directed Bulfin, also promoted to Major General on 26 October, of 2nd Brigade to do the same. With these additional battalions, Landon attempted a counter-attack but little progress was made, a gap of some 500 yards around the crossroads still being open when the light faded. Landon, Bulfin and Fitzclarence and their battalion commanders conferred near Gheluvelt Chateau about 1600 hours and agreed to dig in on a new line about half a mile from the crossroads and to try and sort out the tangle of units that had become involved during the course of the day. Bulfin recorded, 'Do not like the situation at all. Went back to Landon who did not like situation any more than I did. Raining heavily. Got back to my Headquarters after midnight. Road being heavily shelled, also woods round [Veldhoek] Chateau.'[6]

As in several instances previously, entrenching tools were in short supply and few of the troops had any real rest. Moreover, through the commitment of battalions from brigade and divisional reserves, Haig now had only three battalions – two from 2nd Brigade and one from 21st Brigade – and the remnants of 20th Brigade, which had been pulled back to reorganise, as a reserve for his entire corps. Given the situation, Lomax and Major General Charles Monro of 2nd Division, who now both had their headquarters in Hooge Chateau, agreed with Haig's approval that, in the event of any further break in the line held by 1st Division around Gheluvelt, 2nd Division would launch a counter-attack on Polygon Wood in the hope of taking the Germans in the flank.

Allenby's Cavalry Corps had not been seriously engaged but Allenby appeared reluctant to weaken his own line further. In the event, Johnnie Gough contacted his brother and Hubert sent five squadrons and an RHA battery under Colonel Bulkeley Johnson of the Royal Scots Greys to Klein Zillebeke. Johnnie was duly thankful, writing to Hubert, 'Very many thanks for your support. It was like you. I have been up to the front and organised a big counter-attack of close up to 8000 to 12,000 men!! I fancy this will do the trick. Things look better than they did already.' Johnnie had actually been out of corps headquarters when Hubert's cavalry arrived and Neill Malcolm had been the first to pen a note of thanks to Hubert, adding, 'Johnnie, I need hardly say, is splendid on these occasions.'[7] At this stage, however, the cavalry were not needed after all and were sent back to Hubert at 1700. During the retreat from Mons, when Hubert Gough commanded a brigade and Allenby a division, Gough had managed to detach himself from Allenby's immediate supervision. It was typical of his impulsive character, as so readily shown in his defiance of the government during the Curragh incident, that he would now act on his own initiative again. Ironically, he was to be rather less lenient to so many of his own subordinates in the future as he rose to corps and then army command.[8]

The ad hoc plugging of gaps with whatever troops were available was to become known as 'puttying up' or, less prosaically to the French, *'boucher le trou'*. The British line remained thin, not least where Allenby's cavalry, supported by 57th Wilde's Rifles and 129th Baluchis from the Ferozepore Brigade of the Lahore Division, stretched over almost 9 miles with little artillery support though Allenby managed to form a corps reserve of a horse artillery battery and three regiments, one drawn from each brigade of Gough's 2nd Cavalry Division.

That night of 29 October, Lieutenant B.H. Waddy, a Special Reserve officer posted to the 2nd Bedfordshires in 21st Brigade, joined the battalion at Gheluvelt. He reported to the acting CO, Major J.M. Traill, and his adjutant, Captain C.C. Foss: 'The picture they presented gave me a distinct shock; my vague and somewhat theatrical visions vanished; my disillusionment began. For the first time I realised the dirt and discomfort that war means and was brought face to face with that utter weariness which, when experienced, seems almost a material thing. All of them, and especially Foss, were drawn and haggard and their eyes shone out of their pale faces as if fevered. Obviously they had not shaved for days, they were filthy and their clothes were soaked. They were too tired to talk, or even smoke, almost too tired to sleep. Even then, I think, I understood how extreme exhaustion became a tangible object, a shroud enveloping the whole body almost stifling the life within, to the man who has been called upon to display intense mental and physical energy for days and nights on end. I was tired myself after my long day and the uncomfortable march up from the transport lines over the rough and slippery road, but the sight of their faces almost drugged with want of sleep made one feel strangely fresh and wakeful in comparison.'[9]

In gaining the Gheluvelt crossroads, the Germans had obtained a favourable position for a further attack on Gheluvelt itself since there was a dip in the ground there to conceal the massing of German infantry. The positions the Germans held on the higher ground between Gheluvelt and Kruiseecke also gave them good observation for artillery support. Fortunately, however, the enclosed nature of the country with its multitude of farm buildings, hedges, ditches and woods concealed much of the weakness of the British line. French, meanwhile, was sufficiently encouraged by the end of the day to issue orders for the BEF to again attempt an offensive on 30 October, telling Kitchener on the basis of the limited counter-attack by Landon that 'if the success can be followed up, it will lead to a decisive result'. In a private letter to Churchill, who confided it to the Cabinet, French had even spoken of being in Bruges and Ostend in a week.[10]

A visit to Foch at Cassel, at which Foch had spoken of the good progress being made by the French, had proved what has been nicely characterised as a 'salvo of unrealistic optimism'. Only later did French claim that he knew a resumption of the British offensive improbable.[11] Haig wisely resolved instead to hold his ground and, indeed, once more, clear sounds of a considerable amount of movement were heard from the British positions that night. Some improvements were carried out to the trenches though only the men of 2nd Division were really fresh enough to do much and they at least were able to put up some barbed wire. Similarly optimistic, d'Urbal had directed Dubois to continue to advance on Poelcappelle.

The reality, of course, was that *Army Group Fabeck's* five divisions and 266 heavy guns had now moved up to starting positions, their presence not even identified for some days since they had moved by night. Fabeck's order of the day looked forward confidently to a breakthrough that would enable Germany to 'settle for ever with the centuries-long struggle, end the war, and strike the decisive blow against our most detested enemy'. An operational order from *XV Corps* for 30 October subsequently recovered from the body of a German officer also suggested the Germans regarded the offensive as the most important of the war to date.[12]

As indicated previously, Fabeck intended to break through between Zandvoorde and Messines to reach the higher ground at Kemmel, while *Fourth* and *Sixth Armies* staged diversionary attacks, which in the case of *XXVII Reserve Corps* of *Fourth Army* was intended to take Zonnebeke to draw in immediate allied reserves. The main effort by Fabeck's divisions would thus fall on the already exhausted 7th Division between the Menin Road and Zandvoorde, and Allenby's three cavalry divisions stretched out between Zandvoorde and Messines. The initial attack, however, was the diversion against Zonnebeke, which commenced with an artillery bombardment at

0600 on 30 October. At about 0630 – still 20 minutes before sunrise – the German infantry from *54th Reserve* and *30th Division* attacked under cover of mist as well as the gloom. Nowhere, however, did the Germans manage to break through or even compel 1st and 2nd Divisions to put in their reserves, the wire put up by 2nd Division preventing the Germans from closing. Moreover, as the mist cleared, the British had clear visibility, causing the Germans heavy casualties.

Matters were rather different opposite 7th Division and 7th Cavalry Brigade (3rd Cavalry Division) when Fabeck's main effort began about 0645 with another bombardment. While the heavy guns were distributed all along the front, most were concentrated against the defenders around Zandvoorde. Mostly sited on forward slopes in full view of the German observers, many of the British trenches were blown in during the course of a 75-minute bombardment. Indeed, many men were forced back to the support line. It has been suggested that, given Haig's previous criticism of Rawlinson allowing Capper to occupy such forward trenches, he had done singularly little to prevent a recurrence. The same fault was observed with Byng's cavalrymen and even some units of 1st and 2nd Divisions on 29 and 30 October though Byng at least had recognised the dangers but felt unable to further expose Capper's division by altering his own dispositions.[13]

Some men of the machine-gun section of the Royal Horse Guards and two squadrons from each of the 1st and 2nd Life Guards stayed forward but they were overwhelmed by a mass infantry attack by two regiments of the *39th Division* and three *Jäger* battalions at about 0800. By 1000 hours the Germans had occupied Zandvoorde although this was not immediately apparent to I Corps since telephone communications were scarce and easily disrupted. In the case of 7th Division, two of its three cable wagons were lost though one was subsequently recovered.[14] Indeed, due to the isolated nature of many British positions, messages were often passed back through division to corps and then forward again to adjacent units.

In this particular case, Byng had been watching the action and sent an officer to Haig's headquarters in the so-called White Chateau on the Gheluvelt Road – close to what was to become known as Hellfire Corner – and Allenby was informed by telephone from there. Once atop the Zandvoorde ridge the Germans were able to enfilade the positions of 21st Brigade to the extent that the brigade headquarters came under direct artillery fire as did the trenches of 1st Royal Welch Fusiliers from the neighbouring 22nd Brigade. The battalion was completely overrun, only eighty-six men surviving death or capture. Of those lost, 276 officers and men, including Lieutenant Colonel H.O.S. Cadogan, had been killed and only fifty-four taken prisoner. The 2nd Royal Scots Fusiliers also took heavy losses.

Byng meanwhile moved two regiments up to Klein Zillebeke as a stop line for those retiring from Zandvoorde while Lawford of 22nd Brigade sent two of his battalions that had been in reserve to try and regain Zandvoorde. Allenby also moved his corps reserve up to join in the counter-attack. Haig additionally sent two more battalions from 2nd Brigade under Bulfin to help out. In keeping with his worries of the previous day, Bulfin felt even less reassured: 'Don't feel a bit happy, no sort of reserve.' Even with all these forces being sent forward at about 1000 hours, however, no progress could be made in face of the large numbers of German troops and their artillery support. Rees of the 2nd Welch watched these efforts from a farm near Gheluvelt: 'I couldn't make head or tail of the situation. I saw three battalions one after the other try to cross an open stretch by an orchard about 800 yards in front and all three get driven back by machine-gun fire, after losing very heavily. They advanced from the Zandvoorde direction and probably belonged to 7th Division.'[15]

The best that could be done, therefore, was to form a new line about 1200 yards behind Zandvoorde, Haig using the units sent up to counter-attack to plug gaps instead and also moving up other available reserves since the line remained perilously thin. Lieutenant Waddy, who as previously related had joined the 2nd Bedfordshires only on the night of 29 October, heard hostile rifle fire for the first time in his career while in reserve at about 1600: 'The crack of a bullet passing close to one is so vicious and the loud drawn scream of a ricochet so eerie that one feels an utter helplessness, feels the supreme futility of attempting to dodge and such feeling is only intensified by the entire absence of any visible sign of force such as the earth splash and smoke cloud of a high explosive shell, or the curling, cream and white puff of a shrapnel.' Inexperienced as he was, Waddy pulled back the company he had found himself commanding after a brief consultation with his CSM, digging a rough line of rifle pits with farm implements and holding them throughout the following day.[16]

Meanwhile, Haig had also asked Dubois for assistance during the course of the morning for fear that the strength of the German effort might enable them to punch right through to Ypres. Despite his own continuing attack, Dubois immediately placed units from his own corps reserve at Haig's disposal. As a result, d'Urbal instructed Dubois to stop the advance and consolidate his line. In the event, the French were not needed for, as noted on previous occasions, the Germans were extremely cautious in following up their initial successes. The Germans were later to acknowledge that 'there were men of real worth opposed to us who did their duty thoroughly'. Indeed, the Germans seemed constantly to believe that fresh British forces were being thrown in. At the same time they were increasingly apprehensive of the damage being done by the British rifle fire to the extent that some of the divisional commanders protested against continuing the offensive. According to Colonel Max Bauer, Rupprecht who had nominal command over Fabeck overruled his commanders' wishes in 'hard words'.[17] In any case, Falkenhayn was determined to continue the attack and it was announced that the Kaiser himself would visit Rupprecht's headquarters on 31 October.

To the south of 7th Division and 3rd Cavalry Division, Gough's 2nd Cavalry Division was not initially much troubled by *II Bavarian Corps* but, at about 1200 hours, more German artillery was shifted to support its assault towards Hollebeke. Gough normally slept at Kemmel and usually had his advanced headquarters in an estaminet at Wytschaete though he had relocated to the White Chateau for the two previous days to be closer to the scene of action when Capper and Byng were under pressure. His 1500 or so men with just ten guns supported by approximately 1000 Indian infantrymen were holding some $3\frac{1}{2}$ miles of front, a task Gough estimated would have realistically needed 10,000 men and fifty guns. With trenches being blow in, 3rd Cavalry Brigade was forced back about 1230 hours with the Germans being at this point less than 3 miles from Ypres itself. Fortunately, the Germans made no real effort to force the issue further and Gough was able to form a new defensive line though companies of both his Indian battalions were cut off.[18]

Further south again, 1st Cavalry Division repulsed attacks towards Messines. The overall British situation, therefore, was reasonable in the circumstances though it was still not possible to identify what fresh German forces if any had been committed, the bad weather having prevented much aerial reconnaissance during the course of the day. Visiting Allenby and Haig that evening, French decided not to issue any orders for the following day other than to direct Smith-Dorrien to start sending battalions north to be fed into the line as necessary. Haig intended to launch a counter-attack on Hollebeke and Zandvoorde with 1st and 2nd Cavalry Divisions, six battalions led by Bulfin, and three French battalions sent by Dubois with some modest artillery support. Indeed, only a total of 837 shells would be available for the variety of weapons allocated including a naval armoured train.[19] In the event, a late attack developed on Messines and Allenby withdrew 1st Cavalry Division from the equation and, as will be seen, Bulfin's counter-attack was stillborn.

Foch meanwhile had received disturbing news during the day from one of his staff officers, Captain Requin, that there were not sufficient British troops available to cover a gap in the line around Hollebeke, notwithstanding the fact that Dubois was sending reinforcements to Haig. Consequently, being told over the telephone that nothing definite was known, Foch visited GHQ at St Omer just after midnight, asking Wilson to have Sir John French awakened. French appeared with a tunic hastily pulled over his nightshirt. According to Foch, French was panicking. 'We are for it,' Sir John said, to which Foch replied, 'We shall see. In the meantime, hammer, hammer away, keep on hammering, and you will get there.' Also saying that if the line was pierced, all would be lost, Foch promised to send eight battalions from XVI Corps to Hollebeke and 32nd Division to St Eloi that day, French thanking him warmly.[20]

The night before what was to be the single most important day of the entire battle for Ypres was surprisingly quiet. Indeed, south of Hollebeke, Allenby's cavalrymen could hear a German band playing light opera tunes in the chateau.[21] The brunt of the German attack would fall on the cavalrymen between Messines and the Comines Canal, Fabeck moving up the *6th Bavarian Reserve Division* between *II Bavarian Corps* and the *26th Division* for the purpose, though the best known action of the day was that which developed around Gheluvelt. As the morning dawned unusually warm with the mist rapidly clearing, in the memorable words of the British official history, 'the line that stood between the British Empire and ruin was composed of tired, haggard and unshaven men, unwashed, plastered with mud, many in little more than rags'.[22]

At Messines, there had been some intermittent shelling and fairly frequent sniping during the night. Around 0245 hours on 31 October, it was agreed between the staffs of 1st Cavalry Division and 4th Division to bring up the 2nd Inniskilling Fusiliers from 12th Brigade to relieve two companies of the 57th Rifles from the Ferozepore Brigade in support of the cavalrymen in the village. This relief was under way when the Germans attacked at about 0430 hours, the two regiments from the *51st Brigade* of Duke Wilhelm of Urach's *26th (Württemberg) Division* cheering and blowing bugles as they advanced. Those Indians not already relieved were quickly overrun after all their white officers had been killed, but men from the 5th Dragoon Guards manning a barricade at the crossroads in Messines held on as did other dragoons in support trenches behind the Indians. Assorted cavalry reinforcements, those men of the 57th Rifles who had been relieved and the Inniskillings mounted a counter-attack and the Germans were driven off. Similarly, an attack to the north of the village was pushed back by men of the Queen's Bays.[23]

Around 0800 hours a heavy German bombardment opened, followed by a renewed infantry assault at 0900 hours in which some twelve German battalions, comprising some 6000 men, faced not much more than 900 cavalrymen. The Germans broke into the north of the village and the defenders steadily withdrew, fighting from house to house. A German battery from the *65th Field Artillery Regiment* was dragged into the village to demolish the convent, which was then taken by the *125th (Stuttgart) Infantry Regiment*. Around noon, elements of 9th and 13th Brigades from II Corps arrived and began to advance on either side of the Wulverghem to Messines road, supported by the Inniskillings and also the first Territorial Force battalion to see action during the war, the 1/14th London Regiment (London Scottish), which attempted to push north of Messines to the left of 2nd King's Own (Yorkshire Light Infantry) from 13th Brigade.

The London Scottish, with some 700 men, was stronger than either the KOYLI or the other battalion from 13th Brigade, the 2nd King's Own Scottish Borderers, and far fresher, having only reached Ypres late on 29 October. Ironically, when meeting officers of the 2nd Royal Welch Fusiliers at St Omer, the commanding officer of the London Scottish, Lieutenant Colonel George Malcolm, had been indignant at his battalion being sent out 'too late to have a look in'.[24]

The battalion had arrived in France on 16 September but had been tasked with work on lines of communication. Both J.K. Wilson and Duncan Balfour, for example, had found themselves helping to load and unload wounded at the railway junction of Villeneuve St Georges near Versailles. Dressed in their distinctive Hodden Grey kilts, the London Scottish had frequently caused a stir. Sent into Paris to collect 'stragglers', Balfour and two colleagues were 'encircled' by a crowd outside Les Invalides. On another occasion, when on policing duty in the capital, every time the London Scottish patrol stopped to examine soldiers' passes, more crowds gathered: one group explained that they were attracted by the 'delicate' costumes.[25]

Similarly, having delivered three German prisoners – 'miserable almost starving little Bavarians' – to St Nazaire, Wilson and another soldier arrived at St Omer ahead of the battalion. Invited to play golf at the local course by the resident Scottish professional, the two were accompanied by two young women acting as caddies: 'Dicky's full swing from the tee reacted rather violently on his shortish kilt, giving it an upward kick much to the feigned embarrassment of the mademoiselles who modestly shielding their eyes with their hands exclaimed "Oh la la!".'[26]

Suddenly ordered up to Ypres, the battalion had moved in open-top buses, many men getting thoroughly damp in the foggy conditions before being put into the Cloth Hall to have a few hours' rest. The Germans, however, were shelling the town as the battalion arrived on 29 October and one of Wilson's friends spent a worrying night under what in the darkness seemed to be two large orbs that he expected to crash down on him at any moment. The first few streaks of dawn showing through a shell hole in the wall revealed he had been sleeping under a statue of one of the Belgian Kings 'and the black orbs which had given him cause for so much concern were simply the appendages which denoted the sex of the superb charger upon which his imperial majesty was elegantly mounted'. Marched up to Sanctuary Wood on 30 October, the battalion was not needed and marched back to Ypres, the men expressing their frustration with their own version of 'Pop Goes the Weasel': 'Up and down the Menin Road, in and out the Eagle, what a way to run a war and what a bloody fatigue O.' By contrast to the quarters in the Cloth Hall on the previous night, Private A. Moffat's company now occupied a pigsty.[27]

Then, on 31 October, came the summons to Wytschaete. Apart from still having the old eight company organisation, Malcolm's men also had the major handicap of still being armed with the outdated 'Long' or Mark I Lee-Metford, the magazine of which was defective. At least half of the battalion's rifles were incapable of being used for rapid fire, rounds having to be inserted singly by hand.[28] Ordered forward to reinforce the cavalry on the road between Messines and Wytschaete, the battalion's first casualties occurred as they skirted Wytschaete, shells bursting on the roofs showering tiles down on soldiers and civilians alike. Some British artillery batteries were concealed nearby and Wilson's section passed close to one as it suddenly opened fire, Wilson recalling that they were 'airborne for a few seconds; one of the occasions when breeches can claim superiority over the kilt'.[29]

Moving out from the cover of a wood, the London Scottish had to move up a hill to reach the road and press on into beet fields beyond. The men had assumed an attack was intended and deployed accordingly rather than 'dribbling up', advancing in short rushes. Once over the crest at about noon, they were spotted and heavy artillery and machine-gun fire was directed at them. A confused situation ensued as men were forced to find what cover they could in the open, given the scattered nature of the cavalry trenches. Ordered to try and turn round as he dropped to the ground after each short rush to see if any signals were being made by battalion headquarters to the rear, one officer's runner announced, 'If I am going to be shot, Sir, I would prefer not to be shot up the arse.' Both Balfour and Wilson were with groups that became separated from the rest of the battalion. Balfour spent much of the rest of the day in a ditch with some sixty men 'huddled together and cramped up on my knees' under constant shellfire and 'one just sat there wondering when the one that was coming in would come in, with the noise of the bursting shells slowly driving one mad'. After darkness had fallen, Balfour and his colleagues came under attack from elements of the *6th Bavarian Division*, which was launching a night-time attack against the 4th Cavalry Brigade. The Germans were not seen until they were within 30 yards, and were then mistaken as British: 'They were only about ten yards off and every one dropped. It was quite horrible as it was absolute blue murder, and their moans and groans were beastly.'[30]

Moffat's company had spent much of the day in reserve before facing the same attack, the German advance apparently being accompanied by a band playing the Austrian National Anthem with German officers' whistles adding to the din. Hearing an officer calling for an advance, Moffat's company went forward in the belief it applied to them but soon found themselves mixed up with cavalrymen in a ditch well forward of the line: 'Some of the Carabiniers [6th Dragoon Guards] want to retire, but are ordered back. Then a man feeling fed up shouts out "Let's charge the Beggars", so up we get, or rather some of us do, and go forward, but it's useless as they run away, and we can't chase them as we should be shot down by our own men, who have not come on with us. Return to ditch again, and someone shouts "Reinforce on the left", so move there, as there is a big gap. Still the enemy are coming up in masses in spite of the "rapid fire" which is going on. All round there are farms and haystacks burning.' Eventually, they were ordered to withdraw, but Moffat turned back to try and help a wounded man. Finding he could not carry the man and the Germans now very close,

Moffat ran back to rejoin the rest 'and as I neared them shouted out all the available English I could think of through the pitch darkness in order that they shall know that it is really one of their own men'.[31] Fortunately, Moffat made sufficient noise to survive.

By contrast, Wilson found himself in a trench with some other Carabiniers under a young officer, having no idea what had happened to the rest of his battalion. Towards dawn Wilson and the cavalrymen found they were in an exposed position and the young officer ordered them to make a dash for it. Wilson made it and was directed to rejoin the battalion at Wulverghem. Finding themselves close to a field hospital, the surviving London Scottish were at least able to exchange their defective rifles for those of the wounded. Some 321 of the London Scottish became casualties. Treating some of them, Captain Henry Owens of the RAMC was told, 'it was quite alright but were surprised that volunteer troops were sent actually into the fighting line – they hadn't expected it'.[32]

The London Scottish were not the only Territorials to come under fire that day for, after its time at Dunkirk and another period at St Omer, the 1/1st Queen's Own Oxfordshire Hussars had also been ordered up to Ypres, arriving behind Messines at about 0830 on 31 October. After they had dug some reserve trenches, de Lisle appeared to order the yeomen up to some forward trenches. According to Captain Valentine Fleming, MP this 'was disagreeable as projectiles of every variety were exploding with a disquieting regularity all over the ground of our advance'. Three squadrons of the yeomen moved in a succession of rushes in extended lines but, on reaching the supposed trenches, found only sufficient room for one squadron, the others having to lie out on the ground and try and scratch some cover with their bayonets. Fortunately, the German artillery tended to overshoot the yeomen, who remained in their exposed position for some hours before being relieved and sent back into Messines. It had been 'a very trying day for the men, they were d-d hungry, cold, and kept seeing wounded men come hopping back bleeding and howling, and swearing the G's had broken through (which they v nearly did!)'.[33]

The other battalions committed alongside the London Scottish on 31 October had also come under heavy fire and, exhausted by their exertions in reaching Messines, they could make little progress. Nonetheless, at least it took some pressure off the cavalry and the defenders of Messines hung on under heavy fire with much of that part of the village still in British hands set ablaze. Archibald Home of 1st Cavalry Division, who calculated shells falling at about fifty a minute, was in a house in Messines when it was hit: 'It was a curious sensation, it felt rather like the earthquake scene in a Drury Lane Drama – the whole thing came down like a house of cards – It was pitch dark and we got out through the window thinking every minute another was coming in the same place.'[34] The Germans, however, had also taken heavy losses and, during the night, it proved possible to relieve the 1st Cavalry Brigade.

Meanwhile, back to the north of Messines, Gough's 2nd Cavalry Division had also come under attack at Wytschaete from *3rd Bavarian Division* and *6th Bavarian Reserve Division*. The Germans wore white armbands to distinguish themselves from each other in the darkness. As indicated earlier, there were still mistakes made and at one point Colonel Hofmann of the *17th Reserve Infantry Regiment* withdrew from the village until the German artillery could be informed that his men had reached it. Gough was now supported by six French artillery batteries and one and a half Indian battalions but the Germans still deployed some 16,000 men against his force. During the course of the day, Gough sent the 18th Hussars and the London Scottish, who had initially been sent to him, to help out at Messines, but received in turn two squadrons of the 1st Life Guards and, more significantly, a French cuirassier brigade and a brigade from the French 32nd Division. Unfortunately, the French cuirassiers still wore their cuirasses and had only an ineffectual carbine for a weapon so that, according to Hubert Gough, after a time sitting on their horses behind hedges, they simply rode off.[35] Fortunately, despite the heavy German artillery bombardment, which began at about 0600 hours, the Germans did not actually press an infantry assault until 1445 hours and this primarily as a response to the advance by the London Scottish to Gough's right. At one point, Gough came across a young subaltern from the London Scottish and congratulated him on his battalion's work. The youngster said he thought it had been 'an awful disaster', Gough exclaiming, 'Disaster be damned, you have done splendidly.'[36]

Major Philip Howell of the 4th Hussars, who had taken a radically different view of the events at the Curragh to that of Hubert Gough, had been forced away from the canal bridge at Wytschaete by the German fire: 'I've never seen or heard such a hell of shell fire as they poured upon our hill and wood! They must have had dozens of every kind of gun, both large and small.' When the fire slackened, Howell led his men back to the canal bridge, which they had been unable to destroy. Seeking reinforcements at one point in case the Germans rushed the bridge, he came across about 200

French troops hiding out in the wood. Howell managed to persuade them to take up supporting positions by telling them 'all in shocking French but enough to be understood' that he had surrounded a German company and they could help massacre it![37]

French later suggested that the defence of Messines and Wytschaete by the cavalry was crucial to the survival of the BEF.[38] By far the most serious situation of the day, however, was that which developed at Gheluvelt, significant as being one of the last observation points on the ridge line east of Ypres in British hands following the loss of Becelaere and Zandvoorde. Landon's 3rd Brigade held Gheluvelt with the addition of two battalions from 2nd Brigade. Rather as in the case of the cavalrymen at Messines, the night of 30–31 October passed with occasional shelling and sniper fire, the area bathed by moonlight until it clouded over in the early hours. Assisted for the first time by observation balloons directing artillery fire, the German attack began at about 0600 hours, a little rainfall having given way to a clear dawn.

The initial attack was beaten off along the whole front of 1st Division with the exception of elements of *XXIV Reserve Corps* getting into a small orchard forming part of the sector held by the 2nd King's Royal Rifle Corps. The matter-of-fact diary entry by the battalion's Company Quartermaster Sergeant, H.J. Hopper, conveys at least something of the pressure of the day: 'Our art[illery] started firing early, the enemy replied with a murderous attack from their big guns. There are many casualties both in men & horses. The troops had to retire. They then reorganised & fought again. I hear poor [2nd Lieutenant F.] Dean is killed. 4 p.m. Staff officers trying to get men together; weather getting colder. Heaps of wounded everywhere. Alders has just passed, wounded in the left shoulder. Co, Adj, Seymour [and 2nd Lieutenant P.S.] St Aubyn wounded. [2nd] Lt [A.J.] Fisher killed. I had to bring my horse to Halte for the night 2 kilo E of Ypres. Horse wounded.'[39]

It proved impossible to force the Germans out of the orchard in face of the increasing bombardment, which became heavier after 0800 hours. Indeed, half of the 2nd Welch Regiment holding the line to the east of Gheluvelt church in front of the Menin road were 'blown out' of their positions and withdrawn. Lieutenant Colonel C.B. Morland of the Welch informed the commanding officer of the 1st South Wales Borderers to his left that he would keep that part of his battalion in touch with them in the front line. However, the message failed to reach the 1st Queen's Regiment (West Surrey) and two companies of the 2nd King's Royal Rifle

Corps to the right that a gap had opened between them and the Welch. Lieutenant J.F.E. Goad of 2nd KRRC did not believe it when men of the Queen's ran past him saying the Germans had broken through: 'To my amazement a few minutes later I saw a large body of the enemy running towards me from the direction of the farm. I ordered the men by me to face round and open fire at them, but it did not check the German progress and a few minutes later I found myself on the point of being bayoneted by one of the enemy. He however fired at me instead and the bullet only grazed the top of my ear. There was nothing to be done by this time and all the men near me were either killed or taken.'[40]

Morland then discovered that his new position on the support line was just as exposed as the original front line trenches and ordered his men to pull back through the village as a whole. Rees, commanding D Company, tried desperately to extract two of his platoons when Morland ordered the retirement but nearly all who attempted to run across a 50-yard gap between their position and a sunken lane were killed. Rees had to withdraw himself under heavy shellfire, losing more of his remaining men. Having lost contact with Morland, Rees reported to Major Peel of the 54th Battery, RFA that he believed only 100 of the battalion had survived: 'He obviously disbelieved me, and I fancy seriously thought of putting me under arrest for spreading alarmist reports. I confess to being very badly shaken, the stock of my rifle had been shot through in two places and the strap of my water bottle cut.' Peel ordered Rees to stand by as escort to the guns and he collected a number of assorted stragglers before an officer from brigade directed him to lead them back into Gheluvelt. Many of his small force had already disappeared when Rees suddenly came across Morland and the two of them tried to rally some more men to fall back towards Peel's battery. Then a shell burst in the village street mortally wounding Morland, leaving Rees the senior surviving officer but with barely twenty-five men under command. Indeed, Rees later calculated that about twenty shells burst within 100 yards inside a minute: 'It was a day one doesn't wish to live ever again.' As Rees recorded, the battalion 'was annihilated. No other term can describe the casualties.' In all, the battalion suffered the loss of sixteen officers and 514 other ranks dead, wounded or missing on 31 October. Rees was awarded the DSO for his services, going on to command both 94th and 150th Brigades, being captured in May 1918.[41]

Aware of a gap having appeared in the line, Landon sent a company of the 1st Gloucestershires forward but, under heavy fire, it had dwindled to just thirteen men from the original eighty by the time it managed to reach the front. The Queen's, meanwhile, were coming under increasing pressure, those runners sent back to request artillery support all being killed. Cheering and singing, four battalions from the *54th Reserve Division* under Colonel von Hügel and three battalions from the *30th Division* began a concerted advance north and south of the Menin Road at around 1000 hours, supported by three more battalions from *30th Division* with *16th Bavarian Reserve Regiment* also available in reserve. During the day, the Bavarians' commander, Colonel List, was to be killed in action and, at one point, as they were wearing caps rather than helmets, the Bavarians were shelled from the rear by their own artillery.

The advance was watched by von Deimling of *XV Corps*, who was soon wounded by a shell splinter. Since the Germans had lifted their own artillery fire from the British front trenches to try and catch any reinforcements coming up from the rear, the German infantry was caught by sustained rapid rifle fire. It was of such intensity that the Germans later claimed they had faced lines of non-existent British machine guns or equally non-existent automatic rifles, 'and over every bush, hedge and fragment of wall floated a thin film of smoke, betraying a machine-gun rattling out bullets'.[42]

After an hour, however, the Germans moved up two artillery batteries to close range and, with their position now untenable, the survivors of the KRRC retired west of Gheluvelt. His commanding officer having been mortally wounded at an early stage, Major C.F. Watson of the Queen's tried to hold on, but the other units to the right of the Queen's had also been driven back. The Queen's were totally surrounded: only two officers and twelve men escaped death or capture, many of those taken prisoner being robbed and some bayoneted or clubbed to death by men from the *143rd Infantry Regiment*. Subsequently, as Watson was needed to take over as brigade major of the 3rd Brigade, Rees of the 2nd Welch was also directed to take over 1st Queen's, his combined force swelling to two officers and sixty men.[43]

It was now about 1130 hours. Gheluvelt was a shambles of burning buildings, surviving defenders making their way back down the Menin Road towards Hooge either singly or in groups. Two field artillery brigades were also moving back, having abandoned six of their guns, which had been disabled by German fire. The news that Gheluvelt had fallen was brought to Haig from the 1st Division headquarters by the GSO3 in I Corps's

Intelligence Section, Captain R.J. Collins, who assured Haig that at least the retirement appeared to be orderly. Landon, meanwhile, had moved up his few reserves, but no progress could be made and, learning that the Queen's had been overwhelmed, Landon ordered the line held in front of Veldhoek. The Germans, however, did not press down the Menin Road, but moved to roll up the defence to the south of the position formerly held by the Queen's, overrunning in turn two companies of the 1st Loyals and a detachment from the 2nd Royal Scots Fusiliers. Private F.A. Bolwell of the Loyals was one of those who escaped, recalling, 'I had a run for my life that day. A chum of mine who was with us had a cock fowl in his valise that morning from the farm but he had not quite succeeded in killing him; and as we ran this bird began to crow.'[44]

Similarly, to the north of the village, there had also been a heavy opening German bombardment, with a substantial attack developing around 1000 from the battalions of the *54th Reserve Division*. The South Wales Borderers and the 1st Scots Guards to their immediate left had both established their headquarters in the stables of Gheluvelt Chateau. They were aware from Morland's earlier message of the situation developing to their right and, in turn, had intermittent telephone communications with the headquarters of Fitzclarence's 1st (Guards) Brigade in a farm near Veldhoek. Fitzclarence himself and his staff captain, A.F.A.N. 'Bulgy' Thorne, also appeared from time to time to assess matters. Shortly after the Germans broke into Gheluvelt at around 1130, the portion of the Welch Morland had left in contact with the Borderers were overwhelmed, the thirty-seven survivors being captured. By 1230 the Borderers, in turn, had been pushed back to the chateau grounds but a counter-attack by the Borderers and a few men of the Scots Guards forced the Germans out of the chateau grounds, though not before some of the Scots Guards had been firing standing on the chateau front steps.[45]

Lieutenant Colonel H.E.B. Leach, commanding the Borderers, recognised that he had too few men available to attempt to reoccupy the original front line outside the chateau and decided to go no further than the wall surrounding the grounds. Fitzclarence appears to have momentarily considered a withdrawal to Polderhoek Wood but promptly cancelled the orders to the Scots Guards. The orders given to Leach were not rescinded but, fortunately, he decided to ignore them in view of the cancellation of those sent the Scots Guards.[46] Fitzclarence ordered up his only reserve, consisting of a few men of the 1st Black Watch and a company of the 2nd

Worcesters, lent by 5th Brigade, and informed his divisional commander, Lomax, of the critical situation that had now arisen at Gheluvelt.

As it happened, Lomax had been in close contact all morning with Monro of 2nd Division, Monro having released the whole of 2nd Worcesters to Lomax at about 1015 hours. It had also been agreed by Lomax and Monro that, in the event of a major German breakthrough, 2nd Division's reserves, being held near Polygon Wood, would be used to mount a flanking counter-attack from the north. Having heard from Fitzclarence that Gheluvelt was lost, Lomax informed Fitzclarence that he could make use of 2nd Division's reserve and rode with virtually his whole staff from his own battle headquarters at what was to become known as Clapham Junction to Monro's headquarters in Hooge Chateau. The three remaining companies of 2nd Worcesters and also the 1st King's Regiment were warned to ready themselves for a counter-attack, but Monro judged that the line around Polygon Wood itself was weak and, consequently, only the Worcesters were made available to Fitzclarence. Though the organisation of the counter-attack was very much the initiative of Fitzclarence, some thought had been given on the previous evening by Lieutenant Colonel A.C. Lovett of the Gloucesters to possible emergencies. Accordingly, Lovett had sent his adjutant, J.A.L. Caunter, to consult with the Worcesters and point out on the map the best direction of attack in the event of a counter-attack towards Gheluvelt being required.[47] Now, however, Fitzclarence sent Thorne forward to reconnoitre the ground and consulted with the Worcesters' adjutant, Captain B.C. Senhouse Clarke, and at about 1300 hours issued an order to the battalion's acting commander, Major Edward Hankey, to launch an immediate counter-attack 'with the utmost vigour against the enemy who was in possession of Gheluvelt, and to re-establish our line there'. Hankey was apparently initially reluctant 'to obey this direct order from the Brigadier of another Division' though largely because he had been designated to act as the reserve to 2nd Division.[48]

At almost the same moment that the Worcesters were setting off, Lomax and Monro were still conferring in Hooge Chateau, using a small room with a glass veranda in an annexe on the western side of the chateau, which Monro had been occupying as his office. As indicated earlier, Monro and Lomax were both using the chateau, Haig having suggested Lomax co-locate his staff with that of Monro as they would be more comfortable in the larger accommodation than in the two cottages Lomax had previously occupied.[49] It had just been agreed that a new reserve had to be created for

2nd Division by withdrawing as many men as possible from the division's left. Shells were falling in the vicinity as the Germans were continuing to bombard the Menin Road back towards Ypres. About 1315 hours a cluster of four shells straddled the chateau, the second bursting immediately outside Monro's office. Five staff officers were killed outright including the GSO1 of 1st Division, Colonel F.W. Kerr, and the GSO2 of 2nd Division, Lieutenant Colonel A.J.B. Perceval. Lomax was severely wounded, later dying of his injuries in April 1915, by which time he had been promoted to Lieutenant General. Two further officers were mortally wounded and three wounded. Monro, who had been standing in the doorway between the office and the adjoining studio, in which another of the shells burst, was fortunate to escape, albeit badly stunned. Monro's GSOI, Colonel R. Whigham, though rendered unconscious, alone escaped injury among the staffs of the two divisions, having just gone into the adjoining office to find a map. Mowbray of 2nd Division's artillery staff had not been present, having been sent to carry a message out to the batteries. He returned soon after the shell had fallen: 'The killed were all instantaneously killed I judged. [Captain F.M. Chenevix] Trench [Brigade Major, RA] had no sign of suffering on his face. Little trace of Perceval. Trench still breathing when I returned. The Clerk (B[ombardie]r. Hinton) who behaved well replied to me that Trench's pockets had been searched and that the medical officer had contents. [Lieutenant H.M.] Robertson [ADC, RA] was got off in a car.'[50]

Haig was at once informed and at 1350 Johnnie Gough sent a message to Bulfin that he was appointed to succeed Lomax: 'Regret things very bad. 1st Division knocked about and retiring down road passed [sic] Hooge. Come up line yourself at once leaving Lord Cavan to take over your command. General Lomax wounded & Kerr killed & you must take over command but Sir D. Haig wants to see you first. Tell Cavan to hold on tight with right to canal and to throw left back northwards towards Hooge. Keep French informed on your left.' In the circumstances it was a clear and concise order for all that it was hastily scribbled in pencil. Indeed, during this crisis day, Sidney Clive, on liaison duties with the French, passed Haig's headquarters in the White Château near Halte, noting, 'Johnny Gough was there – an absolute model of a GSO.' Clive also noted that, despite the situation, I Corps staff were 'working very quietly in different rooms, the talking was almost in whispers'.[51]

Bulfin, however, was conducting the battle around Hollebeke and, in his absence, Landon was directed to take temporary charge of 1st Division. In the event, Landon, too, could not be immediately located. Monro and Whigham, however, were able to send other staff officers off to ensure resistance continued at the front, while Mowbray helped supervise the movement of the two divisional headquarters to Westhoek, some three-quarters of a mile to the north of Hooge Chateau. The very last reserves available to 1st Division, two Royal Engineer field companies, were sent towards Gheluvelt, one being used to form a line of posts to collect stragglers.

At the White Chateau, the news worsened from about noon onwards. Collins, sent forward to assess the situation, had reported the loss of Gheluvelt and at 1230 Lomax had reported the line had been broken and that Landon's counter-attack had failed though the Worcesters were on their way. In response, Haig sent messages to both Foch and Dubois and moved up his last corps reserve, the 6th Cavalry Brigade. Allenby had asked for both his 6th and 7th Cavalry Brigades from 3rd Cavalry Division back early that morning and had declined a request from Haig around 0655 to send Byng's division north to support I Corps on the Menin Road. Nevertheless, Haig had unilaterally appropriated Byng's brigades and, when Allenby called for Byng's support at about 0835, showing his anxiety, Haig apparently made it clear that he 'did not consider the situation justified this, and ordered the division to remain as originally ordered'. In the event, 7th Cavalry Brigade responded to direct orders from Allenby and turned southwards once more, only 6th Cavalry Brigade proceeding immediately to support I Corps.[52] Haig and some of his staff had also ridden some way up the Menin Road towards Hooge at about 0800 to observe the situation more closely before returning to the White Chateau.

It had now been confirmed that 1st Division had broken and at 1330 Haig directed that a new last line of defence be held from Hollebeke to Frezenberg prior to a possible retirement. In fact, rear positions had already been reconnoitred by Haig and Gough during the morning ride, Gough having returned ahead of Haig, and partly marked by the CRE of I Corps, Brigadier General S.R. Rice. Indeed, even earlier, when meeting d'Urbal at 0700 to arrange for the deployment of the reinforcements Foch had agreed to send the previous evening, some preliminary decisions had been made in the event of any forced retirement for I Corps to hold east and south of Ypres and the French to the north. According to Collins, Johnnie Gough had been 'very difficult to approach as regards making any arrangements for a possible retreat', but some survey of possible retirement routes had also been undertaken by Rice, Neill Malcolm and Collins on 29 October. Rice had ordered some preliminary work on a line from Klein Zillebeke to Steen-becke and another from Klein Zillebeke to Potijze, the first between 1000 and 4000 yards behind the front line and the second somewhat further back. News of the disaster that had befallen the staffs of Lomax and Monro was then given to Haig at about 1350 hours.

As already indicated, orders were issued at 1330 directing I Corps to hold the first line previously designated as long as possible, but if necessary to withdraw to the second position from Verbrandenmolen to Potijze, just 2000 yards from Ypres, which must be held at all costs. In the event, the orders never reached Monro, who was informed about them only at about 1540 hours, by which time the situation had changed. Presumably it was these orders that formed the basis of the official historian, James Edmonds, later telling Basil Liddell Hart in 1931 that Haig had lost his head and had drawn up plans for a general withdrawal 'to the line of the ramparts and canal at Ypres', only for 'one of his staff' – presumably Gough – to recall all copies and order them destroyed. According to a soldier servant at Haig's head-quarters, whose recollection may or may not be accurate, Johnnie Gough had placed secret Corps papers in Haig's car ready for 'an emergency flit' but there is no apparent evidence for Edmonds's assertion that a general withdrawal to Ypres was intended. There is some confusion in British sources as to whether the French were fully informed of the prelimin-ary orders to withdraw, though, as already indicated, messengers went to both Foch and Dubois. The latter later suggested he had learned of Haig's decision from a member of the French liaison section with I Corps, Commandant Jamet, at about 1430. Jamet, however, appears to have exag-gerated the situation, suggesting a retreat was already under way and that he had seen artillery batteries retiring.[53]

At one point, Haig's GSO2 in I Corps intelligence section, John Charteris, was sent forward to find out what was happening: 'You cannot imagine the scene. The road was full of troops retreating, stragglers, wounded men, artillery and wagons, a terrible sight. All the time there was the noise of a terrific bombardment. It was impossible to get any clear idea of the situation. Nobody knew anything except what was happening on his immediate front and that was always the same story. The Germans were attacking in overwhelming strength and our men were being driven back but fighting every inch of the way. The only glimmer of hope was that a counter-attack was being organised.' Charteris returned to the White Chateau to find Haig out and Johnnie Gough organising the mess servants for its defence. Gough, though, 'was quite unruffled, and amused me by saying, "It don't matter a damn what happens here. God won't let those b...win."' Another version used by the *Sunday Pictorial* as a rallying call in the equally grim days of March 1918 was that as Gough 'watched the enemy swarming over a low ride one of his staff said the fight was decided. Gough turned with his eyes ablaze and exclaimed: "God will never let those devils win."'[54]

At about 1400 hours, Sir John French appeared at the White Chateau, having left his car a short distance away. French had already visited Allenby and Hubert Gough and, driving out of Ypres, had encountered a mass of wounded, stragglers and vehicles coming back down the Menin Road. In Ypres itself, French had seen Belgian civilians leaving the town and 'gathered in groups about the streets chattering like monkeys or rushing hither and thither with frightened faces'. Of the scenes on the Menin Road French later commented that 'heavy howitzers were moving west at a trot – always a most significant feature of a retreat – and ammunition and other wagons blocked the road almost as far as the eye could see. In the midst of the press of traffic, and along both sides of the roads, crowds of wounded came limping along as fast as they could go, all heading for Ypres. Shells were screaming overhead and bursting with reverberating explosions in the adjacent fields.' As French also later remarked, 'When a heavy field gun trots you may be sure things are pretty bad.' It has been questioned, however, how far heavy howitzer batteries could have realistically broken into a trot on such a crowded road. Moreover, it would appear that only two of 1st Division's four 60-pounders were apparently pulled back during the afternoon, the other two remaining near Veldhoek all day. In the case of 2nd Division, its siege battery and one section of a heavy battery were actually ordered forward. Also according to French's own later account – he actually confused the White Chateau and Hooge Chateau in his memoirs – he found a white-faced Haig and Johnnie Gough sitting at a table on which a glass chandelier had fallen. They were pouring over maps and were 'evidently disconcerted'. Indeed, Haig remarked, 'They have broken us right in and are pouring through the gap.' French later recalled it as the worst half-hour spent in 'a life full of vicissitudes'. Though 2nd Division appeared to be holding its own, the situation continued to appear desperate around Gheluvelt but French had no reinforcements to offer. Nonetheless, Haig recorded that French 'could not have been nicer at such a time of crisis'.[55]

Accordingly, at about 1430 or 1440 Sir John left, apparently hurriedly, to return to his car in order to find Foch and get French reinforcements. French had just left and Haig had decided to ride over to the 1ˢᵗ Division headquarters when Rice, who had been sent forward to bring back definite news about an hour previously, rode up at the gallop, 'as red as a turkey-cock' according to Charteris, with the dramatic news that the Worcesters had retaken Gheluvelt. Haig, either still standing on the steps of the chateau or having just mounted his horse, sent his ADC, Lieutenant G.H. Straker, to inform French, Straker catching the CinC just as he got to his car. Haig and Gough now rode forward up the Menin Road to find Landon and Fitzclarence at the crossroads beyond Hooge. According to Rice, who accompanied Haig and Gough, a retirement was still contemplated but Haig intended to issue any necessary orders verbally once he had seen the situation for himself. Haig then rode on to see Monro at Westhoek. Bulfin's counter-attack got under way at about 1600 and Jeudwine, who had been liaising between Bulfin and Cavan and was sent for reinforcements, found Haig and Gough soon after this beyond Hooge near the eastern end of what became later known as Sanctuary Wood, the war diary of 3ʳᵈ Cavalry Division also recording Haig's presence on the Menin Road a little earlier at 1530.[56]

Much has been made of Haig's ride up the Menin Road but some confusion has also surrounded it. Contemporary histories by Sir Arthur Conan Doyle and John Buchan did not mention it at all while one recent biographer of Haig, Gerry de Groot, has suggested that Haig intentionally set out in a dramatic gesture even though he knew Gheluvelt had been retaken. Denis Winter has even claimed, quite preposterously, that it never took place at all, Haig transforming his early morning ride into a dramatic event in the afternoon. In part, Winter follows one of Haig's earliest biographers, Duff Cooper, who suggested that only the earlier ride had taken place, though at about noon rather than after breakfast, and that the second had not taken place because French's arrival at the White Chateau had prevented it. Haig's later correspondence with the official historian, James Edmonds, makes it clear that he had ridden out after breakfast at 0800 but had returned to the White Chateau by about 1400 to be told the news by Gough that the 1ˢᵗ Division had broken and that French's arrival had then prevented the second ride until after French's departure. In view of the overwhelming evidence of Haig's staff, who corresponded with Edmonds after the war, there is no doubt that the second ride took place after French's departure though the typed version of Haig's diary certainly errs in suggesting French's visit to the White Chateau did not take place until 1500 and, therefore, that the second ride took place later than was actually the case. Haig himself only ever suggested that he intended 'to see if I could do anything to organise stragglers & push them forward to attack enemy'. What can be questioned, however, as Nikolas Gardner has most recently pointed out, is the actual utility of a corps commander attempting this and, in the process, removing himself from any real control of the situation when, in any case, few men of I Corps were close enough to the Menin Road to have actually seen Haig. Clearly, therefore, if Haig did not actually panic, anxiety certainly clouded his judgement and his anxiety had been communicated to French.[57]

Having learned of the retaking of Gheluvelt from Straker but still alarmed by the situation – according to Edmonds, French's car had apparently almost run down Lieutenant Colonel Moore, the CRE of 7th Division, in the hurry to be off – French motored through Ypres to Foch's headquarters some 19 miles away at Cassel. As he drove through Vlamertinghe en route to Poperinghe, however, he was recognised and flagged down by Jamet, Haig's French liaison officer, who told him that Foch was in the town conferring with d'Urbal and Dubois. Jamet's own report of the situation had clearly alarmed Foch and, according to the latter, French was in a gloomy mood, saying indeed that I Corps was 'in full retreat on Ypres, the heavy artillery was retiring at the trot towards the west, the roads were blocked by ammunition wagons and vehicles of every description, as well as by crowds of wounded streaming back towards Ypres'. In this version, French even maintained that without reinforcements, 'there is nothing left for me to do but go up and be killed with I Corps'. Another version had it that French exclaimed that the only men he had left were the sentries at GHQ and that he would take them 'to where the line is broken, and the last of the English will be killed fighting'. According to the French accounts, Foch either replied 'We must stand firm first, we can die afterwards' or, 'You must not talk of dying, but of winning.' Yet another rendition of events had Foch also urging French, 'Marshal your lines are pierced. You have no troops available. You are finished. Then you must advance. If you retreat voluntarily, you will be swept up like straws in the gale.' French himself merely suggested in his own memoirs that 'we all went thoroughly into the situation' and there is no other account from the British side.[58]

Foch promised to counter-attack on both flanks of I Corps on the following day, 32nd Division operating on Haig's left and IX Corps on his right,

Dubois having already ordered his own reserves to assist I Corps at about 1430. Foch also issued an immediate memorandum for Haig at 1505 hours that it was 'absolutely imperative that no retirement is made', stressing that 'every movement rearward made by a considerable body of troops ensures an advance of the enemy and certain disorder among the retiring troops'. Foch insisted that 2nd Division must hold but he did, however, say that this did not prevent Haig organising a rear position to connect with IX Corps at Zonnebeke. Technically, Foch had no authority to issue such a direct order to Haig and initially gave it to French saying, 'There, if I were in your shoes, those are the orders I'd send to Haig.' Accordingly, the order was carried by French's ADC, Lieutenant Colonel Barry, and his private secretary, Colonel Fitzgerald, to Haig at 1535 hours with a further endorsement by French that it 'is of the *utmost* importance to hold the ground you are now on' and promising to see what troops he could send.[59]

Foch then issued orders at 2100 hours for IX Corps to attack towards Becelaere and for d'Urbal to attack Hollebeke, the battalions under General Moussy either remaining with Haig or joining in d'Urbal's attack as appropriate since he believed reinforcements should not be used to plug gaps but to mount offensives. Dubois, meanwhile, sent a cavalry brigade and three battalions, two from the 68th Infantry Regiment and one from the 268th Infantry Regiment. French accounts tend to suggest that their intervention stopped a British retreat – a correction was later made in the French official history – but, of course, the situation had already been retrieved.[60]

As previously related, one company of the Worcesters – A Company – had earlier reinforced 1st Guards Brigade. Consequently, just three companies were available for Fitzclarence's counter-attack, consisting of seven officers and 350 men. One of their officers described them as dog-tired, cold, wet, plastered with mud and unwashed and unshaven for days.[61] Hankey had sent out scouts to try and cut any wire that might obstruct the advance – most were killed – and the men had discarded their packs and picked up additional ammunition after receiving a rum ration. Hankey spoke a few words of encouragement to his men, 'The 2nd Worcesters will take Gheluvelt. We can and will do it. Good luck to you all.' There was some artillery support from XLI Brigade, RFA, from the corner of Polygon Wood. Moving on Gheluvelt from the north-west, for the first 600 yards or so, the Worcesters were covered by woods. Once they had reached Polderhoek, to which Fitzclarence accompanied them, the Worcesters faced a 1000-yard stretch of country – mostly rank grass and rough stubble – devoid of cover and intersected by fences sloping up to Gheluvelt Chateau and the village beyond. A stream of stragglers passed them, Clark recalling, 'parties from various regiments in the 1st Division (the majority of whom were severely wounded men, and all of whom were completely exhausted by the constant bombardment, and massed attacks on their line) having been driven in by overwhelming odds retired actually through the ranks of the Battalion, even warning them that it was impossible to go on, and that it was murder, etc. to attempt it'.

Hankey, who was carrying his hunting horn, deployed two of his companies in a first line with the third some 50 yards behind, one small group being detached to cover the right flank of the advance. The men came into view as soon as they left Polderhoek, almost 100 casualties occurring as they did so. The advance took place under heavy artillery fire at a steady double pace, officers in front and the men in long irregular lines with fixed bayonets. In the village and chateau grounds, however, about 1200 Bavarians from the *16th*, *244th*, and *245th Reserve Regiments* were too intent on looting to immediately notice the Worcesters and they put up little resistance to the sudden appearance of the battalion among them. Somewhat to his surprise, Hankey found survivors of the Borderers and the Scots Guards still holding out in the south-west corner of the chateau grounds, exclaiming to Leach, 'My God, fancy meeting you here!' to which Leach replied, 'Thank God, you've come.' Leach was accompanied by Major A.J. Reddie, whose brother, Major J.M. Reddie, was in the Worcesters. Leach later described the chateau grounds as being 'littered with bodies and debris of equipment, rifles, caps and helmets of the discomforted enemy'.[62]

Hankey established a line in the sunken road between the chateau and the village. The Germans appeared shaken by the counter-attack and abandoned much of the village. Subsequently, Hankey's fourth company rejoined the battalion about 1545 hours and extended his line to the village church. Two companies of the 1st Royal Berkshires, representing the only other part of Monro's original reserve at Polygon Wood, were then moved up to Gheluvelt to the left of the surviving Borderers and Scots Guards. In all, the remarkable effort by the Worcesters had cost them three officers and 189 men. Fitzclarence, variously characterised as the 'man who saved Calais' and the 'man who turned the tide', noted the day's events laconically in his diary, 'Enemy shelled the Welsh & Queen's out of their trenches at 12.30. I send Worcesters with Thorne guiding them to counter attack & retake village & trenches – Worcesters did very well. Situation critical & our line fight them back to Veldhoek. Black Watch & particularly Scots Guards hung on well & never gave way.'[63] In fact, the Germans had done remarkably little to exploit the advantage they had gained around Gheluvelt, only one large group, mostly from the *105th Saxon Regiment*, pushing westwards south of the Menin Road about the same time the Worcesters' attack was developing. These Germans, however, were halted by fire from those former defenders of Gheluvelt who had been rallied under the command of Lovett of the Gloucesters, now also in command of the brigade once Landon had stepped up to replace Lomax. Lovett occupied the small woods a few hundred yards away from the Germans with support from three artillery batteries firing some of the new 18-pounder high explosive shells that had arrived in France only on 19 October and been issued only on 31 October. Lovett's men also advanced back towards the village though Lovett was apparently 'rattled' and fed his companies in piecemeal rather than launching a more effective attack with his whole battalion.[64]

Those who had held Gheluvelt that morning had taken heavy losses. Once more stragglers had come in and available drafts such as transport men brought up, but the Welch were still down to seventy men, the Queen's to barely fifty under the command of Lieutenant John Boyd, and the Loyals to just one officer and thirty-five men. In view of the overall situation including the losses sustained to the south of Gheluvelt, therefore, Haig concluded that Gheluvelt had to be abandoned and a new line should be occupied on the reverse slope about 600 yards west of the village after dark. This was duly accomplished at the same time that efforts were also made to find troops that could be moved back into reserve. Indeed, the thinning of the line of 6th Brigade on the left of I Corps may have been the movement which suggested to the French that the British were intending a general retirement since 6th Brigade communicated its movements but not the reasons for it to a liaison officer from IX Corps at about 1400 hours.[65] Hence, the anxiety of Foch when he met French at Vlamertinghe, even before Sir John had delivered his message of woe.

The events further south which influenced Haig's decision concerned the situation between Gheluvelt and the Comines Canal, the line held here by 7th Division, five French battalions lent by Moussy and the so-called Bulfin Group, comprising three battalions from 2nd Division commanded by Lord Cavan, a battalion from 20th Brigade and two battalions from 2nd Brigade, the whole under the orders of Bulfin. Moussy also appears to have included his own escort, and 200 volunteers drawn from engineers and the French military train. Subsequently, Haig was to express his thanks to the French, notably to Dubois and Moussy, but also singling out the efforts of Lieutenant Colonels Payerne of the 68th Regiment and Potier of the 32nd Regiment who went into action near Gheluvelt and a number of officers of Zouaves who assisted the BEF at Zillebeke.[66]

As already indicated, following Haig's orders of 30 October, Bulfin, Cavan and the French were to mount a counter-attack at 0630 hours to retake Hollebeke Chateau and Zandvoorde. The French were intended to lead off but soon stalled in face of strong opposition and, in turn, Bulfin and Cavan felt it prudent not to continue the attack. As further north, a heavy German bombardment began at about 0800 hours but it was only about 1225 that a German infantry attack developed. At some stage, the Germans got in between the 2nd Oxford and Bucks Light Infantry, now attached to Bulfin's group, and a neighbouring battalion and into a wood behind the position. Moving up to the front, C.S. Baines, the only officer left in his OBLI company, had encountered a cavalry officer who had advised him that 'if we wanted any more men in the front line we had better go across and see if the Germans would lend us some as they seemed to have so many, whereas he did not think there was any on our side between us and Calais'. Baines had been apprehensive of the responsibility resting on him, 'with a line consisting of hastily dug holes in the ground, and no other shelter, very few men, not much chance of seeing any supports or reserves and a suspicion of there being none, and no wire in front'. Now, 'swarms of Germans' had got into the wood behind the battalion.

Baines's fellow OBLI officer, Harry Dillon 'thought that to do something unexpected might upset their apple-cart, so fixed bayonets and went straight in'. According to Dillon's letter to his family on 4 November, which was significantly not reproduced in the regimental chronicle like his others, his men 'came on some fifty of the grey swine, went straight in and annihilated them. We were very quickly into the next lot and in a few minutes we were shooting, bayoneting and annihilating everything that we came across'. As Baines recalled, some of the Germans surrendered but 'they had a nasty habit of shooting at us from the undergrowth just before turning to run, or throwing down their arms and putting up their hands'. At one point, indeed, Baines and Dillon found some of their men running back and fearing a retreat hastened to try and prevent it. In fact, the Oxford and Bucks had come under fire from Germans in the rear who had taken up their rifles again. No mercy was shown, Baines recalling, 'The whole lot suffered from the folly of a few, and our men did not wait for an apology, nor did they waste their ammunition on them.' By the end of the day, however, Dillon, who according to Baines, had twenty bullet holes in his coat, had lost seventy-three out of his remaining 136 men.[67]

What was left of 7th Division was increasingly hard-pressed, both Capper and Lawford of 22nd Brigade at one point leading some of their staffs forward to rally the brigade and the very last reserve of just eighty men of the 1st Grenadier Guards being committed. As recorded by Captain F.S. Garwood commanding the 7th Signal Company, RE, while Capper was out at the front, the division's CRA, Brigadier General Jackson, ordered a withdrawal by 7th Division's headquarters from Zillebeke Chateau at about 1330 to what later became known as Hellfire Corner once it was heard that Gheluvelt had fallen, moving to a small estaminet. Capper had moved his advanced headquarters some 2000 yards in front of Zillebeke Chateau and the signallers were endeavouring to keep him informed through motor-cycle dispatch riders. Generally, indeed, Capper's habit of getting too far forward compromised communications since his proximity to the firing line made it difficult to run cables to brigades and exposed the signallers' horses: by 5 November they were to lose only two men dead but eighteen horses, a cable wagon and two light spring wagons. While moving back, Garwood also noted the same phenomenon witnessed by Sir John French: 'Large numbers of wounded were coming in to Ypres down the Menin road, along which there passed a steady stream of vehicles, consisting of our heavy batteries and our first line transport.'[68] It can be noted that Garwood confirms French's account with regard to at least some heavy batteries on the road.

At about the same moment Jackson had pulled back his headquarters, Capper was trying to push 22nd Brigade forward. Bulfin, however, ordered his force to retire in conformity to preserve the line once he heard Gheluvelt had fallen, though he had also seen 7th Division giving way: 'I saw them going from where I stood, also the Germans in long lines coming over the top of the ridge lately held by the 7th Division. . . . Streams of Germans in unending numbers kept pouring over the ridge. As far as I could see to my north, there were endless glinting of spikes of German helmets. The roar of guns and rifles was incessant.'[69]

Bulfin's retirement exposed 22nd Brigade's flank and forced it back once more. By 1500 Capper felt it necessary to issue a warning order to fall back if necessary to that part of the line designated by Haig's orders of 1330 hours, in this case, the Klein Zillebeke-Frezenberg line. Bulfin, however, decided to attempt one last counter-attack in view of the fact that the German advance was slowing through the momentum being broken by many officers being killed by the British rifle fire. Accordingly, he instructed the two battalions under his immediate command, 1st Northamptonshires and 2nd Royal Sussex, that when they heard cheering behind them, they were to fire one minute's rapid fire – the celebrated 'mad minute' that British troops had occasionally practised – and advance with the bayonet. The cheering would be the signal that the reserve battalion, 2nd Gordon Highlanders, had arrived. In fact, only eighty-four Gordons including cooks and clerks arrived at about 1615 hours when Bulfin had anticipated at least 200 Gordons, but the woods concealed the paucity of their numbers and the noise clearly confused the Germans further. Fortuitously, too, the 1st Royal Dragoons from 6th Cavalry Brigade also arrived in time to participate.

As already indicated, Jeudwine, who had been sent to report on the situation, had ridden back to Haig and got the cavalrymen released from reserve to support Bulfin. So successful was the counter-attack, in which 26th Field Company, Royal Engineers, also participated, and so disorganised the Germans by it, that Bulfin had great difficulty in bringing his men to a halt before they went too far. According to Bulfin, 'No prisoners were taken but hundreds of Germans were lying bayoneted all through the wood, or shot by our people.'[70] About a half-mile was regained, with 7th Division also being able to retake some of the ground it had lost.

The cost of this relative success had been heavy, 20th Brigade now being reduced to 940 men, 21st Brigade to 750 and 22nd Brigade to less than 800. It had been a confusing day, many details of which were 'scanty, imperfect, often incomplete and confused, often hard to reconcile with one another' and a story of 'isolated stands by little parties, individuals fighting to the last with their backs to the wall, a platoon sticking grimly to its battered trenches till the last man was hit'. How varied the experience could be is illustrated, however, by the case of Waddy of 2nd Bedfordshires in 21st Brigade. His own company's position was not threatened all day and, through his inexperience, he felt no fear or uneasiness and, 'until evening I was more or less completely ignorant of the general situation and of my position in relation to other troops'. Indeed, it was only when he opened fire on a German patrol in the evening that Waddy was located by a brigade major and his small command of fifty or sixty men brought back to be told he was the only surviving officer. In the event, the adjutant, Foss, subsequently turned up with 150 men. Of the twelve original battalion commanding officers in 7th Division, four were now dead, four prisoners and four wounded.[71]

Bulfin readjusted his line after dark to conform to the situation at Gheluvelt. In view of this success, Haig wanted the attack continued, Johnnie Gough issuing orders to this effect at 2315. Bulfin felt it impracticable 'as we were only clinging to the ground by our eyelids' and rode over to the White Chateau at 1300: 'I found Johnnie Gough in bed in the chateau. I told him he must cancel the order, that if we were able to hold our line tomorrow it was as much as we could do, but to advance was madness and we should lose all the ground and Ypres into the bargain. He said all right, the order was cancelled, and I left him falling off to sleep at 1.30 a.m.'[72]

Elsewhere on 31 October, 2nd Division was heavily shelled. For a short time it appeared that the 1st Irish Guards had been broken. A message from Haig relayed through Cavan reached them in the early afternoon that the situation was critical, that they were to hold at all costs, and that he relied on them 'to save the 1st Corps, and possibly the army'. In the event, however, the position was soon restored, the battalion having merely 'bent back' though the adjutant, Trefusis, thought it 'one of the worst days I ever spent, both with anxiety as to what was going to happen, and the great strain on one's nerves to saying nothing of want of food'. In the early hours of 1 November, however, shelling blew in a number of trenches and one company forced back, the subsequent disorganisation of the battalion taking almost all day to sort out. One man, indeed, was court-martialled for running to the Grenadiers claiming all the Irish trenches had been overrun and all killed. At one point, French troops approached the 2nd Grenadiers deeply entrenched in ploughed fields in front of Klein Zillebeke. They 'seemed to have no definite objective and just stumbled forward through the shellfire in little groups, which never reached our front line and dumped down in shell-holes and depressions in the ground wherever they could find any shelter'.[73]

Haig issued orders at 1900 hours for I Corps to hold their positions but to be prepared to assist the French offensive the following day. French meanwhile appealed to London for more ammunition and reported the increasing strength of the German forces. Some II Corps units were available though all were weak in numbers and exhausted by their own exertions. Indeed, of the BEF's eighty-four infantry battalions on 1 November, eighteen were considered at only cadre strength (below 100 all ranks), thirty-one very weak (100 to 200 men), twenty-six weak (200–300) and only nine of middling strength (300 to 450): a battalion's war establishment was 1007 all ranks.[74] Kitchener could do little more than promise six more Territorial battalions.

As it happened, Kitchener was visiting Dunkirk on 1 November – again wearing his Field Marshal's uniform – to meet Poincaré, Millerand, Joffre and Foch, as well as de Broqueville. French sent his military secretary, Brigadier General 'Billy' Lambton, to report on the BEF's situation, as he felt unable to go himself. Kitchener was unimpressed with the mood of optimism among the French, remarking, according to Foch, 'Well, so we are beaten!' Kitchener, however, made it clear that he was not prepared to send untrained troops to Flanders and that fresh British forces would be unlikely to take the field before the spring of 1915. He also raised the possibility of replacing French with General Sir Ian Hamilton but Joffre declined the offer as he felt it inappropriate to remove French in mid-campaign though he would certainly have liked to see the more co-operative Wilson replace Murray as Chief of Staff. The news of the offer reached French via Henry Wilson, who was told what had happened by Foch. Foch himself had been erroneously told by someone on French's staff that Hamilton spoke even worse French than the Field Marshal.[75]

As might be imagined, French was extremely angry and sent his ADC, Captain Freddy Guest, to London to see both Asquith and Churchill. Seeing Asquith, Guest also offered criticism of the leadership of Rawlinson and Capper, making the most unlikely claim that the latter spent most of his time sheltering in a 'bomb proof'. Both Asquith and Churchill expressed their confidence in French, which only partly reassured Sir John, Asquith noting that these 'noxious weeds only grow in prepared soil – in this case, apparently an estrangement, or any rate a coldness, of long standing between French and K'. On 6 November, French motored over to see Foch and thank him personally, saying that he intended seeing Joffre as well to thank him. It had done little, however, for French's relationship with Kitchener, whom French personally blamed for the shortages of shells. In the spring of 1915, indeed, French deliberately tried to undermine Kitchener through publicising the shell shortage, the resulting political crisis contributing to the fall of Asquith's government and the creation of a coalition.[76]

Meanwhile, on 1 November, in accordance with Foch's instructions, there were actually to be three French counter-attacks. From General Taverna's XVI Corps, 32nd Division, corps troops and the 9th Cavalry Division were to attack towards Houthem; four battalions from IX Corps were to attack

Becelaere; and the remainder of IX Corps, 31st Division and 7th Cavalry Division were to demonstrate an offensive intention. To the north XXXII Corps was to attack eastwards from Dixmude. None was successful. The Germans, having failed to consolidate their success at Gheluvelt, resolved to continue to attack between Messines and Wytschaete but to do so in the early hours in an effort to avoid yet heavier casualties.

Wytschaete was held by only 415 men drawn from the Composite Household Cavalry Regiment while the ridge between Wytschaete and Messines was similarly weakly held by under 600 men comprising the 6th Dragoon Guards and the survivors of the London Scottish. Faced with some six German battalions, representing odds of about twelve to one, the defenders were steadily forced back from both village and ridgeline. The last to retreat were two squadrons of the 6th Dragoon Guards (Carabiniers) and some groups of the London Scottish. With the Germans occupying the London Scottish trenches, the latter tried to line a hedge but it was so exposed that they could not hold it and fell back at about 0400. About two hours later, a mass German attack developed, Duncan Balfour recording in his diary, 'We came out and lined the field for about fifteen minutes potting away at them. They were coming up in line, about four paces between each man, but line after line like a piece of paper that had been ruled out.'[77]

The village itself fell into Germans hands at about 0245 hours though they were not in possession of the ridgeline until about 0735 hours on what proved to be a fine and warm day after the early mist had cleared. Sir Philip Chetwode of 5th Cavalry Brigade committed his reserve unit, the 12th Lancers, as did Hubert Gough, who sent in the two battalions – 1st Lincolns and 1st Northumberland Fusiliers from 9th Brigade – previously allocated to him as a reserve. The two infantry battalions each lost about 30 per cent of their remaining strength trying to regain the ridgeline but the 12th Lancers were successful in re-entering Wytschaete.

Captain B.T. St John of the Northumberland Fusiliers had been told little of the intended operation beyond the need to do what he could to support the Lincolns. His company got hung up trying to cross some barbed wire and the leading platoon began to dig in. Having ordered it to keep moving, St John moved back across a ploughed field towards a wood to find his other platoons but came under machine-gun fire. Some 30–40 yards short of the trees, 'I felt as if I had suddenly hit my right arm against a hard obstacle in the dark. It was a very hard and very sharp blow and left a numb sort of tingling sensation in my arm quite different from the stinging of blows of one or two pebbles which had been knocked into my legs by the shots on the ground which had hurt me quite as much.' St John tried to remain still but attracted more fire: 'Suddenly I felt as if someone had gently drawn something rather hot along my shoulder and round my throat. This could not have been the bullet as it appeared to me to take quite an appreciable time to get from my left shoulder to the right side of my throat. I think it must have been the blood flowing. Certainly as soon as it reached my throat I began to cough blood through my mouth and nose and felt as if I were choking and everything looked a sort of blue colour.' St John thought he was dying but then found he could breathe after all not only through mouth and nose but the holes in his neck. After lying out for about five hours, St John managed to attract the attention of some gunners by waving his walking stick with his left hand and also moving his legs. They would not risk crossing the open to him, however, and it was one of his own sergeants who found him about half an hour later and brought up some stretcher bearers. Remarkably, St John subsequently survived septic pneumonia and a tracheotomy performed without anaesthetic.[78]

Hubert Gough came across Lieutenant Colonel W.E.B. Smith of the Lincolns with the remnants of his battalion, having lost eight officers and 298 men: 'He was hatless, and a small trickle of blood was running down his forehead from a scratch where a bullet had gone through his hair and grazed his head.' Smith was reorganising his remaining men to take up a new defensive position: 'He was in no gentle mood; he was the embodiment of energy and stern resolution. I heard him say something about "this b–y disaster," and issue fresh and pre-emptory orders. It struck me as something fine in the nature of the man, that after the shock of being hit in the head (for even a graze by a bullet in the head invariably knocks a man down), and after all the tension to which he must have been exposed during the night, he could rise superior to all terrors.'[79] Smith was later to command 20th Division.

The loss of the central portion of the ridge, however, compelled the withdrawal of de Lisle's 1st Cavalry Division from the western part of the ridge, the cavalrymen falling back to the Wulverghem ridge and abandoning Messines itself. Messines had been significant while there had been the realistic prospect of advancing on Menin. The fading of that hope rendered the retention of Messines of less value and the loss of the ridge merely reinforced this. Having been relieved of their position outside the town the previous day, the 1/1st Queen's Own Oxfordshire Hussars had been sent into the town on the morning of 1 November to help hold one of the barricades. Sent back in the early hours for a rest, they were then suddenly ordered forward once more as the line in Messines gave way. According to Captain Valentine Fleming the 'bloody prospect almost made us sick, however still with empty bellies we began plodding up the usual wire-enclosed ploughed fields on the left of Messines, being pooped at by very high and wild rifle fire, till we found the troops on our left halted and those on our right coming out of Messines, and the whole line fell back about ¹/₂ a mile under v. heavy rifle and Maxim fire'.[80]

Messines was then shelled by the British to discourage any German attempt to follow up the retirement. British artillery and aircraft were also active during the day in attacking Gheluwe and Hollebeke, an intercepted wireless message suggesting, erroneously as it turned out, that the Kaiser would spend the afternoon in their vicinity. Aircraft had also dropped bombs on likely locations the following day 'in the hope of finding them a good billet'. Elsewhere the Germans were less successful though Bulfin was severely wounded in the head by a shell splinter in the fighting to hold on to the line held by his force, command of which devolved upon Cavan, and that of 7th Division. To Garwood of the 7th Signal Company, who had never previously met him, Cavan was the right man for the situation: 'I was filled with admiration by the calm and quite self-confidence of his manner. Here stood a man whose mere presence seemed equivalent to a brigade.'[81] The loss of the ridge, however, made its recapture from Wulverghem highly problematic since there was no observation from there over the steep valley of the Steenbeek and no easy way to give effective artillery support to troops descending into it.

On the following day, the German *3rd (Pomeranian) Division* was brought up to seize Wytschaete on what proved another fine and sunny day. Further French forces had now also arrived and d'Urbal, who had determined a matter of honour not to uncover the flank of I Corps, intended 32nd Division to reinforce Wytschaete and the fresh 39th Division to recapture Messines. In the event, not only were the French unable to make any progress but they were also forced out of Wytschaete by a brigade of the *6th Bavarian Reserve Division*. According to the German semi-official history, 'The church was in flames, and the windmill flared like a beacon in the darkness. Friend and foe lay wounded side by side among the smouldering ruins.' Surprisingly, many of the inhabitants were still in the village and refused to leave their devastated properties.[82]

The French, whose troops had now been effectively interposed between Haig's I Corps and Pulteney's III Corps, were also intended to attack towards Gheluvelt, following much the same line of advance as had the Worcesters two days previously. Unfortunately, in order to allow the French to pass through 1st Division, the British artillery had been instructed to cease firing from 1030 hours onwards, enabling the German *30th Division* to push along the Menin Road towards a barricade held by an understrength company of the 1st Coldstream Guards. The Coldstream were overwhelmed about 1100 and the Germans then turned on three companies of the 1st King's Royal Rifle Corps, of whom nine officers and 437 men were either killed or captured. A hasty counter-attack by three companies of the 1st Black Watch had some effect and Landon was able to move up 2nd King's Royal Rifle Corps to cover the gap. The French troops who had been allocated for the planned attack also arrived to stem the German tide and, though not every position was recovered, the allied line was again stabilised.

An attack had also developed against the junction between Cavan's force and Ruggles-Brise's 20th Brigade. This, too, was stopped, though Ruggles-Brise was severely wounded. Young Waddy of the 2nd Bedfordshires in 21st Brigade came under shellfire in a wood: 'The crash of the explosion is shut in by the trees and so magnified immensely like the bark of a revolver fired in a small room, whilst every trunk and branch seems to echo it backwards and forwards until it almost resembles thunder among the hills. In addition to splinters and pellets, leaves, branches and even whole trees are hurled in all directions and the tangle of undergrowth becomes even more impassable than before. Such a bombardment may not be more dangerous than one suffered in the open but it is infinitely more demoralising, and as control is harder to exercise in enclosed, wooded country it demands a high stand-ard of individual discipline to endure it steadily.' Late that same day, Waddy also took part in a counter-attack: 'We scrambled out with a ringing cheer, that would certainly have rejoiced the hearts of the writers of Field Service Regulations, but which almost as certainly foredoomed our attack to failure by robbing it of the element of surprise.' Nonetheless, the attack reached the German trench, only for a number of men to stop to pick up German helmets. Then a machine gun, which may have been from a French unit they had passed earlier, opened up on them from the rear and stopped the attack.[83]

By now, 7th Division mustered only about a fifth of its original strength and 2nd Division, which also came under pressure, was down to about two-thirds of its original numbers. French again called for reinforcements, especially the 8th Division, which, like the 7th, was being assembled from battalions coming back from overseas garrisons. A yeomanry division was offered by Kitchener and accepted by French although, in the event, it did not materialise.

The check of the German army before Warsaw and the subsequent retreat of the German and Austro-Hungarian armies in the east had compelled Falkenhayn to consider withdrawing some of his divisions from Flanders to bolster the Eastern Front. He was also contemplating the possibility of attempting an offensive elsewhere in France: he had considered Artois, Picardy and Champagne back in September 1914 before determining on the effort in Flanders and now again considered Artois and Picardy. Nonetheless, Fabeck's efforts to break through continued over the next three days, albeit with such little success that the allied commanders began to feel that the German effort as a whole had come to an end. Indeed, Joffre also contemplated withdrawing troops for service elsewhere, going on to direct Foch on 4 November to abandon any offensive plans, stabilise the front and reconstitute the army's reserves.[84]

Foch himself told d'Urbal there was little chance of any breakthrough now and yet still ordered him to continue the offensive in what Liddell Hart nicely called a 'self-exhausting impulse'. D'Urbal's attempt to throw all available forces including his 17th, 18th and 31st Divisions into the attack between Zonnebeke and Langemarck on 3 November, however, was frustrated by the attempted German advance. Haig, meanwhile, endeavoured to collect a new reserve for I Corps but could scrape together only 300 men from the 1st Gloucesters, two companies from each of the 2nd Coldstream and 1st King's, the much depleted 1st Northants, and 500 assorted survivors of 22nd Brigade. Rice also toured the front of I Corps to advise on the construction of small strong points in the rear that might sufficiently delay any German penetration to avoid the need for a counter-attack or act as a pivot on which such a counter-attack could be mounted if necessary. Generally, each strongpoint was intended for about ten men, being wired all round. The 2nd Grenadiers, for example, dug a series of new redoubts behind their trenches at Klein Zillebeke, also clearing the undergrowth from the front of their positions on the edge of the woods.[85]

Haig was also compelled to withdraw about a third of his field artillery from the front so that they should not be exposed to shellfire to which they could not respond with the limited stocks of ammunition now available. Indeed, even for those guns that remained, it was impossible to supply more than ten rounds per 4.5-inch howitzer or twenty rounds per 18-pounder. On 4 November, Johnnie Gough was dispatched to GHQ to impress on French that both 1st and 7th Divisions needed urgent relief. Haig's own head-quarters and advanced headquarters had both come under repeated shellfire and that same day the AA&QMG, the able Lieutenant Colonel Raymond Marker, was mortally wounded. Consequently, the headquarters was moved back to the Chateau des Trois Tours at Brielen. A few days later, Gough wrote to Frederick Oliver, a journalist and old friend, that 'our men were so dead beat that they could only just hang on and he did not believe they had the physical strength to retreat to the next prepared position, and if the Germans made yet another attack he did not see how they could stand up to it'. Aware of Gough's ill health, Oliver put this assessment down to 'over-depression'. Others, however, felt Gough kept his anxieties to himself and 'gave a brave lead to the rest of us', Hubert also noting that Johnnie was 'very fit & doing a lot to keep up courage & resolution in others'.[86]

Pulteney also reported the need to relieve 4th Division. At least French had now been promised 8th Division and further Territorial battalions. On the night of 5 November, it did prove possible to relieve the remnants of 7th Division and 3rd Brigade, battalions of II Corps replacing the former and the 6th Cavalry Brigade the latter. The battalions from II Corps, however, were no longer strong enough to be formed into proper brigades and were accordingly organised into three groups under Brigadier Generals F.C. Shaw, McCracken and Count Gleichen. The increasing privations of the infantry were noted by Sister Jentie Paterson of the Queen Alexandra's Imperial Nursing Service Reserve, who with other nurses had volunteered to join No. 5 Clearing Station at Hazebrouck on 5 November and thus get closer to the front than any other nurses except those serving on ambulance trains: 'One kilt the other day was white with lice. He had been in the trenches for weeks. If they think they are "alive" and heaps are, they always beg us not to remove their shirts but to send an orderly and the most severely wounded apologises before he allows us to remove his socks and explains the condition of his feet. Poor souls, we assure them not to worry; they've done their share of the work and now it is our turn.'[87]

The state of the BEF was perhaps best illustrated by Capper's 7th Division, which had suffered enormously since its arrival at Ghent on 12 October, at one point being called upon to cover a 7-mile front without reserves. It came out of the line with only 4149 men remaining from its original infantry establishment of 12,522 and this after absorbing reinforcing drafts. In the case of the four battalions of 22nd Brigade – 2nd Queen's, 2nd Royal Warwicks, 1st Royal Welch, and 1st South Staffs – they now mustered a composite battalion of just two composite companies. True to his inclinations, Capper had been heard to say at one point during the battle for Ypres that, 'No good officer has a right to be alive during a fight like this.' On 1 November, while searching for Cavan, 'Ma' Jeffreys had come across Capper in woods to the north of Klein Zillebeke. Jeffreys remarked that Capper's division had had a bad time, 'He replied, "Yes, so bad that there's no Division left, so that I'm a curiosity – a Divisional Commander without a Division." He seemed to treat it almost as a joke.'

Some days later, Captain A.N.S. Roberts of the 2nd Queen's arrived with a draft of approximately 1500 men for 7th Division. When Roberts told Capper how many men he had brought, 'The general produced a mirthless laugh. "If it were fifteen thousand," he said grimly, "it still wouldn't be enough. . . .' Roberts himself caught the mood when asked by a newly arrived young subaltern of the Royal Welch who was in command of the dishevelled party that purported to be the battalion: 'I suspect that you are.'[88]

It was generally felt, however, that the worst was now over, French and his corps commanders even discussing winter and leave arrangements when meeting at Bailleul on 5 November. Falkenhayn, however, had resolved to make one last effort to break through north and south of Ypres.

Notes and references

1 PRO, WO95/1227, Fitzclarence Operational Report for 27 October to 2 November 1914.

2 PRO, CAB45/141, Rice to Edmonds, 6 November 1922.

3 IWM, Owen Mss, 90/37/1, Owen to 'AEM', 28 October 1914.

4 PRO, CAB45/140, Boyd to Sutton, 18 May 1922.

5 PRO, CAB45/140, Statement of WO R.H. Fitz-Roy; LUBLLC, Green Mss, GS0657, diary, 29 October 1914.

6 IWM, Thorne Mss, DS/MISC/11, Account by Leach, no date; PRO, CAB45/140, Bulfin diary, 29 October 1914.

7 IWM, I Corps Mss, MISC/3/43, J.E. Gough to GHQ, 29 October 1914; Beckett, *Johnnie Gough*, p. 191; Gough, *Fifth Army*, pp. 62–3.

8 Ian F.W. Beckett, 'Hubert Gough, Neill Malcolm and Command on the Western Front' in Bond, *Look to Your Front*, pp. 1–12.

9   NAM, Waddy Mss, 8311-71-1, Account of First Ypres, 1 July 1916.

10 OFH, p. 276, French to Kitchener, 30 October 1914; Brock and Brock, *Asquith*, pp. 295–6.

11 Holmes, *Little Field Marshal*, p. 248; French, *1914*, p. 242.

12 OFH, p. 282; IWM, Wilson Mss, HHW 3/8/9, Huguet to Wilson, 31 October 1914.

13 Gardner, *Trial by Fire*, pp. 213–14.

14 IWM, Garwood Mss, 91/23/1, diary, 30 October 1914.

15 PRO, CAB45/140, Bulfin diary, 30 October 1914; IWM, Rees Mss, 77/179/1, 'Record', 29 October 1914. Rees admitted in his account that he could not be sure of the date and he clearly saw this incident on 30 October 1914.

16 NAM, Waddy Mss, 8311-71-1, Account of First Ypres, 1 July 1916.

17 *Ypres, 1914*, pp. 71–2; OFH, p. 301.

18 Gough, *Fifth Army*, pp. 61, 63–5.

19 Farrar-Hockley, *Ypres 1914*, p. 156.

20 Ratinaud, *Course*, p. 309; Foch, *Memoirs*, p. 156; Aston, *Foch*, p. 138; Palat, *Ruée vers Calais*, p. 188; Liddell Hart, *Foch*, pp. 140–1; French, *1914*, p. 245; *Armées Françaises* I, Pt. IV, Annexes Vol. IV, p. 322 'Note on Relations between GHQ and GQG', 30 October 1914; IWM, Wilson Mss, DS/MISC/80, diary, 31 October 1914.

21 Farrar-Hockley, *Ypres 1914*, p. 153.

22 OFH, p. 304.

23 IWM, Home Mss, 82/18/2, Report on Action of 1st Cavalry Division at Messines, compiled 7 November 1914.

24 *War Infantry Knew*, p. 69.

25 R.F.K. Goldsmith, 'Territorial Vanguard: A London Scottish Diary', *Army Quarterly* 103 (2), 1976, pp. 230–8.

26 IWM, Wilson Mss, PP/MCR/100, memoir, p. 33.

27 LUBLLC, Moffat Mss, GS1124, diary, 29 and 30 October 1914; IWM, Wilson Mss, PP/MCR/100, memoir, pp. 35–6, 38.

28 J.H. Lindsay (1925), *The London Scottish in the Great War*, London: Regimental Headquarters, p. 49; OFH, p. 350, n. 3.

29 IWM, Wilson Mss, PP/MCR/100, memoir, p. 39.

30 IWM, Wilson Mss, PP/MCR/100, memoir, p. 40; Goldsmith, 'Territorial Vanguard', pp. 230–8.

31 LUBLLC, Moffat Mss, GS1124, diary, 31 October 1914.

32 IWM, Owens Mss, 80/23/1, memoir, 1 November 1914.

33 IWM, Fleming Mss, 90/28/1, Fleming to 'Randolfo', 6 December 1914.

34 IWM, Home Mss, 82/18/1, diary, 31 October 1914.

35 Gough, *Fifth Army*, p. 66.

36 Gough, *Fifth Army*, p. 68.

37 Simpson, *Evolution of Victory*, pp. 25–6.

38 French, *1914*, p. 266.

39 Hopper, 'Diary of Old Contemptible', p. 16.

40 OFH p. 314; PRO, CAB45/140, Goad diary, 31 October 1914.

41 IWM, Rees Mss, 77/179/1, 'Record', 31 October 1914; ibid., Rees to mother, 6 and 15 November 1914.

42 *Ypres, 1914*, pp. 74, 76.

43 IWM, Rees Mss, 77/179/1, 'Record', 31 October 1914.

44 Farrar-Hockley, *Ypres 1914*, p. 170.

45 IWM, Thorne Mss, DS/MISC/11, Shepherd to Tate, 14 March 1932 (also in NAM, Thorne Mss, 8703-31-458); ibid., account by Sergeant Macdonald, no date.

46 IWM, Thorne Mss, DS/MISC/11, Account by Leach, no date (also PRO, CAB45/140).

47 IWM, Thorne Mss, DS/MISC/11, Account by Caunter, 15 March 1930.

48 X (1917), 'Gheluvelt 1914: The Man Who Turned the Tide', *Blackwood's* MCCXXII, pp. 209–21 (also in NAM, Thorne Mss, 8703-31-451); ibid., 8703-31-456, Gheluvelt File; Colonel A.F.A.N. Thorne (1932), 'Gheluvelt Cross Roads, October 29th, 1914', *Household Brigade Magazine*, Summer, pp. 174–81 (also in NAM, 8703-31-453); PRO, CAB45/140, Statement by C.E. Corkran, 14 August 1915; ibid., Account by B.C. Senhouse Clarke, 6 June 1922.

49 John Bourne (1989), *Britain and the Great War, 1914–18*, London: Edward Arnold, p. 25; G.J. de Groot (1988), *Douglas Haig, 1861–1928*, London: Unwin Hyman, p. 165.

50 IWM, Mowbray, 82/16/1, memoir, 31 October 1914; ibid., Smallwood Mss, 97/4/1, diary, 31 October 1914; ibid., Lomax Mss, 90/1/1, Smith Dorrien to Lomax, 10 November 1914; ibid., War Diary, 1st Division, 31 October 1914; Wyrall, *Second Division*, p. 136.

51 NLS, Haig Mss, Acc 3155/99, Gough to Bulfin, 31 October 1914; IWM, MISC/3/43; PRO, WO95/588; CAB45/140 Bulfin diary, 31 October 1914; LHCMA, Clive Mss, II/1, diary, 31 October 1914.

52 Gardner, *Trial by Fire*, pp. 215–16.

53 NLS, Haig Mss, Acc 3155/99, diary, 31 October 1914; PRO, CAB45/183, Haig
to Edmonds, 10 August 1923; ibid., CAB45/140, Note by Collins, 22 January
1923; Beckett, *Johnnie Gough*, p. 193; Sergeant Secrett (1929), *Twenty-Five Years
with Earl Haig*, London: Jarrolds, p. 100; Palat, *Ruée vers Calais*, p. 196; LHCMA,
Liddell Hart Mss, 11/1931/4 'The Inner Truth of October 31st 1914 at Ypres
(as told to me by General Edmonds)', 17 February 1931; Dubois, *Deux Ans*, II,
p. 54; Hussey, 'Hard Day at First Ypres, pp. 70–89.

54 John Charteris (1931), *At GHQ*, London: Cassell, pp. 52, 76–7; Beckett, *Johnnie
Gough*, p. 194.

55 French, *1914*, pp. 252–7; Holmes, *Little Field Marshal*, p. 251; IWM, Mowbray
Mss, 82/16/1, memoir, 31 October 1914; NLS, Haig Mss, Acc 3155/99, diary,
31 October 1914.

56 PRO, CAB45/141, Rice to Edmonds, 6 November 1922; Edmonds to Malcolm,
5 December 1922; Malcolm to Edmonds, 5 January 1923; Straker to Edmonds,
16 December 1923; ibid., CAB45/182, Jeudwine to Edmonds, 11 December
1922; ibid., WO95/588, Note by Jeudwine; OFH, p. 337; Charteris, *At GHQ*,
p. 53; NAM, Thorne Mss, 8703-31-456, Gheluvelt File.

57 PRO, CAB103/76, Haig to Edmonds, 10 August 1923; NLS, Haig Mss, Acc.
3155/99, diary 31 October 1914; de Groot, *Douglas Haig*, pp. 165–6; Denis
Winter (1991), *Haig's Command: A Reassessment*, London: Viking, pp. 36–7;
John Hussey (1995), 'Haig's Ride up the Menin Road at First Ypres on
31 October 1914: Did he invent the Whole Story?' *Bulletin of the Military
Historical Society* 46 (181), pp. 21–9; Gardner, *Trial by Fire*, pp. 220–1.

58 Farrar-Hockley, *Ypres 1914*, p. 175; Edward L. Spears (1930), *Liaison 1914*,
London: Heinemann p. 13; Foch, *Memoirs*, p. 157; Aston, *Foch*, p. 138; Neiberg,
Foch, p. 37; Liddell Hart, *Foch*, pp. 142–3; Dubois, *Deux Ans*, II, p. 55; Hussey,
'Hard Day at First Ypres', pp. 70–89.

59 OFH, pp. 342–3; *Armées Françaises*, I, Pt. IV, p. 353; ibid., Annexes Vol. IV,
pp. 386–9, Foch Note for French, 31 October 1914 and 'Note on the relations
with the BEF', 31 October 1914; Foch, *Memoirs*, pp. 158–9; Liddell Hart, *Foch*,
p. 143; French, *1914*, p. 260.

60 OFH pp. 342–3; Foch, *Memoirs*, p. 160; *Armées Françaises*, I, Pt. IV, p. 347.

61 Ascoli, *Mons Star*, p. 231.

62 Farrar-Hockley, *Ypres 1914*, p. 168; PRO, CAB45/140, Account by Major B.C.S.
Clarke, 6 June 1922; IWM, Thorne Mss, DS/MISC/11, Thorne Account, no date;
ibid., account by Leach, April 1932 (also in NAM, Thorne Mss, 8703-31-458
and PRO, CAB45/140).

63 NAM, Thorne Mss, 8703-31-434, Fitzclarence diary, 31 October 1914.

64 IWM, Thorne Mss, DS/MISC/11, Caunter to Thorne, 31 January 1932; Wyrall,
Second Division, pp. 135–6.

6 ♦ Army Group Fabeck

65 OFH p. 340.

66 Dauzet, *Bataille de Flandres*, p. 114; SHAT, 18N 134, Haig to GQG,
20 November 1914.

67 IWM, P146, Baines Mss, 'Personal Account of 31 October 1914', pp. 3, 5, 7,
10–11; ibid., Dillon Mss, 82/25/1, letter, 4 November 1914.

68 IWM, Garwood Mss, 91/23/1, diary, 31 October and 5 and 8 November 1914.

69 PRO, CAB45/140, Bulfin diary, 31 October 1914.

70 PRO, CAB45/140, Bulfin diary, 31 October 1914.

71 Atkinson, *Seventh Division*, pp. 96, 106–7; NAM, Waddy Mss, 8311-71-1,
Account of First Ypres, 1 July 1916.

72 Beckett, *Johnnie Gough*, p. 194; PRO, CAB45/140, Bulfin diary, 31 October and
1 November 1914.

73 IWM, Trefusis Mss, 82/30/1, diary, 31 October, 1, 2 and 6 November 1914;
Craster, *Fifteen Rounds*, pp. 122–4, 145.

74 Farrar-Hockley, *Ypres 1914*, p. 178.

75 SHAT 1K268/2/9, Foch to Joffre, 9 November 1914; IWM, Wilson Mss,
DS/MISC/80, diary, 5 November; Joffre, *Memoirs*, I, pp. 318–19; Foch, *Memoirs*,
p. 162; Liddell Hart, *Foch*, p. 150.

76 Brock and Brock, *Asquith*, pp. 302–3, 311–12; IWM, French Mss, PP/MCR/C33,
Churchill to French, 6 November 1914; French to Churchill, 9 November 1914
in Gilbert, *Churchill Companion*, p. 259. See also David French (1979), 'The
Military Background to the Shell Crisis of May 1915', *Journal of Strategic Studies*
2, pp. 192–205 and Richard Holmes (1991), 'Sir John French and Lord
Kitchener' in Brian Bond (ed.), *The First World War and British Military History*,
Oxford: Oxford University Press, pp. 113–39.

77 IWM, JS5, Allenby to Haig, 1 November 1914; Goldsmith, 'Territorial
Vanguard', pp. 230–8.

78 IWM, St John Mss, 83/17/1, memoir, 1–2 November 1914.

79 Gough, *Fifth Army*, pp. 68–9.

80 IWM, Home Mss, 82/18/1, diary, 30 October–2 November 1914; ibid., 82/18/2,
Report on 1st Cavalry Division at Messines, 7 November 1914; ibid., Fleming
Mss, 90/28/1, Fleming to 'Randolfo', 6 December 1914.

81 IWM, Home Mss, 82/18/1, diary, 31 October–2 November 1914; PRO,
CAB45/140, Bulfin diary, 2 November 1914; IWM, Garwood Mss, 91/23/1,
diary, 1 November 1914.

82 *Armées Françaises*, I, Pt. IV, p. 361; *Ypres, 1914*, p. 89.

83 NAM, Waddy Mss, 8311-71-1, Account of First Ypres, 1 July 1916.

· 159 ·

84 Falkenhayn, *German General Staff*, p. 35; *Armées Françaises* I, Pt. IV, pp. 370–1.

85 OFH, p. 377; PRO, CAB45/141, Schreiber to Edmonds, 19 November 1922; Wyrall, *Second Division*, p. 147; Craster, *Fifteen Rounds*, p. 129.

86 NLS, Haig Mss, Acc 3155/215(c), I Corps Action Reports, 4 November 1914; ibid., 3155/99, diary, 4 November 1914; Beckett, *Johnnie Gough*, p. 194; Stephen Gwynn (ed.) (1936), *The Anvil of War*, London: Macmillan, pp. 50–1; *Eton College Chronicle*, 30 March 1915.

87 IWM, Paterson Mss, 90/10/1, letter to 'Martha', 16 November 1914.

88 OFH, p. 385; PRO, WO95/706, IV Corps Operational Report for October, 14 November 1914; Charteris, *At GHQ*, p. 58; Craster, *Fifteen Rounds*, pp. 125–6; Tim Carew (1971), *The Vanished Army*, London: Corgi, pp. 211, 228–9.

chapter 7

Nonnebosschen

In preparation for one last great German effort at Ypres, it had been possible to withdraw *Fourth Army* troops from opposite the inundated area in the north and Rupprecht had also shifted troops and artillery to Fabeck in the belief that a decision south-east of Ypres was no longer possible. Other formations were also on the move including Lieutenant General von Winckler's newly constituted *Guards Division*, two brigades having been detached from the existing Guards divisions in Artois. Unlike other German formations, which were territorial in character, the Guard was recruited from all parts of the German Empire except Bavaria and stationed at Potsdam: recruits had to be a minimum of 5 feet 6 inches tall and of superior physique and bearing: indeed, its reserves were classified as on a par with the active army. Moreover, it had received far better training than, say, the reserve corps committed to Langemarck. Yet, its tactics were to prove no better, the same close order formations just as fatal to their practitioners.

Pending the arrival of the Guard and the *4th Division* from La Fère, Albrecht and Fabeck were directed to continue to attack, a new *Group Gerok* being formed by Fabeck from elements of *3rd Division*, the *25th Reserve Division*, the *11th Landwehr Division* and *6th Bavarian Reserve Division* to apply pressure north of the Ypres-Comines canal. Further north, *Group Urach*, consisting of some elements of *3rd Division* and *26th Infantry Division*, would maintain pressure on Kemmel. On 6 November the French lost Zwarteleen and the Germans, bands playing, closed on St Eloi. At one point, the Germans had advanced to within 3000 yards of Ypres, being stopped only by a counter-attack at Zwarteleen by Charles 'Black Jack' Kavanagh's 7th Cavalry Brigade, in the course of which the Household Cavalry lost seventeen officers including

Lords Gerard and Northampton wounded and the Hon. Hugh Dawnay killed.

Having been a GHQ liaison officer with corps, Dawnay had only recently returned to his regiment, having repeatedly asked to do so. Reports differed as to whether Dawnay had been killed leading the clearing of the village or trying to rally demoralised Frenchmen. Archibald Home largely blamed the French, believing that they were too ready to retire and then advance again: 'It seems to me that they would rather do this and lose 100 men doing it, than stick it out and lose 25 men – I think that it is a matter of numbers – the French fight in depth and can do it, we fight in a thin line and cannot afford to give an inch because we have not enough men to retake a position once it is lost.' In this case, the French withdrawal had cost Kavanagh unnecessary losses.[1]

With the weather now taking a decidedly wintry turn amid heavy mist and falling temperatures on 7 November, Ypres and Armentières both came under heavy shellfire, the Germans later claiming that the towers of Ypres were being used by British artillery observers. This was not the case since they did not offer in fact a commanding view over the plain. Foch had promised to restore the line that day and claimed that this had been achieved by 0930 hours. In reality, the French did not appear until well into the afternoon, Foch subsequently removing the commander of the XVI Corps and replacing him with Grossetti. Realising that the French would not appear in time, Cavan had already launched a counter-attack by 22nd Brigade on Zwarteleen but it was unable to make much progress.

Elsewhere, German attacks upon Le Touquet, Ploegsteert and Herenthage Woods, and Broodseinde were all repulsed and, indeed, there was often little co-ordination in the German effort. Haig was appalled, however, to find that men from the 1st Lincolnshires, 1st Northumberland Fusiliers and 1st Bedfordshires had left their trenches 'on account of a little shellfire'. Some twenty-three men of the 1st Bedfordshires, nine from the Northumberland Fusiliers and two from the 1st Cheshires were apprehended by the Assistant Provost Marshal of 1st Division on the Ypres-Menin Road making their way 'as rapidly as possible to the rear'. Haig 'directed that enquiry should be made into the matter, and the worst offenders brought to trial by Court Martial' while the trenches should be 'reoccupied *at once*'. Much the same kind of isolated attacks occurred on 8 November, with Haig again displeased that some men had left their trenches though the position was restored by the 1st Loyals and the South Lancashires.[2]

Generally, despite the enormous pressures, the BEF's morale had stood up remarkably well. It has been suggested that there was something of a crisis of morale in the months following the end of the Ypres battle with most of the indices of morale employed by GHQ, namely the incidence of trench feet, shell-shock and crime, suggesting increasing difficulties in the winter of 1914–15. The indices, however, were flawed. Military crime did invariably rise after heavy casualties but medical advances progressively reduced the cases of trench feet and shell-shock. Nevertheless, it has been suggested that 7th Division's unhappy experiences at Ypres contributed to problems in it during December and January. In common with so many other cases in the application of the army's system of justice, death sentences were largely commuted. Indeed, the first actual execution in 7th Division was of a private in the 2nd Royal Warwickshires, who had deserted at Zonnebeke on 24 October and was apprehended at Boulogne in January 1915: it was the twentieth sentence passed and the twelfth in the battalion though most of these related to the aftermath of a botched attack in December. It has similarly been suggested problems in the 2nd Border Regiment in January also related to its losses at Ypres in November though it was also heavily engaged in December, two members of the battalion winning the VC that month. After a third change in command since Hubert Hamilton's death, Major General Aylmer Haldane taking over from Wing on 21 November, 3rd Division also saw an increase in death sentences being passed for military offences with three executions in February 1915. Conceivably, this may be related to the belief that 3rd Division had shown want of fighting spirit but the idea that it was directly related to Haig's criticism of the division seems unlikely given that it was in Smith-Dorrien's corps.

Two other death sentences that were carried out in other formations were also related directly to the Ypres battle. A private in the 1st Wilts, who deserted from a party marching up to the line on 18 October, was arrested the next day in civilian clothing and was executed on 28 October. A lance sergeant from the 2nd King's Royal Rifle Corps went missing on 1 November when his unit was ordered up to reinforce the 1st Battalion near Herthenthage Chateau. He was finally apprehended in March 1915 after hiding with a bootmaker in Arques and executed on 23 March 1915. Yet, in the case of the regular Irish regiments, most had a worse disciplinary record in the summer of 1915 than the winter of 1914–15, illustrating the complexity of issues of morale and discipline. Nor was a unit's disciplinary record necessarily a guide to its battle readiness in the Irish case so that, for example, the 2nd

Royal Irish Rifles suffered higher losses than the 2nd Leinsters but the latter had the worst disciplinary record of the two units.[3]

In many cases a kind of routine had been established. On quieter days, especially when early mist and fog delayed the start of the German shelling, the men of the 2nd Oxford and Bucks had breakfast. They then 'retired into the holes which we had dug, taking with us some bread and jam, or something of the kind to eat during the day'. They would then emerge after dark when rations would be brought up. The strain on the BEF, however, was increasing, Trefusis recording of the Irish Guards that most were suffering from nerves 'and we shall do no good till we can be sent somewhere to recoup. We have had a tiring time for the last fortnight, and it is telling on everyone. We are at it night and day without relief and very irregular food, although we always get in supplies. The men have not had a hot meal except tea for a very long time.' Indeed, when sent into corps reserve on 10 November, the battalion had lost sixteen officers and 583 men dead, wounded and missing since 31 October.

For Craig Brown of the 1st Cameron Highlanders, there had been similar privations. On 3 November he noted that he had not washed since 25 October and had changed his socks only once, having already noted on 24 October that he and his men had not washed for five days nor eaten for two. On 8 November he wrote, 'You can imagine what uniforms look like after being day & night in deep, narrow drains for a fortnight, rubbing against the earth walls every movement made. The straw in the bottom of my drain is all sodden & smelly, but there are occasions in which I am jolly glad to get well into the furthest & darkest end.' By 14 November, having still not used soap since 25 October, Craig Brown recorded his daily diet, 'Dry bread, jam & comppie for breakfast at 5 a.m., washed down with rum & water. The other meals exactly the same. Sardines sometimes make a pleasant variety, & one night we had tinned apricots & cold mealy puddings provided by a Black Watch officer.' He was finally relieved on 16 November after twenty-two days without washing. For Jock Bremner, a 31-year-old Scottish corporal in the 115 Heavy Battery, Royal Garrison Artillery, a routine day's work was also becoming tedious: 'More firing during the night and early part of morning. We started off as usual and kept it up all day especially our gun we hardly had a rest, I am just beginning to get fed up, the same thing day after day, one might as well be in a wilderness.'[4]

In meeting Foch on the morning of 8 November, French and Haig raised the need to re-establish the line in the vicinity of the Comines Canal but sufficient French reinforcements were not forthcoming to assist d'Urbal in retaking the ground lost. Some minor progress was made by the French on 9 November but, on the following day, the Germans attacked between Langemarck and Dixmude, the French and Belgian defenders of the latter being forced back over the Yser though the Belgians successfully destroyed the bridges as they retreated. The conditions in this sector as the weather deteriorated were increasingly difficult for both sides. On the German side, trenches were filling with water, insufficient troops were available to effect regular reliefs and there was such insufficient shelter for those who were in reserve to the front line that they had to 'bivouac on sodden fields'.[5]

Joffre was still convinced that the Germans would soon begin to transfer troops to the Eastern Front and that, though this would be masked by a few heavier attacks in the West, these diversionary attacks had already taken place. Thus, although having placed XX Corps at Foch's disposal if needed, on 3 November he had sent only the 11th and 39th Divisions north. The very last reserves Joffre felt he could afford to send went north on 10 November, being some two infantry brigades, ten chasseur battalions and an artillery division culled from four different armies elsewhere. In all, during the course of the battle, Joffre had augmented the original French forces in the north – seven cavalry divisions, two Territorial divisions and a marine fusilier brigade – with nine infantry divisions, a Territorial division, two infantry brigades, two infantry regiments, ten chasseur battalions, and sixteen cavalry regiments.[6]

In reality, the series of German attacks between 6 and 9 November were actually intended to pin the allies in their existing positions and prevent them from either resting or improving their defences. The new effort had been intended for 10 November opposite Gheluvelt and to be accomplished by Winckler's *Guards Division* and *4th Division*, the two forming a corps under the command of General Baron von Plettenberg 'to drive back and crush the enemy lying north of the [Ypres-Comines] canal'.[7] In turn, Plettenberg's new corps and *XV Corps* were constituted as a new Army Group under General von Linsingen, formerly commander of *II Corps*. Fabeck was instructed to support the new offensive by *Army Group Linsingen* while both *Fourth* and *Sixth Armies* would also attack to prevent any allied troops being moved to confront Linsingen's effort. In the event, the deteriorating weather had prevented an adequate reconnaissance being carried out and Linsingen's attack was postponed to 11 November though the intended supporting efforts had gone ahead between Langemarck and Dixmude. It would prove the climax of the battle, the counter-attack by the 2nd Oxford and Bucks Light Infantry being almost as significant an event as that by the Worcesters on 31 October.

The Germans appeared quiet on the evening of 10 November and, though there had been some reports by British aircraft during the day of artillery movements, the scale of the attack would prove unexpected. Moreover, the French had concluded that the increased German efforts suggested any large-scale attack would be against them. Though invariably associated later with the attack by the *Prussian Guard*, the German effort actually embraced twelve and a half divisions over a 9-mile frontage given the inclusion of Fabeck's formations and those of *XXVII Reserve Corps* from *Fourth Army* as well as the remainder of *Army Group Linsingen*. Ironically, too, within the German Army the *4th Division* recruited from Pomeranians and West Prussians was regarded as superior in training to the *Guards Division*.

The day began with the customary mist, which was not really dispersed until the onset of a strong wind around noon. With the wind, however, came rain which became heavier and heavier through the late afternoon and early evening. As on 31 October, the German attack was preceded by a heavy bombardment, indeed one of greater intensity than before from about 0630 hours onwards, reaching its peak about 0900 hours. The worst of the shelling fell on the II Corps battalions from Wing's 3rd Division in the groups commanded by McCracken and Shaw, and upon Fitzclarence's 1st Guards Brigade, which now actually comprised two Scottish line battalions – 1st Black Watch and 1st Cameron Highlanders – and the 1st Scots Guards.

Most of the defenders still had their heads well down when the German infantry began to advance but, fortunately, in many cases, with the exception of the fresh units of Linsingen, the Germans did not attack with the energy their commanders had anticipated. Indeed, neither Allenby's nor Conneau's cavalry came under any pressure at all around Messines. North of the Comines Canal, the French were forced out of their trenches at a time when allied reserves had mostly been committed opposite Gheluvelt. Dubois, however, managed to find the French 7th Hussars to shore up the line. Cavan's mixed detachment of assorted cavalry and infantry also held its own between the French on the canal and Polygon Wood, though at one point Lieutenant Colonel Malcolm of the London Scottish was forced to send his battalion headquarters into the firing line. Holding the line next to the London Scottish, the 2nd Grenadiers suffered twenty-one men killed with thirty-seven wounded and a further sixteen missing in addition to three officers killed and another badly wounded.[8]

The main German thrust was directed towards the front opposite Gheluvelt, extending from the so-called Shrewsbury Forest in the south across the Menin Road to Nonnebosschen (Nun's Copse) and the edge of Polygon Wood beyond it. The centre and right of this sector covering about 3500 yards was held by the three groups from II Corps, men still recovering from their previous exertions. McCracken had some 1754 officers and men, Gleichen some 1600 and Shaw a total of 2714 including a Zouave company from a French battalion Haig had retained. Shaw also controlled a further 846 officers and men around Veldhoek Chateau, while Fitzclarence's brigade of about 800 officers and men held the 900 yards between Veldhoek and Polygon Wood. The line was backed by five of the improvised strong points constructed some days earlier while Haig had a reserve of less than 2000 men. Discounting these reserves, less than 7800 men faced twenty-five German battalions totalling 17,500 infantry.

McCracken and Gleichen's groups were attacked by the twelve battalions of *4th Division* but the attack was stopped almost immediately by the concentrated rifle fire of the British to the extent that German accounts spoke of meeting deep trenches, broad obstacles and machine guns firing in enfilade. Matters became far more serious, however, for Shaw's group and Fitzclarence's brigade, which were attacked by the twelve fresh battalions of the *Guards Division*. The *4th Guards Brigade* attacked Shaw and *1st Guards Brigade* attacked Fitzclarence, advancing 'silently at a jog' in massed columns with officers in front, swords at the carry. For a reason the British Official Historian was never subsequently able to discover, the *1st Foot Guards Regiment* was wearing mitre caps rather than pickelhaubes.[9]

Shaw beat off the first attack and, when the *2nd Guard Grenadier Regiment* got into part of the trenches of 4th Royal Fusiliers and the Zouave company in the Herenthage woods, a counter-attack by the 1st Royal Scots and a company of the 2nd Royal Sussex drove them back out of the support trenches. However, it did not recover the front line. Shaw himself was also wounded during the morning. Similarly, a fusilier battalion of the *2nd (Emperor Franz) Guard Grenadier Regiment* passed over the trenches of the 2nd Duke of Wellington's Regiment in a sudden lull in the artillery bombardment, many of the men having been withdrawn into the cover of Veldhoek woods. The Germans, however, were stopped by the strong point near the chateau stables held by another Zouave company. The reserve company of the Duke's pushed them out of the woods but, again, the original front line was not recovered. The German battalion took some 500 casualties and the Duke's 380 of its 826 rank and file. The most serious breach of the line, however, came with the attack against Fitzclarence.

Fitzclarence's position was in largely open ground overlooked by German observers on the Reutel ridge, with the result that as many men as possible were withdrawn into support positions. Even without the consequent thinning of the front line strength, the defence was overstretched. The 1st King's of 6th Brigade covered a mile of line between Polygon Wood and the Poezelhoek stream with only six officers and 450 men with no reserves available. Moreover, for Fitzclarence's neighbouring 1st Brigade generally, shelling had made it difficult to bring up food, water and ammunition in addition to the problems resulting from the recent rain, which had made the tracks through the wood muddy. Men, indeed, were surviving largely on rum and biscuits with neither washing nor sanitation facilities.

As elsewhere along the front, the Germans advanced at about 0900 hours, coming on in closely arranged lines, apparently at a quick walk. Partly due to the mist and a slight breeze blowing smoke towards the British positions, the Germans were spotted only when about 50 yards from the front trenches. Thus, the Germans passed over them before there was time to bring the men back from their positions under cover to the rear. Craig Brown of the 1st Cameron Highlanders had only just managed to order his men to fire 'but it was throat-racking work trying to make oneself heard above the noise of the shelling'. He saw the Scots Guards begin to run and his own men followed: 'I shouted to them to turn & open fire, but I might just as well have shouted to the wind.' Craig Brown found himself almost alone and dived into a dugout, being joined by one of his lance corporals. A German peered in but did not see them. Some time later a wounded German also came in, whom they bandaged. Two more Camerons appeared after dark and Craig Brown with one of these, the lance corporal and a bandsman they also came across, crawled back and fortuitously found the remains of the battalion.[10]

Nonetheless, Fitzclarence's men put up a sturdy resistance and, abandoning any notion of conserving shells, the field guns supporting the front line managed to lay down sufficient fire to prevent the Germans bringing up further reinforcements. The combination of resistance and the counter-bombardment broke up the cohesion of the German formations, Prince Eitel Friedrich of Prussia's *1st Guards Brigade* drifting into Polygon Wood to deal with the defenders rather than maintaining the intended advance north-westwards between Polygon Wood and Veldhoek woods. A gap also began to widen between the *Guards Division* and *4th Division*.

As the fighting continued, two of the strong points in Fitzclarence's rear, one held only by the cooks and spare details of the 1st Scots Guards, were overwhelmed but a third one at the so-called Northampton Farm continued to hold out. Similarly, about 100 men of the Black Watch, including the battalion staff, managed to hold Verbeek Farm. Some forty men manning the battalion's own designated strong point – 'Black Watch Corner' – in Polygon Wood, comprising simply a trench inside the hedges of a cottage garden protected by a few strands of barbed wire, also held. Trying to find a way round the fire being put down, elements of the *1st* and *3rd Foot Guard Regiments* – perhaps 900 men in all – pushed into Nonnebosschen, a small wood of oaks and chestnuts with hazel and maple undergrowth. Had the Germans but known it, there was little behind Nonnebosschen. They were prevented from getting further forward, however, by fire from some artillery batteries, some also forming improvised firing lines of gunners with rifles, various stragglers from 1st Brigade and the 5th Field Company, RE, including the latter's cooks. One German officer captured on the edge of Nonnebosschen asked a British artillery officer where the British reserves were. The latter pointed to 2nd Division's gun line and, when asked what was behind that, simply replied divisional headquarters. 'God Almighty,' the German exclaimed.[11]

Both Landon and Monro sent what reserves they could to assist Fitzclarence as it became clear that a serious situation had arisen. Haig, too, rode out to the White Chateau and sent Johnnie Gough further forward to see Landon at Hooge and organise a counter-attack. Haig himself sent word to d'Urbal by one of his ADCs, Baird, to inform the French of the situation while Straker was sent to warn Monro. Later that afternoon, with the situation still appearing grave, Baird was sent out to fix a potential line of retreat with Monro but by then the situation had improved materially at the front.[12]

In fact, before Gough reached Landon, preparations were already under way to restore the line. Monro had sent up his only reserves, comprising the Irish Guards and the 2nd Oxford and Bucks. At about noon, Lieutenant Colonel Henry Davies, commanding the latter battalion, was directed to clear Nonnebosschen and then, in conjunction with the 2nd Highland Light Infantry, to retake the trenches lost by the Black Watch at the corner of Polygon Wood. Almost simultaneously with getting these orders through

5th Brigade, Davies also received orders from 1st Brigade to recover the trenches lost by the rest of Fitzclarence's brigade. Davies decided that Non-nebosschen was the first priority and sometime between 1400 and 1500 hours sent his A and B companies into the wood from the north-west, C and D companies following in support. A company of the 1st Northants joined in as did the 5th Field Company, while two batteries from XXXIX Brigade, RFA gave covering fire.

Led by Captain Harry Dillon, the Oxford and Bucks 'charged the Germans out of the trenches, some of the enemy turning and running when the attack was thirty or forty yards off, and others surrendering. Most of those who ran were shot.'[13] The tall Prussian Guardsmen, many in pickel-haubes but some in field caps, were taken by surprise and swept out of the wood, one witness characterising the Germans' emergence from the far side as like pheasants coming out of the trees in ones and twos and then a rush. Having taken few casualties, the Oxford and Bucks paused briefly at the edge of Nonnebosschen then retook the former support trenches and pushed on to the morning's front line. At that point, however, some French batteries near Frezenberg mistook them for Germans and shelled them. By the time the French had been warned, heavy rain was falling and it was too dark to go further. The Oxford and Bucks had suffered just five dead and twenty-two wounded. By contrast, Fitzclarence's brigade had been reduced to barely 300 men. The Prussian Guard, however, had also taken heavy losses. The *1st Foot Guard Regiment* alone, for example, had ten officers and 310 men killed. The *Guards Division* apparently suffered 2134 casualties for the period between 11 and 19 November and *4th Division* had 2932 casualties in November as a whole.[14]

Although it was now dark, Fitzclarence was determined to recover all of his lost trenches. Consulting with 5th Brigade, Fitzclarence resolved to use the Oxford and Bucks and the HLI to make a surprise attack out of Polygon Wood at 2100 hours without prior artillery bombardment from north to south down the trench line. The rain and darkness hampered preparations, however, and the attack was postponed until 0100 hours on 12 November. Meanwhile, Landon had put some 500 men drawn from 2nd Grenadier Guards, 1st Irish Guards and 2nd Royal Munster Fusiliers at Fitzclarence's disposal. Fitzclarence decided to support Davies with these additional men under his own command as he knew where the trench line was.

Lieutenant Colonel Wilfrid Smith of the Grenadiers was uneasy at the whole venture since 'We none of us knew exactly where the trenches were, nor had we seen the country by daylight.' Undertaking a preliminary reconnaissance, Davies, who was also doubtful, discovered that the Germans had dug some new trenches behind the old British front, which were well wired and full of troops, and that an attack north to south down the latter would expose his men to enfilade. Davies therefore concluded that the attack was unwise and sent back a message to this effect to the acting commander of 5th Brigade, Colonel Claude Westmacott. As the Oxford and Bucks pulled back towards Nonnebosschen, however, they met Fitzclarence coming forward at the head of his column sometime between 0200 and 0300. Fitzclarence wanted to go on and went forward to undertake his own reconnaissance accompanied by Trefusis of the Irish Guards, who was acting as brigade major. According to 'Ma' Jeffreys, the Irish Guards were 'shaky', one man suddenly letting off his rifle in the air and starting to run. Jeffreys kicked the man back into place only for the man to dive in a hedge. There was faint moonlight and the shot had attracted the attention of the Germans. Almost at once, as the moon appeared briefly from behind a cloud, Fitzclarence was hit by rifle fire and killed. In the circumstances, after consulting briefly with Wilfrid Smith of the Grenadiers, Davies had the attack called off, though he later claimed it was Westmacott's decision. It left the Germans in possession of the British front line between Polygon Wood and the Menin Road.[15]

Farther south at Armentières, Private Osborne of the 1st East Lancashires had a miserable night, recording the onset of a heavy thunderstorm at about 2200 and torrential rain, 'as being bitter cold, could not sleep for being starved with cold & wet through we have only our overcoats'. Johnnie Gough sensed that the worst was now truly over. According to R.J. 'Jack' Collins, the GSO3 in I Corps, he had remarked at the end of 11 November, 'I am sorry for the Huns on the other side of that hill. They must have had a terrible day. I think they are beat.'[16]

Yet, the situation still seemed grave in view of the British losses and Haig told French that if he could not be sent immediate support then both I Corps and Dubois's IX Corps might be cut off. Neither Landon nor Wing had any reserves left and Monro only a single weak battalion, while the corps reserve consisted of three even weaker battalions and two regiments from Kavanagh's 7th Cavalry Brigade. French could send only drafts of 1500 men without officers, a Territorial battalion, and a yeomanry regiment though 1st Cavalry Division was also made available. Foch, however, had promised to relieve I Corps with French troops from the Alsace sector. It was certainly necessary, I Corps now being short of 90 per cent of its officer establishment and 83 per cent of its men. Haig, indeed, feared that if the French did not keep their promises and exhausted men from II Corps had to fill the gap then the BEF might cease to exist and the 'voice of Great Britain in European strategy would be much diminished'. Generally, indeed, Haig was critical of the French for 'ever since we landed in France they seem ready to drain the last drop of blood out of the British force'.[17]

Rather in keeping with those who had noted growing fatigue even before the attack of 11 November, Archibald Home felt that the BEF was in a pitiful condition: 'Here you can see the results on men of 19 days fighting against hopeless odds, continual fighting and who have not yielded their ground – you see some of them coming in for a rest – their faces tell the story – some look tired, you cannot interest them, they have reached the stage where men hope they will be wounded, killed, captured anything so that they can lie down and sleep, sleep for days, sleep for ever. Others have a half mad look in their eyes – difficult to describe but it is there. A few only are cheerful, these are the men with that great asset – personality – they have each probably kept 20, 40, 50 men in the trenches fighting where otherwise they would have gone back.'[18]

In the event, however, the battle was effectively over. Though Sir John French suggested that he and Foch were equally puzzled by German intentions, the French considered it so as early as 13 November. The Germans decided to abandon the offensive on 17 November, the initial decision being that of Albrecht but immediately confirmed by Falkenhayn.[19] Men like Tappen of the OHL Operations Staff and the Kaiser's Adjutant General, Hans von Plessen, had concluded that it was no longer possible to break through in the West without more men, more artillery and new ideas. Initially, however, Falkenhayn had refused to accede to a request for an immediate reinforcement of the Eastern Front on 9 November and an attack was made on the French IX Corps on 12 and 13 November. This – carried out once more by the *Prussian Guard* – extended to the II Corps groups on 13 and 14 November, but without any serious pressure being applied though the Germans got briefly into Veldhoek Chateau and had to be driven out. Meeting Erich Ludendorff in Berlin on 30 October to discuss the perennial question of East or West, Falkenhayn had still been adamant that victory was possible in the West: all that had now changed. On 10 November, *III Reserve Corps* under Beseler, *XIII Corps* under Fabeck, and *II Corps* under Linsingen and the German cavalry began departing for the Eastern Front, the Russian concentration around Warsaw and the increasingly desperate pleas of the Austro-Hungarian Chief of Staff, Franz Conrad von Hötzendorf, for help proving too serious to ignore. Falkenhayn, too, had experienced what the German official history later characterised as an 'inner change'. Indeed, Falkenhayn had already told the Kaiser that the army was exhausted on 8 November and ten days later he was to suggest to the Chancellor, Bethmann, that it was now time to develop a political strategy to detach Russia from its western allies.

There was much criticism of Falkenhayn's conduct of the offensive, not least for employing badly trained reserve formations, thus wearing out an important resource for the future, and the unnecessary losses. Among the critics was Rupprecht, who had resented *Army Group Fabeck* being established outside his control, and Bethmann. The view of the influential Colonel Max Hoffmann on Hindenburg's staff was that there had been 'useless deaths' at Ypres. The Quartermaster General, Gustav von Freytag-Loringhoven, echoed the judgement when writing to Falkenhayn's eventual successor as Prussian war minister, Wild von Hohenborn, in June 1915. There was perhaps a wider failure, however, in that the astonishment at the fact of stagnation in the West was to continue at OHL. There were attempts to oust Falkenhayn in December 1914 and January 1915 and Bethmann recorded in August 1915 that Falkenhayn would 'never be able to get rid of Ypres'. In the event, however, Falkenhayn was not replaced as Chief of the General Staff until August 1916.[20]

The end of the German offensive was not immediately apparent with the renewed attacks between 12 and 14 November. Indeed, on 12 November Lieutenant 'Jack' Dimmer of the 2nd King's Royal Rifle Corps, a former ranker, won the VC at Klein Zillebeke, continuing to fire his machine gun though hit five times by shrapnel or bullets. As Dimmer later wrote from hospital, 'My face is splattered with pieces of my own gun and pieces of shell, and I have a bullet in my face and four small holes in my right shoulder. It made rather a nasty mess of me at first, but now that I am washed and my wounds dressed I look quite alright.' It was the last of eleven VCs won during First Ypres. Subsequently, while commanding the 2/4th Royal Berkshires, Dimmer was killed on 21 March 1918 while riding his horse in full view of the advancing Germans.[21]

The weather deteriorated markedly after 11 November with the first snowfall on 15 November, the first really hard frost on 18 November and the first serious snowfall on 19 November. The Frenchman, Chamard, recalled holding the trenches in snow and frost, the men unable to wash, with feet frost-bitten, rifle and machine-gun mechanisms seized up and an over-whelming feeling of misery. Between 30 October and 20 November I Corps had 15,083 men evacuated sick, an average of 717 a day.[22] Both sides were equally affected by the mud, which made it all but impossible to keep rifles clean, and contributed to the problems in bringing up supplies to the front line trenches. At least the 8th Division had arrived by 13 November and some work also commenced on the so-called BCD Line to cover the British dis-embarkation ports at Boulogne, Calais and Dunkirk, though it was not com-pleted until the autumn of 1915. The aged Field Marshal Lord Roberts also visited the BEF, coming over with his daughter on 11 November, but caught a chill, leading to congestion of the lungs, and died on the evening of 14 November.

A reorganisation now took place to consolidate the line held by the BEF so that its component parts were no longer separated on the ground by French troops, I Corps being relieved by the French IX and XVI Corps. Agreement was reached between French and Foch on 13 November. But, three days later, French had to request an adjustment, ending the British line close to Wytschaete rather than St Eloi as he did not consider he had a sufficient number of reliable troops: 'Our long line of trenches, with consequent exten-sion and inability to rest the men in positions in rear, our heavy losses (amounting to 48,000 in the last 4 weeks) and our lack of Regimental Officers render it impossible for us to carry out our promise.' Foch agreed and the French took over the sector from Zonnebeke to the Ypres-Comines Canal, with the new British line running for 21 miles from Wytschaete to the La Bassée Canal at Givenchy. The Belgians held 15 miles of front and the French 430 miles: previously, on 31 October the BEF had held 12 miles of line and 9 miles on 5 November.[23] Finally, the movement of German formations to the east was detected on 20 November.

For the BEF the date of 22 November, when the occupation of its new line was completed, became that on which men ceased to be eligible for the 1914 or 'Mons' Star, the bar for which carried the dates 5 August to 22 November. It was also on 22 November that the Germans, who had been shelling Ypres almost continuously since 18 November, set fire to the Cloth Hall. Even earlier, German aircraft had bombed the town. B.H. Waddy of the 2nd Bedfordshires had been in Ypres on 28 October when two air-craft appeared overhead: 'I saw a column of black smoke rise and heard the whistle of fragments over me and then, trembling with excitement rather than fear, went to see what damage had been done. I found a G.S. Wagon, absolutely undamaged but with the two horses harnessed to it lying dead, riddled with splinters and just in front of their heads a hole in the ground three feet deep and about five feet in diameter.' The driver and an officer sitting next to him on the wagon box had been knocked off but were both unharmed.[24]

For some time the inhabitants had been sheltering in the casemets of the old ramparts, only a few elderly residents, some officials such as the police commissioner, and some curates or nuns much in evidence. One group of Irish Benedictine nuns, who had been sheltering and feeding the poor as best they could, had been forced out by the shelling of 6 November. The Yperlee river, which ran underground, was exposed by the shelling while a Belgian Red Cross worker came across one civilian who had apparently crossed the town and found he was at the Grande Place without realising it, whole quarters of the town having disappeared. Sister Marguerite-Marie of the Lamotte School had recorded back on 7 November, a day on which 1st Division's field companies were sent back into Ypres to help fight the fires, that the city already resembled 'an enormous furnace'. The sisters had been burying the bodies of British soldiers killed near their convent in its garden, 'for the shells did not permit us to gain the civil cemetery, and over the graves of the soldiers we raised a poor wooden cross, marked with the names of those beneath'. The first man buried was supposedly a Private Whitehead of the Royal Warwickshires on 22 October. Sister Marguerite also recorded the destruction of the Cloth Hall, 'Heavy fire at about 6 o'clock in the morning. By 9, the Hall was under fire. The first shell fell on the tower, the third on the clock. At about 11 o'clock the carillon collapsed and the Hall was ablaze. It is a horrible spectacle. In a moment the build-ing is a great sea of flame. The St Martin's Church also went up.' The Germans claimed, erroneously, that the 'towers' of Ypres had been used for artillery observation and thus had been destroyed 'for German life is more precious than the finest Gothic architecture'.[25]

Thus, the last attempt to break the increasing deadlock during the 'race to the sea' had ended with German failure despite their superiority in both numbers and artillery and their greater command cohesion over that of the allies. The Germans, however, had failed to co-ordinate their assaults, pushing formations into attack without thought for the need to keep a reserve in hand to exploit the opportunities their massed columns won on several occasions. As the British Official History had it, they had made the mistake of 'seeking for a weak place by trying many'.[26] Conceivably, they consistently took the small numbers of defenders they confronted as representing merely an outpost line since it appears from the evidence of their own wartime semi-official account that they had greatly overestimated allied strength. Indeed, whereas a German infantry brigade consisted of two regiments, each of six battalions, the British equivalent had only four battalions.

It had been an old-fashioned battle in many respects, riflemen being as significant in its outcome as artillery, and the decisions of junior officers as important if not more so than those of senior officers. Indeed, in terms of the impact of men like Fitzclarence, Cavan and Bulfin on the British side, it already suggested that divisions if not brigades would be the level at which innovation would occur. It was rapidly also becoming apparent, of course, that the defensive was superior to the offensive, even lightly armed dismounted cavalry being quite capable of holding a trench line against superior numbers of infantry backed by heavy artillery. In the end, the allied success had been one of defence and not offence.

The cost to both sides was heavy. It is difficult to estimate the precise German losses, but they were at least 134,300 between 15 October and 24 November, of whom approximately 19,600 were killed. The actual figure may have been considerably greater. Certainly, the reserve corps had lost about half of their infantry. Between 19 and 18 November alone, *Fourth* and *Sixth Armies* sustained 23,500 casualties. It was also claimed at the time that 30,000 Germans had been evacuated wounded from Brussels between 31 October and 2 November.[27] The French lost possibly 50,000–85,000 casualties, the figures being obscured within the 104,000 casualties suffered on the Western Front as a whole in October and November 1914. In October 1914 alone, d'Urbal's Belgian Army Detachment had 7122 casualties and Tenth Army 14,440.[28] Belgian strength in what the distinguished historian C.R.M.F. Cruttwell, himself an officer in the Territorials during the war, memorably called the 'flat, naked and oozy country' had declined from 52,683 effectives to 34,161 between 18 and 30 October, a loss of a third of those who had escaped Antwerp in just twelve days.[29]

Between 14 October and 30 November, the BEF had committed twenty-two cavalry and four yeomanry regiments, eighty-eight regular and seven Territorial battalions and ninety-five artillery batteries to the struggle for Ypres. It had suffered 58,155 casualties, including 7960 dead: of these, 7th Division and I Corps had suffered 21,713 casualties, of whom 2621 had been killed. In most cases, there were barely one officer and 30 men left from those who had arrived in France in August 1914.[30]

In the judgement of James Edmonds, the BEF had been 'incomparably the best trained, best organised and best equipped British Army that ever went forth to war'. He was almost certainly correct, but that small colonial constabulary was no more as a result of what Cruttwell characterised as its 'chief glory'. In November 1914 Sergeant John Lucy of the 2nd Royal Irish Rifles commented on the new face of his battalion after receiving the latest batch of drafts as 'shiftless, half-baked in every way, and the non-commissioned officers were very poor stuff. . . . The old army was finished.' In many ways, it was indeed finished, although its ethos was to survive and so were a few of its old soldiers. Indeed, in March 1916 Lieutenant General Richard Haking, who had been wounded on the Aisne while commanding 5th Brigade and had so missed Ypres, inspected the 2nd Royal Welch Fusiliers. To his delight, Haking, who had just been visiting one of the New Army battalions, discovered many old regulars: 'He chatted and chaffed, pinched their arms and ears, asked how many children they had, and if they could be doing with leave to get another. As he passed from one 1914 man to another he dug his elbow into the CO's ribs and exclaimed, "You're a lucky fellow." When he was over he said to the CO, "That's been a treat. That's the sort we've known for thirty years." ' The lesson, however, was well summarised by Cyril Falls's comment on the BEF: '*Armées d'élite* would be invincible if wars were fought without casualties. Things being what they are, *armées d'élite* are unlikely to remain so for long.'[31]

In another sense, the cost was to be heavier yet. The last occasion upon which Douglas Haig would physically intervene in the 'zone of fire', First Ypres had had the most profound impact upon him. On the one hand, it had secured his reputation, Haig allowing Conan Doyle to see parts of his diary in December 1914 for his history of the campaign in France and Flanders as well as consciously embellishing his role in the version sent to the King.[32] On the other, it had led Haig to certain conclusions. Succeeding French in command of the BEF in December 1915, Haig believed that the German error had been to abandon their Ypres offensive prematurely. He would not make the same mistake for the side that prevailed would be that which 'stuck it out'. Indeed, in one subsequent wartime conference on 2 October 1917 Haig specifically drew attention to the events of 31 October 1914 when the Germans had not seized the opportunity: 'We must be careful not to make the same error.' Thus was the gallantry of the men of the old BEF to unwittingly bequeath a murderous legacy to their successors. Moreover, the ground that they had held at such cost was to take on its own symbolic significance over the course of the next four years.[33]

In part, this was a natural consequence of the continuing concern for the strategic implications of the German control of Ostend and Zeebrugge, including the use of these ports as bases for submarines and destroyers that might threaten the control of the Channel and the BEF's lines of communication between Britain and France. Thus, French and Churchill conceived a plan for an amphibious assault on Ostend and Zeebrugge over the winter of 1914/15. Indeed, at one point in December 1914 the Cabinet requested the relocation of the BEF further to the left to facilitate an advance up the coast, a deployment the French always resisted on political grounds partly so that the British could not exercise influence over the Belgian army.[34] The Zeebrugge plan was ultimately eclipsed by other seemingly more attractive strategic options further afield in January 1915, but the northern flank still beckoned. It was effectively revived by Haig's plans for a Flanders offensive in 1917, by which time the exhaustion of the French had made Britain the more dominant partner in the alliance. Haig was always convinced of the importance of safeguarding the Channel ports, which, coupled with concerns about the supposed submarine menace from Zeebrugge and Ostend, led to ideas for what became the Flanders offensive surfacing in November 1916. Indeed, the plans included a scheme for an amphibious assault on the Belgian coast though this was never to materialise. During the German offensives of spring 1918 it was clear that British and French defensive priorities were different, the French concerned to cover Paris and the British Ypres and the Channel ports. The same issue had also arisen in British minds during the second battle for Ypres in April and May 1915, at which time Kitchener had insisted the BEF maintain contact with the French army.[35]

In the event, a partial withdrawal from the salient proved necessary in the face of the German Flanders offensive in April 1918. An allied offensive on 28 September, symbolically conducted under the overall direction of King Albert commanding an army group comprising the Belgian army, the British Second Army and the French Sixth Army, finally won the ground that had been in the allies' grasp four years earlier. Ostend and Lille fell to the Belgians and British respectively on 17 October and Zeebrugge to the Belgians two days later.

Notes and references

1 Beckett, *Johnnie Gough*, p. 195; JEG Mss, papers on death of Hugh Dawnay; French, *1914*, pp. 278–9; NAM, Rawlinson Mss, 5201-33-17, Rawlinson to Wigram, 10 November 1914; IWM, Home Mss, 82/18/1, diary, 8 November 1914.

2 NLS, Haig Mss, Acc 3155/99, diary, 7 and 8 November 1914; PRO, WO154/18, Landon to Wing, 7 November 1914.

3 J. Brent Wilson (1978), 'The Morale and Discipline of the British Expeditionary Force, 1914–1918', Unpub. MA, University of New Brunswick, pp. 67–117, 212–62; Gerard Oram (2003), *Military Executions During World War I*, Basingstoke: Palgrave, pp. 103–4, 134–8; Bowman, *Irish Regiments*, pp. 50–1, 54–5; Anthony Babington (1983), *For the Sake of Example*, New York: St Martin's Press, pp. 8–9, 24–5; Cathryn Corns and John Hughes-Wilson (2001), *Blindfold and Alone*, London: Cassell, pp. 312–16.

4 Mockler-Ferryman, *OBLI Chronicle*, p. 200; IWM, Trefusis Mss, 82/30/1, diary, 6 and 10 November 1914; ibid., Craig Brown Mss, 92/23/2, diary, 24 October, and 3, 8, 14 and 16 November 1914; ibid., Bremner Mss, 94/17/1, diary, 11 November 1914.

5 *Ypres, 1914*, p. 101.

6 *Armées Françaises* I, Pt. IV, p. 279; Joffre, *Memoirs*, I, p. 316.

7 *Ypres, 1914*, p. 103.

8 Craster, *Fifteen Rounds*, p. 134.

9 PRO, CAB45/141, Rochfort-Boyd Account and Thorne Account (also in CAB45/143).

10 IWM, Craig Brown Mss, 92/23/2, 4/3, Account of Nonnebosschen, 2 November 1915.

11 IWM, Mowbray Mss, 82/16/1, memoir, 11 November 1914; OFH, p. 439, n. 1.

12 NLS, Haig Mss, Acc 3155/99, diary, 11 November 1914.

13 Mockler-Ferryman, *OBLI Chronicle*, p. 202 quoting Davies.

14 OFH p. 441; IWM, 87/26/1, Spencer diary, 11 November 1914; PRO, CAB45/143, Hume to Edmonds, 14 April 1924.

15 Craster, *Fifteen Rounds*, pp. 138, 151–2; IWM, Trefusis Mss, 82/30/1, diary, 12 November 1914; X, 'Gheluvelt 1914', pp. 209–21; Mockler-Ferryman, *OBLI Chronicle*, p. 203; PRO, CAB45/141, Thorne Account.

16 LUBLLC, Osborne Mss, GS1206, journal, 11 November 1914; JEG Mss, Collins to Dorothea Gough, 24 April 1941.

17 OFH, p. 449; PRO WO256/2 Haig diary 18 November 1914; de Groot, *Douglas Haig*, p. 168.

18 IWM, Home Mss, 82/18/1, diary, 12 November 1914.

19 IWM, French Mss, PP/MCR/C32, diary, 12 November 1914; *Ypres, 1914*, p. 124.

20 IWM, Horne Mss, 52/54/10, diary, 14 November 1914; Afflerbach, *Falkenhayn*, pp. 195–7; Gerhard Ritter (1972), *The Sword and the Sceptre*, ibid., III, Coral Gables: University of Miami Press, pp. 44, 50, 68; *Der Weltkrieg*, V, pp. 347–50; VI, p. 437; Foley, 'East or West', pp. 117–38.

21 D.J. Harrison (1984), 'Jack Dimmer VC', *Stand To* 12, pp. 18–20.

22 Chamard, 'Zonnebeke', pp. 103–41; Beckett, *Johnnie Gough*, p. 196; JEG Mss, Corps Operational Narrative.

23 SHAT, 18N 134, French to Foch, 16 November and 18 November 1914; Anglesey, *History of Cavalry*, p. 215; Foch, *Memoirs*, p. 175.

24 NAM, Waddy Mss, 8311-71-1, Account of First Ypres.

25 Willson, *Ypres*, pp. 44–5; Barry Bryan (ed.) (1915), *The Irish Nuns at Ypres*, London: Smith, Elder & Co, pp. 75–6; Dominiek Dendooven and Jan Dewilde (1999), *The Reconstruction of Ieper*, Ieper: Openbaar Kunstbezit in Vlaanderen, p. 51; *Ypres, 1914*, p. 15. Only Private George Whitehead of the 1st Loyals is listed on the Menin Gate for 23 October 1914.

26 OFH, p. 464.

27 OFH, pp. 467–8; *Der Weltkrieg*, V, p. 401; ibid., VI, p. 25; Dauzet, *Bataille des Flandres*, p. 119.

28 Ratinaud, *Course*, p. 324; Palat, *Ruée vers Calais*, pp. 358–9; *Armées Françaises* I, Pt. IV, p. 554.

29 Cammaerts, *Albert of Belgium*, p. 200; C.R.M.F. Cruttwell (1991), *A History of the Great War, 1914–18*, 2nd edn., Chicago: Academy Chicago, p. 100.

30 Ascoli, *Mons Star*, p. 191, n. 6; French, *1914*, p. 292; OFH, p. 465.

31 OFH 1914 , I, pp. 10–11; Cruttwell, *Great War*, p. 106; Lucy, *Devil in a Drum*, p. 293; *War Infantry Knew*, p. 185; Cyril Falls (1967), *The First World War*, London: Longman, p. 16.

32 Gardner, *Trial by Fire*, pp. 228–30.

33 LHCMA, Liddell Hart Mss, I/162, Charteris to Liddell Hart, 11 October 1935; Occleshaw, *Armour Against Fate*, p. 342; Shelford Bidwell and Dominick Graham (1982), *Firepower: British Army Weapons and Theories of War, 1904–45*, London: Allen & Unwin, p. 69; de Groot, *Douglas Haig*, pp. 166–7.

34 Philpott, *Anglo-French Relations*, pp. 54–66, 106–8.

35 Philpott, *Anglo-French Relations*, pp. 106–7, 129–49.

Conclusion:
The immortal salient

The remaining civilian population of Ypres had been finally evacuated in May 1915 in the wake of the second battle for the town. By 1918 only a handful of buildings remained. A come-back subsidy was instituted in July 1919 and there were 6000 people back in Ypres by 1920 though less than half had been residents at the war's start. The Belgian artist and war veteran Alfred Bastien commenced work on a panorama of the battle of the Yser that same year, which included a scene of the Cloth Hall and St Martin's Church in flames on 22 November 1914. The town was also awarded the French Croix de Guerre with Golden Palm on 20 January 1920 and the British Military Cross on 19 May 1920.

There were differing views, however, on what should happen to Ypres. One architect, Eugène Dhuicque, appointed by the Belgian government in 1915 to save what he could from those Belgian towns in the front line favoured retaining the ruins, which spoke 'with an eloquence and relief, which no inscription will ever equal of the fierce resistance of an entire race'. His fellow architect, Jules Coomans, criticised those calling for a 'zone of silence' around the Cloth Hall, the Belfry and St Martin's Church on the grounds that misfortune was to be turned into pleasure 'on the pretext of giving them artistic emotions which they wish to enjoy in comfort'. Coomans had been the pre-war town architect tasked in 1895 with a full restoration programme, which had been just about complete by August 1914. As early as 1916, Coomans had begun agitating for a post-war reconstruction, restoring the medieval appearance. Other Belgian modernist architects suggested rebuilding the town in modern style.[1]

The British perspective was projected by the Town Major of Ypres, Lieutenant Colonel Beckles Willson, whose *Ypres: The Holy Ground of the British Army* was published in 1920. Willson was adamant that the ruins must be preserved as they were 'an eternal memorial of British valour', equivalent to Jerusalem for Jews and Mecca for Muslims. To Willson, in Ypres, there was not a 'single half acre that is not sacred'. Similarly, John Buchan had also suggested that the death roll of the sons of prominent families at First Ypres such as Wyndham, Dawnay, Fitzclarence, Wellesley, Cadogan, Cavendish, Bruce, Gordon-Lennox, Fraser, Kinnaird, Hay and Hamilton was 'like scanning the death roll after Agincourt or Flodden'. Apart from Hubert Hamilton and Fitzclarence, another brigadier and eighteen battalion commanding officers had been killed.[2]

For all the suffering associated with the second and third battles for Ypres, it was therefore that first struggle in October and November 1914 that had caught Willson's imagination. Actually a Canadian, Willson envisaged each of the first seven divisions of the old regular army that had fought at Ypres in 1914 having their own memorials in a great marble chapel to be erected opposite the ruins of the Cloth Hall while their cemeteries 'would range along the streets by the eastern Menin Gate, whose cobblestones are worn by the tramp during those four years of our infantry and the restless wheels of our guns'. In pursuance of his grand scheme, Willson did all he could to prevent any rebuilding or repairs. He was especially exercised by the appearance of huts catering for the already developing pilgrimage trade, complaining in July 1919 about six new estaminets, one of which 'is painted sky-blue, boldly calls itself "The British Tavern", which exposes us daily to the rebuke of Belgian and French visitors, who think we are responsible'. Willson also had notices erected on the ruins proclaiming, 'This is Holy Ground! No stone of this fabric to be taken away. It is a heritage for all civilised people.'[3] Willson, however, had also managed to have a smart bungalow for himself erected on the ramparts supposedly as a Canadian information centre, causing the Battle Exploits Memorials Committee in London and the Imperial War Graves Commission to query Willson's precise status with respect to the Canadian government. Willson was promptly demobilised, but then went on a lecture tour in Britain in November 1919 to publicise his vision, inspiring the creation of the Ypres League in 1920.[4]

There were others, however, who shared Willson's vision in some respects. In January 1919 Churchill, then Secretary of State for War and Air, but acting in his capacity as chairman of the governing body of the Imperial War Graves Commission, proposed acquiring the whole of the ruins of the town as a place of pilgrimage. Anticipating difficulties, Fabian Ware, the director of the Commission, tried to temper Churchill's enthusiasm. In July 1919 a delegation from the Battle Exploit Memorials Committee visited Ypres. It learned that the Belgian government itself was minded to preserve the ruins of the Cloth Hall and St Martin's Church but to restore the remainder of the town. The British would be permitted to fence off the area pending a final decision on the nature of the monuments to be erected.[5]

This was not acceptable to the burgomaster, René Colaert, and those who owned properties adjacent to the Grote Markt and the British moved quickly to send sufficient materials for the fences though these were to be erected by the City Council. Meanwhile, on grounds of cost, support was growing for a British monument on the ramparts rather than on the Grote Markt, an idea embraced by Sir Reginald Blomfield, the designated architect for the British monument. It was also endorsed by the new National Battlefield Memorials Committee, whose remit was wider than that of the existing War Office Battle Exploits Memorials Committee. Public opinion still appeared to support the notion of preserving the ruins. In fact, the Cabinet briefly considered protesting to the Belgian government about the scale of reconstruction already under way: not all the ruins had been fenced off, the Belgians having declined to recognise the decision taken locally when the British delegation had visited Ypres back in July. In any case, the Belgian government could not afford compulsory purchase of the land in the town centre and was increasingly tending towards supporting Colaert and the inhabitants. The British tended to view those Belgians in favour of preserving the ruins as 'the educated and well-informed opinion of Belgium' and the locals as older Ypres families anxious to rebuild. Once reconstruction began, the British feared the ruins 'will have to be pulled down for every reason, artistic or otherwise, and, once down, an agitation will be set a foot for money with which to rebuild'.[6]

The dispute continued through 1920, Colaert at one point suggesting that the rebuilding of the Cloth Hall by the British government would be the most suitable monument. Field Marshal Lord Plumer was enlisted to try to put pressure on the Belgians, to which the Belgian government responded by inviting the British to say exactly what they wanted preserved in the salient as a whole. In July 1920 the Army Council produced a list including the Cloth Hall, St Martin's, the Lille Gate and the Menin Gate. The waters were further muddied by the Ypres League suggesting a 'foreign' tower-like structure over the Menin Gate, to which the Belgians objected when the British were declining to see the Cloth Hall reconstructed. In the end, however, it was the refusal of the British to put up any actual money even for preservation of the ruins that effectively ended the debate. In April

1921, therefore, the British government formally withdrew its request for a British monument on the Grote Markt and stated that, in consequence, the Belgians had no obligation to preserve the Cloth Hall in its ruined state.[7]

Slowly life returned to Ypres, work on the Cloth Hall commencing in 1928, St Martin's Church being finished by 1930. The rebuilt belfry was unveiled in 1934 though the wing of the Cloth Hall housing the Town Hall was only completed in 1967.[8] St George's Memorial Church, organised by the Ypres League, had its foundation stone laid on 24 July 1927 by Plumer, an hour after the unveiling of the Menin Gate, Blomfield's masterpiece. Originally, it was intended that the Menin Gate should commemorate those missing during the first battle of Ypres, specifically from 19 October to 22 November 1914 but, subsequently, it was decided to commemorate all those missing in the salient up to 14 August 1917. Further memorials were erected at Tyne Cot for the period after 15 August 1917 and at Ploegsteert for those missing in the Ploegsteert-Armentières sector. The celebrated playing of the Last Post at the Menin Gate began in July 1928 and, since May 1929, has only been interrupted during the German occupation of Ypres between May 1940 and September 1944.

The number of visitors to Ypres, especially after the opening of the Menin Gate, remained high throughout the inter-war period. In July and August 1928, for example, over 23,000 people signed the visitor's book at the Menin Gate, the latter month one in which the British Legion organised the largest of the battlefield pilgrimages. A five-day visit by some 11,000 people culminated in a memorial service at the Menin Gate while others travelled independently so that an estimated 20,000 people attended the service, which was also broadcast by the BBC. The visitor's book similarly recorded 18,832 names in August 1936 and 37,000 for 1937 as a whole.

Apart from the neat and familiar green signs of the Commonwealth War Graves Commission and the beautifully maintained cemeteries, many of which relate only to the later struggles around Ypres, little remains of the 1914 battle. The reconstructed Gheluvelt Chateau is in private hands and not open to the public, while the White Chateau and Hooge Chateau have both disappeared. The latter has gone beneath the Bellewaarde leisure park though the chapel remains and houses a small privately run war museum. At Gheluvelt, the memorials to the Worcesters and the South Wales Borderers are almost hidden down a small lane across the road from the village square. At least the memorial to the London Scottish on the open road between Wytschaete and Messines is rather more prominent. There is also the memorial to the Household Cavalry at Zandvoorde and to the 7th Division at Broodseine. Though it was their victory, too, the French did not choose to locate one of their five large national ossuaries in the salient, all understandably being on French soil. However, there is a French memorial in St Martin's and a plaque on the Cloth Hall and a memorial and small ossuary at Kemmel relating to the battle there in April 1918. The only truly national Belgian monument to the Yser is the equestrian statue of King Albert near the sluices at Nieuport, the Flemish Tower in Dixmude having been a matter of some controversy to the extent that it was at one stage blown up in mysterious circumstances after the Second World War. There is a Flemish Memorial Crypt in Zonnebeke Cemetery, however, as well as a Belgian memorial in Ypres.[9]

Ypres, however, was not just sacred ground to the British for the *kindermord* had had a profound impact in Germany. This was especially among conservative and nationalist circles though an equally mythic view of the Franco-German struggle at Verdun between February and November 1916 was arguably closer to fascist visions of a modernistic machine-age conflict. After a campaign for its restoration after some years of neglect, the German cemetery at Langemarck was rededicated in July 1932, the cemetery commemorating 45,000 Germans killed in the Ypres sector during the war as a whole. The address of the author and Nazi sympathiser, Josef Wehner, was simultaneously read at ceremonies in all German universities. According to Wehner, the 'stormers sang as they were being annihilated: "Deutschland, Deutschland über Alles, über Alles in der Welt". But by singing this song, they were resurrected once more, a thousand times, and they will rise again a thousand times until the end of the Reich.' Subsequently, the address was issued in a schools edition for dissemination to youths throughout Nazi Germany. Similarly, another author, Siegmund Graff, characterised Langemarck as 'the beginning of a new epoch of German history' and a third, Hans Schwarz, had his reflections on the meaning of German history from an address on Langemarck given at the University of Greifswald in 1928 widely distributed.

As suggested earlier, the myth of Langemarck had been begun by the official OHL communiqué on 11 November 1914, notably the emphasis upon the singing of patriotic songs. As early as November 1915 the German press commemorated the supposedly youthful sacrifice, while the Kaiser referred to the episode when reviewing the *205th Infantry Regiment* in January 1916 and the communiqué also surfaced in a wartime history by Hermann Stegeman. So, too, did Langemarck figure in the semi-official German history of the Ypres battle published by Otto Schwink in 1917, an essentially popular account which regarded Ypres as 'a memorial to German courage and the spirit of self-sacrifice around which history and poetry will grow'. A reservist captain who served in *Fourth Army*, Schwink also claimed that the British and French had 'installed their best troops in deep trenches' so that 'every wood, every village or house, every large wood alike gained a bloody celebrity'.

Equally, Philipp Witkop's edition of the war letters of fallen German students published in 1928 celebrated the spirit of Langemarck although also illustrated something of the increasing disillusionment among such young soldiers following the heavy losses. Even the formal German Official History, the Ypres volume of which was published in 1929, referred to the troops singing though without specifying locations or giving sources. The publication of the latter, of course, predated the Nazis coming to power but, even in the Weimar Republic, Langemarck was used as a symbol of nationalism and rejection of the terms imposed upon Germany in 1919, particular celebrations being organised in 1924, 1928 and 1932. The Nazis quickly assimilated the myth as their own, members of the SA attending the rededication of the cemetery at Langemarck in 1932, those regimental histories appearing after 1933 also choosing to stress the 'spirit of Langemarck'. From 1934 onwards, the Hitler Youth became responsible for annual commemoration of Langemarck, involving annual telegrams to Hitler from the organisation, though Hitler's own messages in reply were invariably brief, Langemarck serving the use of the cult of youth as a means of integrating Nazi ideals with traditional power elites.

In 1938 the organisation instituted a compulsory monthly collection, known as the Langemarck Pfennig, to support commemoration activities while there was also a Langemarck Studium, a programme to support students who were acceptable on academic and ideological grounds but unable to support themselves financially at university. Two years earlier, a Langemarck cantata had also been specially composed. During the Second World War, the SS fielded a Langemarck Grenadier Division and, in one broadcast to the encircled *Sixth Army* in Stalingrad in January 1943, Goering also invoked Langemarck as an example of sacrifice. Increasingly, however, Verdun and the 'spirit of the front' had superseded Langemarck as a more suitable model for the idealised warrior of the machine age.[10]

Significantly, on 1 June 1940, a few days after the Germans had occupied Ypres, Hitler visited the town, pausing at the Menin Gate then driving on to the German cemetery at Langemarck. Hitler returned to Ypres on 26 June, accompanied by Goering and the Japanese ambassador to Berlin.[11]

A different German perspective was that of Käthe Kollwitz, whose striking impressionist sculpture of mourning parents, placed at the Vladlso cemetery in 1932, commemorated her son, Peter, killed nearby at Dixmude on 23 October 1914. Kollwitz's vision of war differed also from that of traditional British battle artists such as J.P. Beadle, W.B. Wollen and Fortunio Matania, all of whom produced heroic images of First Ypres. As suggested earlier, it was in many ways a very traditional battle and, though the British survivors had learned lessons, they had done so in the context of a defensive battle. Mounting an offensive from a trench system was not the same thing and the Ypres experience meant relatively little in terms of the army's 'learning curve'. Moreover, the losses of experienced officers and men was hardly helpful.

As is well known, every year farmers in France and Belgium still confront an 'iron harvest' of shells and other wartime debris along the old front line. Bodies are also routinely discovered. In October 2001 such a skeleton was discovered with, unusually, the identity disc intact, the first identifiable body to be recovered in Belgium in 20 years. It proved to be that of Private Harry Wilkinson of the 2nd Lancashire Fusiliers (12th Brigade, 4th Division), a former fire-beater in a Bury cotton mill.[12] He had been recorded as missing after a six-company counter-attack carried out on a group of houses in front of Ploegsteert Wood at 2330 hours on 9 November 1914. The attack had been undertaken by two companies from the Lancashire Fusiliers, and two each from the 1st East Lancashires (11th Brigade, 4th Division) and the 2nd Argyll and Sutherland Highlanders (19th Brigade, 6th Division). Beyond the short paragraph describing this small action, the Official History states that elsewhere 'there is nothing to record except reliefs', having already characterised the day on the III Corps front as 'uneventful'.[13] No less than many others of the old British regular army and their Belgian and French allies, however, Wilkinson had given his life to keep the Germans from the Channel coast. While this and the defence of Belgium had not been necessarily a British obligation, it had assuredly been in the British national interest. The allied victory had been a true soldiers' battle, albeit won at great cost and with undoubted consequences for the future of the war on the Western Front. But then freedom has rarely been won cheaply.

Notes and references

1 'Guide to Quotations', In Flanders Fields Museum, Ypres, p. 36; Dendooven, *Menin Gate*, pp. 9–11.

2 Willson, *Ypres*, pp. xiii; 47; John Buchan (1922), *A History of the Great War*, I, London: Thomas Nelson & Sons, p. 368.

3 PRO, WO32/5569, Willson to de Broqueville, 5 July 1919; ibid., Willson to French, 6 July 1919; Dendooven, *Menin Gate*, p. 30.

4 Dendooven, *Menin Gate*, pp. 28–32.

5 Dendooven, *Menin Gate*, pp. 12–23; PRO, WO32/5569, Minutes of Conference, 14 July 1919.

6 PRO, WO32/5569, Spicer to Battlefields Exploits Memorial Committee, 29 April 1920.

7 PRO, WO32/5569, Phipps to Villiers, 22 July 1920, Parr to Curzon, 2 August 1920; Creedy to Ingpen, 30 July 1920; Grahame to Curzon, 4 November 1920; Dendooven, *Menin Gate*, pp. 32–6, 40–52.

8 Dendooven and Dewilde, *Reconstruction of Ieper*, pp. 7–15.

9 David Lloyd (1998), *Battlefield Tourism: Pilgrimage and Commemoration of the Great War in Britain, Australia and Canada, 1919–39*, Oxford: Berg, pp. 19–48, 101–30, 134–79; Dendooven, *Menin Gate*, p. 89; Mark Derez (1997), 'A Belgian Salient for Reconstruction: People and Patrie, Landscape and Memory' in Peter Liddle (ed.), *Passchendaele in Perspective*, pp. 437–58.

10 Fox, 'Myths of Langemarck', pp. 13–25; Hüppauf, 'Langemarck, Verdun and Myth of New Man', pp. 70–103; Otto Schwink, *La Bataille de L'Yser* (Brussels: Cartographic Institute of the Belgian Army, 1919), p. 31; Unruh, *Langemarck*, pp. 1–17, 61, 169–72, 187–97.

11 H. Bourgeois (1987), 'Hitler et la région de Comines-Warneton en 1914–1918 et en 1940' in *Mémoires de la Société d'Histoire de Comines-Warneton et de la Région*, 17, pp. 381–438.

12 *Daily Telegraph* 1 November 2001, p. 17.

13 OFH, pp. 409–10.

Orders of battle

British Expeditionary Force (October 1914)

Field Marshal Sir John French

I Corps (Haig)

1st Division (Lomax)

1st (Guards) Brigade: 1st Coldstream Guards, 1st Scots Guards, 1st Black Watch, 1st Cameron Highlanders, 1/14th London Regiment (London Scottish).

2nd Brigade: 2nd Royal Sussex Regiment, 1st Loyal North Lancashire Regiment, 1st Northamptonshire Regiment, 2nd King's Royal Rifle Corps.

3rd Brigade: 1st Queen's Regiment, 1st South Wales Borderers, 1st Gloucestershire Regiment, 2nd Welch Regiment.

Mounted Troops: A Squadron, 15th Hussars, 1st Cyclist Company.

Artillery: XXV, XXVI, XXXIX Brigades RFA, XLIII (Howitzer) Brigade RFA, 26th Heavy Battery, RGA.

Engineers: 23rd and 26th Field Companies RE.

2nd Division (Monro)

4th (Guards) Brigade: 2nd Grenadier Guards, 2nd and 3rd Coldstream Guards, 1st Irish Guards.

5th Brigade: 2nd Worcestershire Regiment, 2nd Oxfordshire and Buckinghamshire Light Infantry, 2nd Connaught Rangers, 2nd Highland Light Infantry.

6th Brigade: 1st King's, 2nd South Staffordshire Regiment, 1st Royal Berkshire Regiment, 1st King's Royal Rifle Corps.

Mounted Troops: B Squadron, 15th Hussars, 2nd Cyclist Company.

Artillery: XXXIV, XXXVI and XLI Brigades RFA, XLIV (Howitzer) Brigade RFA, 35th Heavy Battery RGA.

Engineers: 5th and 11th Field Companies RE.

II Corps (Smith-Dorrien)

3rd Division (Hamilton/Mackenzie/Wing)

7th Brigade: 3rd Worcestershire Regiment, 2nd South Lancashire Regiment, 1st Wiltshire Regiment, 2nd Royal Irish Rifles.

8th Brigade: 2nd Royal Scots, 2nd Royal Irish Regiment, 4th Middlesex Regiment, 1st Devonshire Regiment.

9th Brigade: 1st Northumberland Fusiliers, 4th Royal Fusiliers, 1st Lincolnshire Regiment, 1st Royal Scots Fusiliers.

Mounted Troops: C Squadron, 15th Hussars, 3rd Cyclist Company.

Artillery: XXIII, XL and XLII Brigades RFA, XXX (Howitzer) Brigade RFA, 48th Heavy Battery RA.

5th Division (Fergusson/Morland)

13th Brigade: 2nd King's Own Scottish Borderers, 2nd Duke of Wellington's, 1st Queen's Own Royal West Kent Regiment, 2nd King's Own (Yorkshire Light Infantry).

14th Brigade: 2nd Suffolk Regiment, 1st East Surrey Regiment, 1st Duke of Cornwall's Light Infantry, 2nd Manchester Regiment.

15th Brigade: 1st Royal Norfolk Regiment, 1st Bedfordshire Regiment, 1st Cheshire Regiment, 1st Dorset Regiment.

Mounted Troops: A Squadron, 19th Hussars, 5th Cyclist Company.

Artillery: XV, XXVII and XXVIII Brigades RFA, VIII (Howitzer) Brigade RFA, 108th Heavy Battery RGA.

Engineers: 17th and 59th Field Companies RE.

III Corps (Pulteney)

4th Division (Wilson)

10th Brigade: 1st Royal Warwickshire Regiment, 2nd Seaforth Highlanders, 1st Royal Irish Fusiliers, 2nd Royal Dublin Fusiliers.

11th Brigade: 1st Somerset Light Infantry, 1st Hampshire Regiment, 1st Rifle Brigade, 1st East Lancashire Regiment.

12th Brigade: 1st King's Own (Royal Lancaster Regiment), 2nd Lancashire Fusiliers, 2nd Inniskilling Fusiliers, 2nd Essex Regiment.

Mounted Troops: B Squadron, 19th Hussars, 4th Cyclist Company.

Artillery: XIV, XXIX and XXXII Brigades RFA, XXXVII (Howitzer) Brigade RFA, 31st Heavy Battery RGA.

Engineers: 7th and 9th Field Companies RE.

6th Division (Keir)

16th Brigade: 1st The Buffs, 1st Leicestershire Regiment, 1st King's Shropshire Light Infantry, 2nd York and Lancaster Regiment.

17th Brigade: 1st Royal Fusiliers, 1st North Staffordshire Regiment, 2nd Prince of Wales's Leinster Regiment, 3rd Rifle Brigade.

18th Brigade: 1st West Yorkshire Regiment, 1st East Yorkshire Regiment, 2nd Sherwood Foresters, 2nd Durham Light Infantry.

19th Brigade: 2nd Royal Welch Fusiliers, 1st Cameronians, 1st Middlesex Regiment, 2nd Argyll and Sutherland Highlanders.

Mounted Troops: C Squadron, 19th Hussars, 6th Cyclist Company.

Artillery: II, XXIV and XXXVIII Brigades RFA, XII (Howitzer) Brigade RFA, 24th Heavy Battery RGA.

Engineers: 12th and 38th Field Companies RE.

IV Corps (Rawlinson)

7th Division (Capper)

20th Brigade: 1st Grenadier Guards, 2nd Scots Guards, 2nd Rifle Brigade, 2nd Gordon Highlanders.

21st Brigade: 2nd Bedfordshire Regiment, 2nd Alexandra, Princess of Wales's Own (Green Howards), 2nd Royal Scots Fusiliers, 2nd Wiltshire Regiment.

22nd Brigade: 2nd Queen's, 2nd Royal Warwickshire Regiment, 1st Royal Welch Fusiliers, 1st South Staffordshire Regiment.

Mounted Troops: Northumberland Hussars.

Artillery: XIV Brigade RHA, XXII and XXXV Brigades RFA, 111th and 112th Heavy Batteries RGA.

Engineers: 54th and 55th Field Companies RE.

3rd Cavalry Division (Byng)

6th Cavalry Brigade: 3rd Dragoon Guards, 1st Royal Dragoons, 10th Hussars.

7th Cavalry Brigade: 1st and 2nd Life Guards, Royal Horse Guards.

Artillery: XV Brigade RHA.

Engineers: 3rd Field Squadron RE.

Cavalry Corps (Allenby)

1st Cavalry Division (de Lisle)
1st Cavalry Brigade: 2nd Dragoon Guards, 5th Dragoon Guards, 11th Hussars.

2nd Cavalry Brigade: 4th Dragoon Guards, 9th Lancers, 18th Hussars.

Artillery: VII Brigade RHA.

Engineers: 1st Field Squadron RE.

2nd Cavalry Division (Gough)
3rd Cavalry Brigade: 4th Hussars, 5th Lancers, 16th Lancers.

4th Cavalry Brigade: 6th Dragoon Guards, 3rd Hussars, Household Cavalry Composite Regiment, 1/1st Queen's Own Oxfordshire Hussars.

Artillery: III Brigade RHA.

Engineers: 2nd Field Squadron RE.

Indian Corps (Willcocks)

Lahore Division (Watkis)
Ferozepore Brigade: 1st Connaught Rangers, 9th Bhopal Infantry, 57th Wilde's Rifles, 129th Baluchis.

Jullundur Brigade: 1st Manchester Regiment, 47th Sikhs, 59th Scinde Rifles.

Mounted Troops: 15th Lancers (Cureton's Multanis).

Artillery: XVIII Brigade RFA, 109th Heavy Battery RGA.

Engineers: 20th and 21st Companies, 3rd Sappers and Miners.

Meerut Division (Anderson)
Dehra Dun Brigade: 1st Seaforth Highlanders, 6th Jat Light Infantry, 2/2nd Gurkha Rifles, 1/9th Gurkha Rifles.

Garhwal Brigade: 2nd Leicestershire Regiment, 1/39th and 2/39th Garhwal Rifles, 2/3rd Gurkha Rifles.

Bareilly Brigade: 2nd Black Watch, 41st Dogras, 58th Vaughan's Rifles, 2/8th Gurkha Rifles.

Mounted Troops: 4th Cavalry.

Artillery: IV, IX and XIII Brigades RFA, 11th Heavy Battery RGA.

Engineers: 3rd and 4th Companies, 1st King George's Own Sappers and Miners.

French Army (November 1914)

Détachement d'Armée de Belgique (d'Urbal)

IX Corps (Dubois)

17th Division: 33rd, 34th and 304th Brigades.

18th Division: 35th and 36th Brigades

6th Cavalry Division: 5th (Cuirassier), 6th (Dragoon) and 6th (Light) Brigades.

7th Cavalry Division: 6th (Cuirassier), 1st (Dragoon) and 7th (Light) Brigades.

XVI Corps (Grossetti)

31st Division: 61st and 62nd Brigades.

32nd Division: 63rd and 64th Brigades.

39th Division: 77th and 78th Brigades.

43rd Division: 85th and 86th Brigades.

XXXII Corps (Humbert)

38th Division: 75th and 76th Brigades.

42nd Division: 83rd and 84th Brigades.

89th (Territorial) Division: 177th and 178th Brigades.

4th Cavalry Division: 3rd (Cuirassier), 4th (Dragoon) and 4th (Light) Brigades.

Marine Fusilier Brigade.

XX Corps (Balfourier)

11th Division: 21st and 22nd Brigades.

26th Division: 51st and 52nd Brigades.

I Cavalry Corps (Conneau)

1st Cavalry Division: 2nd (Cuirassier), 5th and 11th (Dragoon) Brigades.

3rd Cavalry Division: 3rd Light, 4th (Cuirassier), and 13th (Dragoon) Brigades.

10th Cavalry Division: 10th and 15th (Dragoon) Brigades.

II Cavalry Corps (de Mitry)

87th (Territorial) Division: 173rd and 174th Brigades.

5th Cavalry Division: 3rd (Cuirassier), 7th (Dragoon) and 5th (Light) Brigades.

9th Cavalry Division: 1st (Cuirassier), 9th and 16th (Dragoon) Brigades.

German Army (October–November 1914)

Fourth Army (Albrecht)

III Reserve Corps (Beseler)

5th and 6th Reserve Divisions.

4th Ersatz Division.

XXII Reserve Corps (Falkenhayn)

43rd and 44th Reserve Divisions.

XXIII Reserve Corps (Kleist)

45th and 46th Reserve Divisions.

XXVI Reserve Corps (Hügel)

51st and 52nd Reserve Divisions.

XXVII Reserve Corps (Carlowitz/Schubert)

53rd and 54th Reserve Divisions.

Attached at Times

9th Reserve Division.

6th Bavarian Reserve Division.

Marine Division.

Sixth Army (Rupprecht)

II Corps (Linsingen)
3rd and 4th Divisions.

VII Corps (Clear)
13th and 14th Divisions.

XIII Corps (Fabeck)
26th Division.
25th Reserve Division.

XIX (Saxon) Corps (Laffert)
24th and 40th Divisions.

XIV Reserve Corps (Loden)
26th Reserve Division.
6th Bavarian Reserve Division.

Army Group Fabeck

XV Corps (Deimling)
30th and 39th Divisions.

II Bavarian Corps (Martini)
3rd and 4th Bavarian Divisions.

26th Division (from XIII Corps).

Group Gerok
3rd Division.
6th Bavarian Reserve Division.
11th Landwehr Brigade.
25th Reserve Division.

Army Group Linsingen

XV Corps (from Group Fabeck)

Plettenberg's Corps (Plettenberg)
4th Division (from II Corps).
Composite Guards Division.

Cavalry

I Cavalry Corps (Richthofen)
Guards and 4th Cavalry Divisions.

II Cavalry Corps (Marwitz)
2nd and 7th Cavalry Divisions.

IV Cavalry Corps (Hollen)
6th and 9th Cavalry Divisions.

V Cavalry Corps (Stetten)
3rd Cavalry Division.
Bavarian Cavalry Division.

Bibliography

Manuscripts

British Library, London

Hunter-Weston Mss

Churchill College Archives Centre, Cambridge

Rawlinson Mss

Imperial War Museum, London

Baines Mss

Bremner Mss

Craig Brown Mss

Dillon Mss

Edgington Mss

Fleming Mss

French Mss

Garwood Mss

Geddes Mss

Home Mss

Horne Mss

Jackson Mss

Knight Mss

Loch Mss

Lomax Mss

Milton Mss

Misc Mss

Mowbray Mss

Owen Mss

Owens Mss

Paterson Mss

Price-Davies Mss

Quinton Mss

Rees Mss

Reeve Mss

St John Mss

Scott-Tucker Mss

Simpson Mss

Smallman Mss

Smith-Dorrien Mss

Snow Mss

Spencer Mss

Thorne Mss

Trefusis Mss

Henry Wilson Mss

J.K. Wilson Mss

Leeds University Brotherton Library – Liddle Collection

Acland Mss

Bradshaw Mss

Green Mss

McDougall Mss

Moffat Mss

Osborne Mss

Patterson Mss

Ritchie Mss

Saumarez Mss

Liddell Hart Centre for Military Archives, King's College, London

Clive Mss

Edmonds Mss

Liddell Hart Mss

National Archives (formerly Public Record Office), Kew

CAB44 (Material on Official Histories)

CAB45 (Material on Official Histories)

CAB103 (Cabinet Office Historical Section Papers)

PRO30/57 (Kitchener Mss)

WO32 (War Office Miscellaneous)

WO79/62 (Murray Mss)

WO95 (War Diaries)

WO138 (Selected Personnel Files)

WO153 (Maps and Plans)

WO154 (Supplementary War Diaries)

WO157 (Intelligence Summaries)

WO158 (Military Headquarters Papers)

WO159 (Kitchener Private Office Papers)

WO256 (Haig Diaries)

National Archives (US), College Park, Maryland

RG165 Reports of US Military Attachés

National Army Museum, London

Hunter-Weston Mss

Rawlinson Mss

Thorne Mss.

Waddy Mss

National Library of Scotland, Edinburgh

Haig Mss

Private collections

Hubert Gough Mss

John Gough Mss

Royal Archives, Windsor Castle

King George V Mss

Service historique de l'armée de terre, Vincennes

18N 134

1K 268

Books

Official publications

Belgian Army (1915), *The War of 1914: Military Operations of Belgium*, London: W.H. & L. Collingridge.

Edmonds, Sir James (1925), *Official History of the Great War: Military Operations France and Belgium, 1914: Volume II: Antwerp, La Bassée, Armentières, Messines and Ypres, October-November 1914*, London: HMSO.

Ministère de la Guerre, État-Major de l'Armée – Service Historique (1934), *Les Armées Françaises dans la Grande Guerre*, Volume I, Part IV, Paris: Imprimerie Nationale.

Raleigh, Walter (1922), *The War in the Air*, Volume I, London: HMSO.

Reichsarchiv (1929), *Der Weltkrieg, 1914–1918*, Volume V, Berlin: Mittler & Sohn.

Ypres, 1914: An Official Account published by Order of the German General Staff (1919), London: Constable.

Divisional and regimental histories

Atkinson, C.T. (1927), *The Seventh Division, 1914–1918*, London: John Murray.

Dunn, J.C. (ed.) (1987), *The War the Infantry Knew, 1914–19*, 2nd edn., London: Jane's.

Gleichen, Count Edward (1917), *The Doings of the Fifteenth Infantry Brigade, August 1914 to March 1915*, London: Blackwood.

Hamilton, Lord Ernest (1916), *The First Seven Divisions*, London: Hurst and Blackett.

Lindsay, J.H. (1925), *The London Scottish in the Great War*, London: Regimental Headquarters.

Marsden, T.O. (1920), *A Short History the Sixth Division, 1914–18*, London: Hugh Rees.

Mockler-Ferryman, A.F. (ed.) (1920), *The Oxfordshire and Buckinghamshire Light Infantry Chronicle, 1914–1915*, London: Eyre and Spottiswoode.

Wyrall, Everard (1921), *The History of the Second Division, 1914–18*, London: Thomas Nelson & Sons.

Memoirs, biographies and printed primary sources

Afflerbach, Holger (1996), *Falkenhayn: Politisches Denken und Handeln im Kaiserreich*, 2nd edn., Munich: R Oldenbourg Verlag.

Aston, Sir George (1930), *The Biography of the Late Marshal Foch*, London: Hutchinson.

Beckett, Ian F.W. (1989), *Johnnie Gough VC*, London: Tom Donovan.

Beckett, Ian F.W. (ed.) (1993), *The Judgement of History: Sir Horace Smith-Dorrien, Lord French and 1914*, London: Tom Donovan.

Binding, Rudolf (1929), *A Fatalist at War*, London: Allen & Unwin.

Brock, Michael, and Brock, Eleanor (eds.) (1982), *H.H. Asquith: Letters to Venetia Stanley*, Oxford: Oxford University Press.

Cammaerts, Emile (1935), *Albert of Belgium: Defender of the Right*, New York: Macmillan.

Charteris, John (1931), *At GHQ*, London: Cassell.

Churchill, Winston S. (1923), *The World Crisis*, Volume I, New York: Scribner's Sons.

Craster, J.M. (1976), *Fifteen Rounds a Minute: The Grenadiers at War, August to December 1914, Edited from the Diaries and Letters of Major 'Ma' Jeffreys and Others*, London: Macmillan.

Dubois, A. (1920), *Deux Ans de Commandement sur le Front de France, 1914–16*, Paris: Charles-Lavauzelle.

Falkenhayn, Erich von (1920), *The German General Staff and its Decisions, 1914–16*, New York: Dodd, Mead & Co.

Farrar-Hockley, Anthony (1973), *Goughie*, London: Hart-Davis, MacGibbon.

Flemalle, Gabriel de Libert de (1915), *Fighting with King Albert*, London: Hodder & Stoughton.

Foch, Ferdinand (1931), *The Memoirs of Marshal Foch*, New York: Doubleday.

Fraser, Pamela and Thornton, L.H. (1930), *The Congreves: Father and Son*, London: John Murray.

French, Field Marshal Lord (1919), *1914*, Boston: Houghton Mufflin.

Galliéni, Joseph (1920), *Mémoires du Général Galliéni*, Paris: Payot.

Gilbert, Martin (1972), *Winston S. Churchill*, Volume III Companion Pt. I, London: Heinemann.

Groot, Gerard de (1988), *Douglas Haig, 1861–1928*, London: Unwin Hyman.

Gough, General Sir Hubert (1931), *The Fifth Army*, London: Hodder & Stoughton.

Gwynn, Stephen (ed.) (1936), *The Anvil of War*, London: Macmillan.

Haldane, General Sir Aylmer (1948), *A Soldier's Saga*, Edinburgh: Blackwood & Sons.

Hamilton, Nigel (1981), *Monty*, New York: McGraw-Hill.

Holmes, Richard (1981), *The Little Field Marshal: Sir John French*, London: Cape.

Hyndson, J.G.W. (1933), *From Mons to the First Battle of Ypres*, London: Wyman.

Joffre, Joseph (1932), *The Personal Memoirs of Joffre*, Volume I, New York: Harper & Brothers.

Kuhl, Hermann von (1929), *Der Weltkrieg 1914–1918 dem deutschen Volke dargestelt von Hermann von Kuhl*, Berlin: Verlag Tradition Wilhelm Kolk.

Liddell Hart, Basil (1931), *Foch: Man of Orleans*, London: Eyre & Spottiswoode.

Lloyd George, David (1933), *War Memoirs*, Volume I, London: Ivor Nicholson & Watson.

Lucy, John (1938), *There's a Devil in the Drum*, London: Faber & Faber.

Maze, Paul (1934), *A Frenchman in Khaki*, London: Heinemann.

Neiberg, Michael (2003), *Foch*, Washington: Brasseys.

Palat, General (1922), *La Ruée vers Calais*, Paris: Librarie Chapelot.

Prior, Robin and Wilson, Trevor (1992), *Command on the Western Front: The Military Career of Sir Henry Rawlinson, 1914–18*, Oxford: Blackwell.

Rawlinson, Toby (1925), *Adventures on the Western Front: August 1914 to June 1915*, London: Andrew Melrose.

Richards, Frank (1964), *Old Soldiers Never Die*, 2nd edn., London: Faber & Faber.

Secrett, Sergeant (1929), *Twenty-Five Years with Earl Haig*, London: Jarrolds.

Smith-Dorrien, General Sir Horace (1925), *Forty-Eight Years' Service*, London, John Murray.

Spears, Edward (1930), *Liaison 1914*, London: Heinemann.

Terraine, John (1963), *Haig: The Educated Soldier*, London: Hutchinson.

Terraine, John (ed.) (1964), *General Jack's Diary, 1914–18*, London: Eyre & Spottiswoode.

Thielemans, Marie-Rose and Vandewoude, Emile (eds.) (1982), *Le Roi Albert: Au Travers de ses lettres inédites, 1882–1916*, Brussels: Office International de Librarie.

Thielemans, Marie-Rose (ed.) (1991), *Albert Ier: Carnets et Correspondance de Guerre, 1914–1918*, Paris: Éditions Duculot.

Winter, Denis (1991), *Haig's Command: A Reassessment*, London: Viking.

Monographs

Allen, G.H. and Whitehead, H.C. (1916), *The Great War: The Mobilisation of the Moral and Physical Forces*, Philadelphia: George Barrie's Sons.

Anglesey, Marquess of (1996), *A History of the British Cavalry, 1816–1919: VII: The Curragh Incident and the Western Front, 1914*, London: Leo Cooper.

Ascoli, David (1981), *The Mons Star*, London: Harrap.

Babington, Anthony (1983), *For the Sake of Example*, New York: St Martin's Press.

Bailey, Jonathan (1996), *The First World War and the Birth of the Modern Style of Warfare*, HMSO: Strategic and Combat Studies Institute.

Beckett, Ian F.W. (1991), *The Amateur Military Tradition, 1558–1945*, Manchester: Manchester University Press.

Beckett, Ian F.W. (2001), *The Great War, 1914–1918*, London: Longman.

Beckett, Ian F.W. (ed.) (1986), *The Army and the Curragh Incident, 1914*, London: Bodley Head.

Beckett, Ian F.W. and Gooch, John (eds.) (1981), *Politicians and Defence*, Manchester: Manchester University Press.

Beckett, Ian F.W. and Simpson, Keith (eds.) (1985), *A Nation in Arms: A Social Study of the British Army in the First World War*, Manchester: Manchester University Press.

Bidwell, Shelford and Graham, Dominick (1982), *Firepower: British Army Weapons and Theories of War, 1904–45*, London: Allen & Unwin.

Bond, Brian (ed.) (1991), *The First World War and British Military History*, Oxford: Oxford University Press.

Bond, Brian (ed.) (1999), *Look to Your Front: Studies in the First World War*, Staplehurst: Spellmount.

Bond, Brian and Roy, Ian (eds.) (1975), *War and Society: A Yearbook of Military History*, London: Croom Helm.

Bond, Brian and Cave, Nigel (eds.) (1999), *Haig: A Reappraisal 70 Years On*, Barnsley: Leo Cooper.

Bourne, John (1989), *Britain and the Great War, 1914–18*, London: Edward Arnold.

Bowman, Timothy (2003), *The Irish Regiments in the Great War: Discipline and Morale*, Manchester: Manchester University Press.

Brose, Eric Dorn (2001), *The Kaiser's Army: The Politics of Military Technology in Germany During the Machine Age, 1870–1914*, Oxford: Oxford University Press.

Brown, Ian Malcolm (1998), *British Logistics on the Western Front, 1914–19*, Westport: Praeger.

Bryan, Barry (ed.) (1915), *The Irish Nuns at Ypres*, London: Smith, Elder & Co.

Buchan, John (1922), *A History of the Great War*, Volume I, London: Thomas Nelson & Sons.

Carew, Tim (1971), *The Vanished Army*, London: Corgi.

Chickering, Roger (1998), *Imperial Germany and the Great War, 1914–18*, Cambridge: Cambridge University Press.

Cecil, Hugh and Liddle, Peter (eds.) (1996), *Facing Armageddon: The First World War Experienced*, London: Leo Cooper.

Corns, Cathryn and Hughes-Wilson, John (2001), *Blindfold and Alone*, London: Cassell.

Corrigan, Gordon (1999), *Sepoys in the Trenches: The Indian Corps on the Western Front, 1914–15*, Staplehurst: Spellmount.

Cruttwell, C.R.M.F. (1991), *A History of the Great War, 1914–18*, 2nd edn., Chicago: Academy Chicago.

Dauzet, Pierre (1917), *La Bataille des Flandres*, Paris: Charles-Larauzelle.

Dendooven, Dominiek (2001), *Menin Gate and Last Post: Ypres as Holy Ground*, Koksijde: De Klaproos.

Dendooven, Dominiek and Dewilde, Jan (1999), *The Reconstruction of Ieper*, Ieper: Openbaar Kunstbezit in Vlaanderen.

Doyle, Peter (1998), *Geology of the Western Front, 1914–18*, London: Geologists' Association.

Dungan, Myles (1995), *Irish Voices from the Great War*, Dublin: Irish Academic Press.

Essen, Léon Van Der (1917), *The Invasion and the War in Belgium from Liège to the Yser*, London: T. Fisher Unwin.

Evans, R.J.W. and Strandemann, H. Pogge von (eds.) (1999), *The Coming of the First World War*, 2nd edn., Oxford: Oxford University Press.

Falls, Cyril (1967), *The First World War*, London: Longman.

Farrar-Hockley, Anthony (1967), *Death of an Army*, London: Arthur Barker.

Ferris, John (1992), *The British Army and Signals Intelligence during the First World War*, Stroud: Sutton.

Ferro, Marc (1973), *The Great War, 1914–18*, London: Routledge.

French, David (1982), *British Economic and Strategic Planning, 1905–15*, London: Allen & Unwin.

French, David and Holden Reid, Brian (eds.) (2002), *The General Staff: Reform and Innovation, 1890–1939*, London: Frank Cass.

Gardner, Nikolas (2003), *Trial by Fire: Command and the British Expeditionary Force in 1914*, Westport: Praeger.

Goffre, Charles le (1916), *Dixmude*, Philadelphia: J.B. Lippincott.

Griffith, Paddy (ed.) (1996), *British Fighting Methods in the Great War*, London: Frank Cass.

Gudmundsson, Bruce (1995), *Stormtroop Tactics: Innovation in the German Army, 1914–18*, Westport: Praeger.

Herwig, Holger (1997), *The First World War: Germany and Austria-Hungary, 1914–18*, London: Arnold.

Horne, John (ed.) (1997), *State, Society and Mobilisation in Europe during the First World War*, Cambridge: Cambridge University Press.

Horne, John and Kramer, Alan (2001), *German Atrocities 1914: A History of Denial*, New Haven: Yale University Press.

Howard, Michael (ed.) (1965), *The Theory and Practice of War*, London: Cassell.

Hughes, Matthew and Seligmann, Matthew (eds.) (2000), *Leadership in Conflict, 1914–18*, Barnsley: Leo Cooper.

Leed, Eric (1979), *No Man's Land: Combat and Identity in World War I*, Cambridge: Cambridge University Press.

Liddle, Peter (ed.) (1985), *Home Fires and Foreign Fields*, London: Brasseys.

Liddle, Peter (ed.) (1997), *Passchendaele in Perspective: The Third Battle of Ypres*, London: Leo Cooper.

Lloyd, David (1998), *Battlefield Tourism: Pilgrimage and Commemoration of the Great War in Britain, Australia and Canada, 1919–39*, Oxford: Berg.

Madelin, Louis (1919), *La Mêlée des Flandres: L'Yser et Ypres*, Paris: Librarie Plon.

Michalka, Wolfgang (ed.) (1994), *Der Erste Weltkrieg: Wirkung, Wahrnehmung, Analyse*, Munich: Seehamer Verlag.

Millett, Allan and Murray, Williamson (eds.) (1988), *Military Effectiveness: The First World War*, London: Unwin Hyman.

Omissi, David (1994), *The Sepoy and the Raj: The Indian Army, 1860–1914*, London: Macmillan.

Occleshaw, Michael (1989), *Armour against Fate: British Military Intelligence in the First World War*, London: Columbus Books.

Oram, Gerard (2003), *Military Executions during World War I*, Basingstoke: Palgrave.

Paret, Peter (ed.) (1986), *Makers of Modern Strategy*, 2nd edn., Oxford: Oxford University Press.

Perry, F.W. (1988), *The Commonwealth Armies: Manpower and Organisation in Two World Wars*, Manchester: Manchester University Press.

Philpott, William (1996), *Anglo-French Relations and Strategy on the Western Front, 1914–1918*, Basingstoke: Macmillan.

Porch, Douglas (1981), *The March to the Marne: The French Army, 1871–1914*, Cambridge: Cambridge University Press.

Ramsay, M.A. (2002), *Command and Cohesion: The Citizen Soldier and Minor Tactics in the British Army, 1870–1918*, Westport: Praeger.

Ratinaud, Jean (1967), *La Course à La Mer*, Paris: Fayard.

Ritter, Gerhard (1972), *The Sword and the Sceptre*, Volume III, Coral Gables: University of Miami Press.

Samuels, Martin (1995), *Command and Control?: Command, Training and Tactics in the British and German Armies, 1888–1918*, London: Frank Cass.

Schwink, Otto (1919), *La Bataille de L'Yser*, Brussels: Cartographic Institute of the Belgian Army.

Sheffield, Gary (2000), *Leadership in the Trenches*, London: Macmillan.

Simkins, Peter (1988), *Kitchener's Army: The Raising of the New Armies, 1914–16*, Manchester: Manchester University Press.

Simpson, Andy (1995), *The Evolution of Victory*, London: Tom Donovan.

Simpson, Keith (1981), *The Old Contemptibles*, London: Allen & Unwin.

Snyder, Jack (1984), *The Ideology of the Offensive Military Decision-making and the Disaster of 1914*, Ithaca: Cornell University Press.

Strachan, Hew (2001), *The First World War: To Arms*, Oxford: Oxford University Press.

Travers, Tim (1993), *The Killing Ground: The British Army, the Western Front and the Emergence of Modern Warfare, 1900–1918*, London: Routledge.

Turner, J.M. (ed.) (1988), *Britain in the First World War*, London: Unwin Hyman.

Unruh, Karl (1986), *Langemarck: Legende und Wirklichkeit*, Koblenz: Bernhard & Graefe Verlag.

Willson, Beckles (1920), *Ypres: The Holy Ground of British Arms*, Bruges: Charles Beyaert.

Wilson, Keith (ed.) (1987), *Empire and Continent*, London: Mansell.

Wilson, Keith (ed.) (1995), *Decisions for War, 1914*, London: UCL Press.

Winter, Jay and Robert, Jean-Louis (eds.) (1997), *Capital Cities at War: London, Paris, Berlin, 1914–19*, Cambridge: Cambridge University Press.

Wohl, Robert (1979), *The Generation of 1914*, Cambridge MA: Harvard University Press.

Articles

Badsey, Stephen (1991), 'Mounted cavalry in the Second Boer War', *Sandhurst Journal of Military Studies* 2.

Bourgeois, H. (1987), 'Hitler et la region de Comines-Warneton en 1914–18 et en 1940', *Mémoires de la Société de Comines-Warneton et de la Région* 17.

Chamard, Élie (1935), 'Zonnebeke', *Revue des Deux Mondes*.

Cowley, Robert (1989), 'Albert and the Yser', *Military History Quarterly* 1 (4).

Deedes, Sir Charles (1984), 'The view from GHQ', *Stand To* 12.

Ferris, John (1988), 'The British army and signals intelligence in the field during the First World War', *Intelligence and National Security* 3/4.

Fox, Colin (1995), 'The myths of Langemarck', *Imperial War Museum Review* 10.

French, David (1979), 'The military background to the shell crisis of May 1915', *Journal of Strategic Studies* 2.

French, David (1984), 'Sir John French's secret service on the Western Front, 1914–15', *Journal of Strategic Studies* 7.

Goldsmith, R.F.K. (1976), 'Territorial vanguard: a London Scottish diary', *Army Quarterly* 103 (2).

Greenhut, Jeffrey (1981), 'Race, sex and war: the impact of race and sex on morale and health services for the Indian corps on the Western Front', *Military Affairs* 45 (2).

Greenhut, Jeffrey (1983), 'The imperial reserve: the Indian corps on the Western Front, 1914–15', *Journal of Imperial and Commonwealth History* 12 (1).

Harrison, David (1984), 'Jack Dimmer VC', *Stand To* **12**.

Hopper, H.J. (1984), 'The diary of an Old Contemptible', *Stand To* **12**.

Hüppauf, Bernd (1988), 'Langemarck, Verdun and the myth of a new man in Germany after the First World War', *War and Society* **6** (2).

Hussey, John (1994), 'A hard day at First Ypres: the allied generals and their problems, 31 October 1914', *British Army Review* **107**.

Hussey, John (1995), 'Haig's ride up the Menin Road at First Ypres on 31 October 1914: did he invent the whole story?' *Bulletin of the Military Historical Society* **46**.

Philpott, William (1989), 'The strategic ideas of Sir John French', *Journal of Strategic Studies* **12**.

Prete, R.A. (1989), 'French strategic planning and the deployment of the BEF in France in 1914', *Canadian Journal of History* **24**.

Richardson, Matthew (2004), 'Tigers at bay?: The Leicestershire Regiment at Armentières', *Stand To* **69**.

Simpson, Keith (1973), 'Capper and the offensive spirit', *Journal of the Royal United Services Institute for Defence Studies* **118** (2).

Spiers, Edward (1981), 'Reforming the infantry of the line, 1902–14', *Journal of the Society for Army Historical Research* **59**.

Spiers, Edward (1984), 'The British Cavalry, 1902–14', *Journal of the Society for Army Historical Research* **57**.

Thorne, A.F.A.N. (1932), 'Gheluvelt cross roads, October 29th, 1914', *Household Brigade Magazine*, Summer.

Wilson, Keith (1977), 'The War Office, Churchill and the Belgian option, August to December 1911', *Bulletin of the Institute of Historical Research* **50**.

Wilson, Trevor (1979), 'Britain's moral commitment to France in July 1914', *History* **64**.

X (1917), 'Gheluvelt 1914: the man who turned the tide', *Blackwood's* **MCCXXII**.

'A guards officer at war: the diary and letters of Lieutenant Colonel H.M. Pryce-Jones', *The Great War, 1914–1918* **3** (3).

Dissertation

Brent Wilson, J. (1978), 'The Morale and Discipline of the British Expeditionary Force, 1914–1918', Unpub. MA., New Brunswick.

Index

Bremner, Jock 164
British Expeditionary Force (BEF) 1,
    4–5, 8–11, 15–18, 29–35, 41–2,
    51–2, 59–61, 63–4, 74–5, 83, 88,
    130, 147–8, 154, 163–4, 171,
    174, 176–8
Army,
    1st Army 75
    2nd Army 56, 178
Corps,
    I Corps 1–2, 17, 44, 51, 61, 63,
        67, 72, 74–5, 79, 81–3, 89, 91–2,
        94, 108–9, 111, 114, 117, 132,
        135–7, 140–1, 143, 147, 151–3,
        171–2, 174, 176
    II Corps 1, 16, 44, 51–6, 58–9, 63,
        67, 70, 74, 88, 101, 104, 108–10,
        125, 147, 154, 166–7, 172
    III Corps 1, 16, 44, 52, 55–8, 62–3,
        68–70, 74, 108, 110–11, 152, 187
    IV Corps 1, 24, 52, 58–60, 62–3,
        70, 72, 74, 91, 94
    Cavalry Corps 1, 44, 52, 70, 74, 91,
        94, 103, 118
Divisions,
    1st Cavalry Division 1, 3, 57, 71,
        77, 123–4, 128, 150, 171, 175
    2nd Cavalry Division 1, 58, 70–1,
        77, 119, 123, 129
    3rd Cavalry Division 1, 20–1, 24,
        33, 57, 70, 94, 121, 123, 136
    1st Division 1, 4, 70, 72–3, 76, 79,
        81–3, 94, 114–15, 117–18, 121,
        130, 135–6, 138–9, 142, 152,
        154, 162
    2nd Division 1, 3, 45–6, 70, 72,
        80–4, 89, 91–2, 94, 114, 118,
        120–1, 134–5, 138, 141, 143,
        147, 152, 169
    3rd Division 1, 54–5, 67–8, 103–8,
        163, 166
    4th Division 1, 3, 56–8, 102,
        110–11, 124, 153, 187
    5th Division 1, 53, 55, 67, 104–5
    6th Division 1, 3, 57–8, 69, 107,
        110–11, 187

7th Division 1, 15, 18, 20–1, 24–5,
    32–3, 44, 59, 61, 71, 73, 81–4,
    91, 94, 114, 120–3, 140, 143,
    145–7, 151–5, 163, 176, 185
8th Division 15, 94, 153–4, 174
20th Division 150
Brigades,
    1st (Guards) Brigade 73, 77, 93,
        114–15, 118, 133, 141, 166,
        168–70
    2nd Brigade 74, 80, 118, 122, 130,
        143
    3rd Brigade 4, 77, 82–3, 115, 117,
        130, 132, 154
    4th (Guards) Brigade 73, 91, 118
    5th Brigade 2, 72, 80–1, 84, 170–1,
        177
    6th Brigade 91, 143, 168
    7th Brigade 106–7
    8th Brigade 67, 103, 108
    9th Brigade 55, 108, 125, 149
    10th Brigade 57
    11th Brigade 70, 187
    12th Brigade 124, 187
    13th Brigade 53, 55, 103–4, 125
    14th Brigade 103, 106–7, 109
    15th Brigade 53, 55, 106
    16th Brigade 110
    17th Brigade 69
    18th Brigade 69
    19th Brigade 45, 69–71, 187
    20th Brigade 3, 72, 83, 91, 93, 114,
        118, 143, 146
    21st Brigade 59, 72, 81, 83, 118–19,
        121, 146, 152
    22nd Brigade 61, 72–3, 121–2,
        145–6, 153, 155
    29th Brigade 115
    1st Cavalry Brigade 129
    2nd Cavalry Brigade 107
    3rd Cavalry Brigade 10, 56, 58,
        71–2, 123, 139
    4th Cavalry Brigade 127
    5th Cavalry Brigade 149
    6th Cavalry Brigade 33, 71, 136,
        146, 154